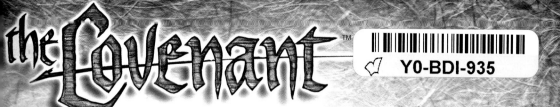

# the Covenant™



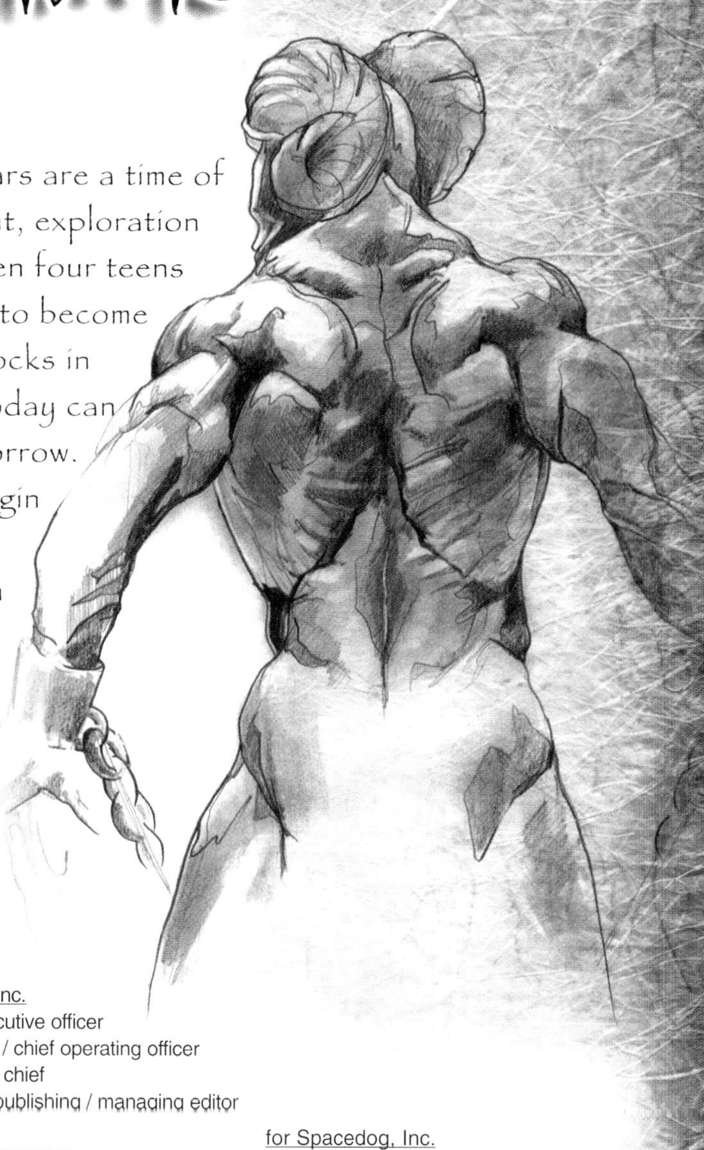

Your teenage years are a time of carefree fun, excitement, exploration and discovery. But when four teens discover they're about to become the most powerful warlocks in the world, a little fun today can mean big trouble tommorrow.

When murders begin near the boys' summer camp, suspicion falls on one of their own. Can they retain their bond and find the truth? Or will the covenant be broken?

for Top Cow Productions, Inc.
**Marc Silvestri**_chief executive officer
**Matt Hawkins**_president / chief operating officer
**Jim McLauchlin**_editor in chief
**Renae Geerlings**_vp of publishing / managing editor
**Scott Tucker**_editor
**Chaz Riggs**_production manager
**Annie Pham**_marketing director
**Peter Lam**_webmaster
**Phil Smith**_trades and submissions
**Rob Levin and Zach Metheny**_production assistants
**Jacques David**_marketing assistant
**Corey Teblum, Jef Harmatz and Scott Newman**_interns

for Spacedog, Inc.
**Roger Mincheff**_chief executive officer
**Hal Burg**_director of business development and marketing

**ISBN # 1-58240-556-5**
**Published by Image Comics®**
**The Covenant 2005 First Printing.**
Office of Publication: 1942 University Ave., Suite 305, Berkeley, CA 94704. 
**Printed in The U.S.A.**

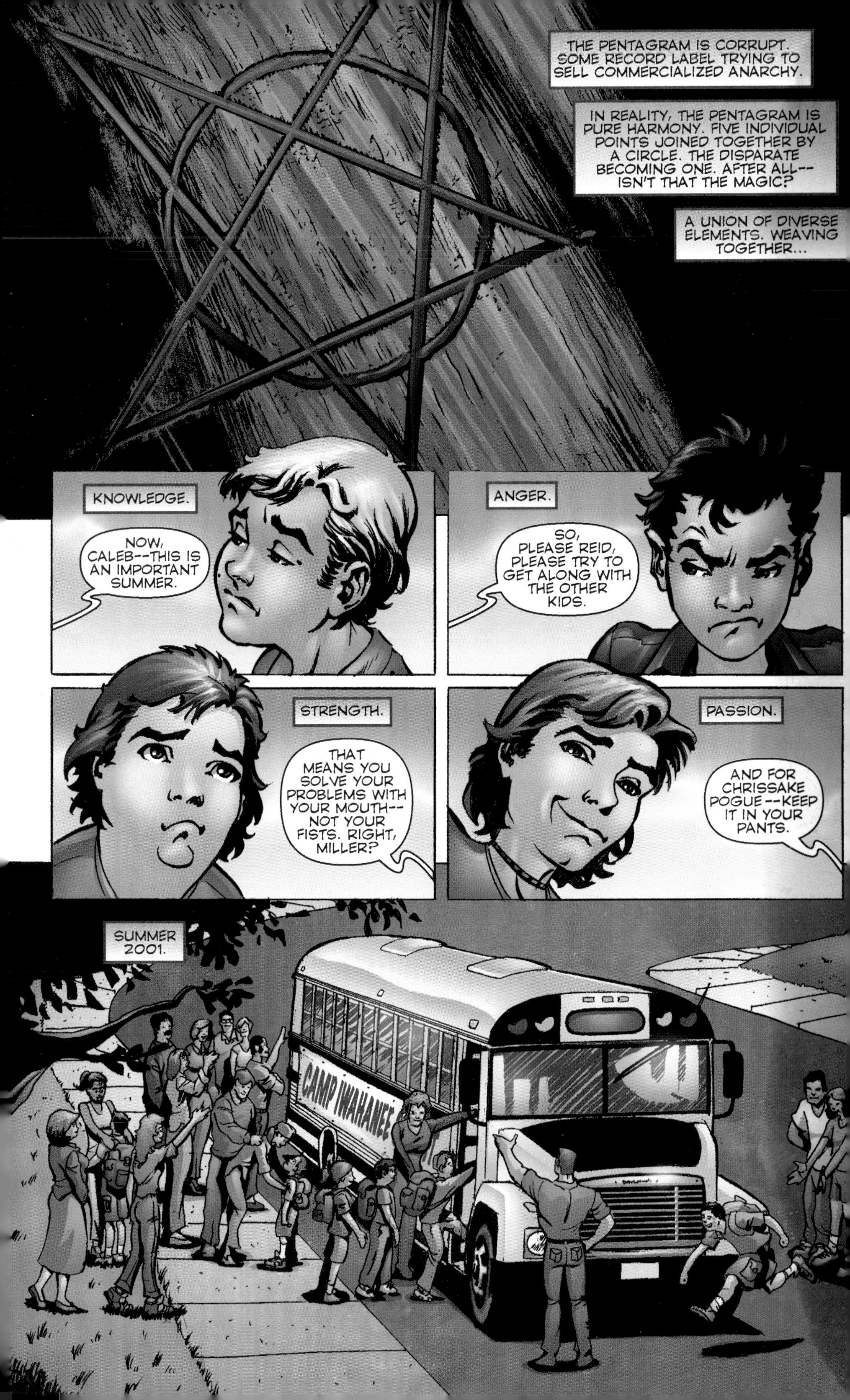
THE PENTAGRAM IS CORRUPT. SOME RECORD LABEL TRYING TO SELL COMMERCIALIZED ANARCHY.
IN REALITY, THE PENTAGRAM IS PURE HARMONY. FIVE INDIVIDUAL POINTS JOINED TOGETHER BY A CIRCLE. THE DISPARATE BECOMING ONE. AFTER ALL-- ISN'T THAT THE MAGIC?
A UNION OF DIVERSE ELEMENTS. WEAVING TOGETHER...
KNOWLEDGE.
NOW, CALEB--THIS IS AN IMPORTANT SUMMER.
ANGER.
SO, PLEASE REID, PLEASE TRY TO GET ALONG WITH THE OTHER KIDS.
STRENGTH.
THAT MEANS YOU SOLVE YOUR PROBLEMS WITH YOUR MOUTH-- NOT YOUR FISTS. RIGHT, MILLER?
PASSION.
AND FOR CHRISSAKE POGUE--KEEP IT IN YOUR PANTS.
SUMMER 2001.
CAMP IWAHANEE

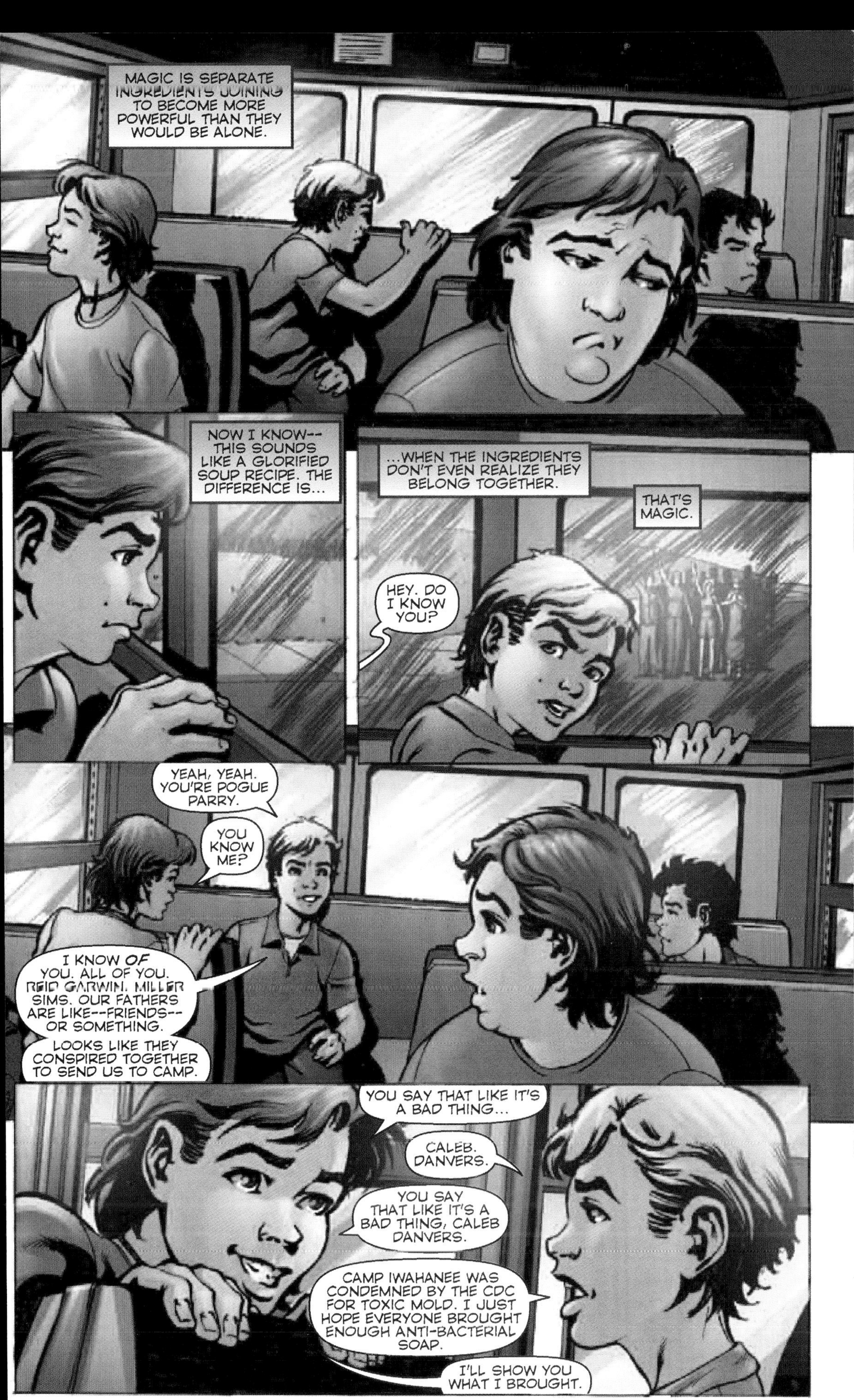
MAGIC IS SEPARATE INGREDIENTS JOINING TO BECOME MORE POWERFUL THAN THEY WOULD BE ALONE.
NOW I KNOW-- THIS SOUNDS LIKE A GLORIFIED SOUP RECIPE. THE DIFFERENCE IS...
...WHEN THE INGREDIENTS DON'T EVEN REALIZE THEY BELONG TOGETHER.
THAT'S MAGIC.
HEY. DO I KNOW YOU?
YEAH, YEAH. YOU'RE POGUE PARRY.
YOU KNOW ME?
I KNOW *OF* YOU. ALL OF YOU. REID GARWIN. MILLER SIMS. OUR FATHERS ARE LIKE--FRIENDS-- OR SOMETHING.
LOOKS LIKE THEY CONSPIRED TOGETHER TO SEND US TO CAMP.
YOU SAY THAT LIKE IT'S A BAD THING...
CALEB. DANVERS.
YOU SAY THAT LIKE IT'S A BAD THING, CALEB DANVERS.
CAMP IWAHANEE WAS CONDEMNED BY THE CDC FOR TOXIC MOLD. I JUST HOPE EVERYONE BROUGHT ENOUGH ANTI-BACTERIAL SOAP.
I'LL SHOW YOU WHAT I BROUGHT.

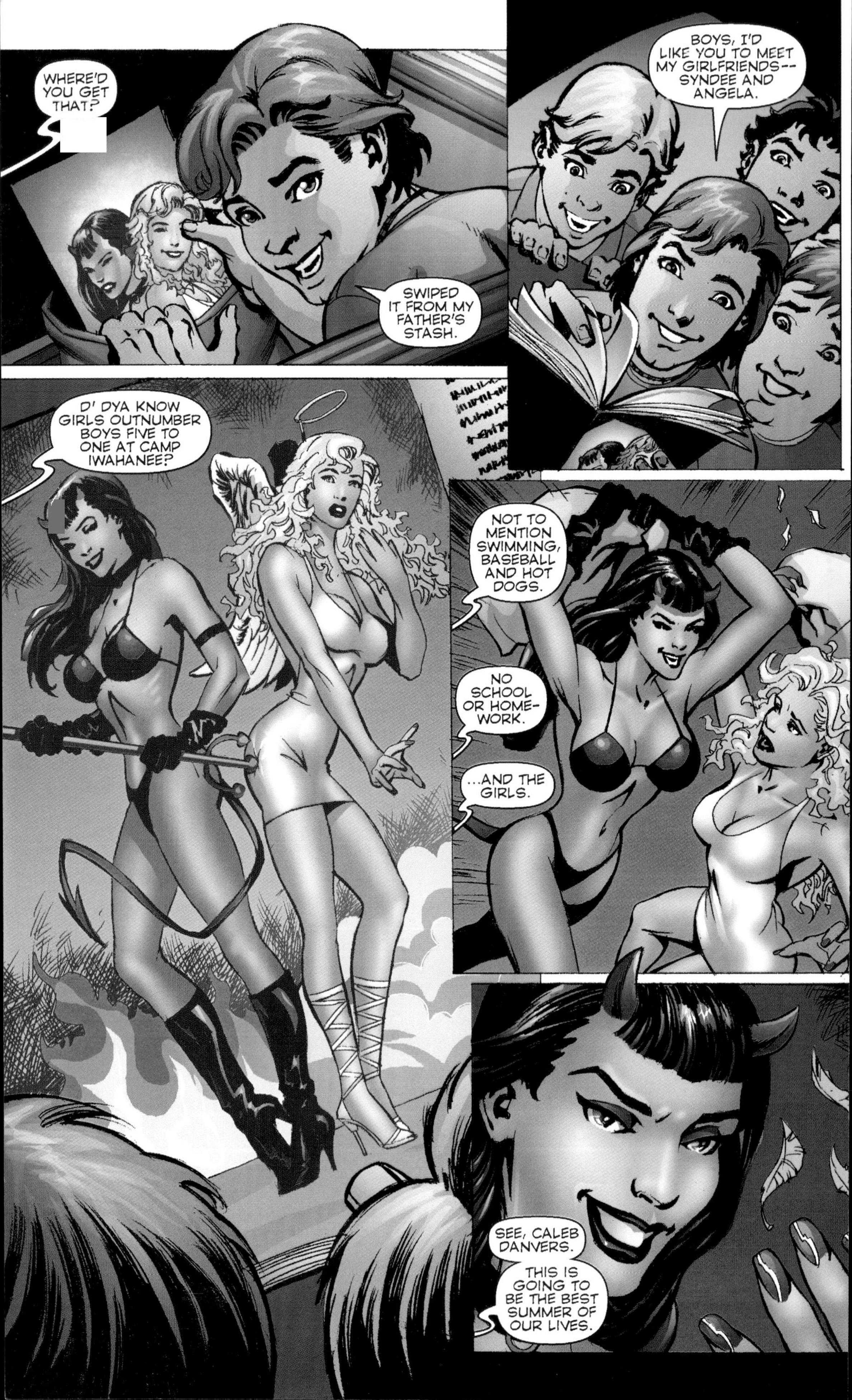
WHERE'D YOU GET THAT?
SWIPED IT FROM MY FATHER'S STASH.
BOYS, I'D LIKE YOU TO MEET MY GIRLFRIENDS-- SYNDEE AND ANGELA.
D' DYA KNOW GIRLS OUTNUMBER BOYS FIVE TO ONE AT CAMP IWAHANEE?
NOT TO MENTION SWIMMING, BASEBALL AND HOT DOGS.
NO SCHOOL OR HOME-WORK.
...AND THE GIRLS.
SEE, CALEB DANVERS.
THIS IS GOING TO BE THE BEST SUMMER OF OUR LIVES.

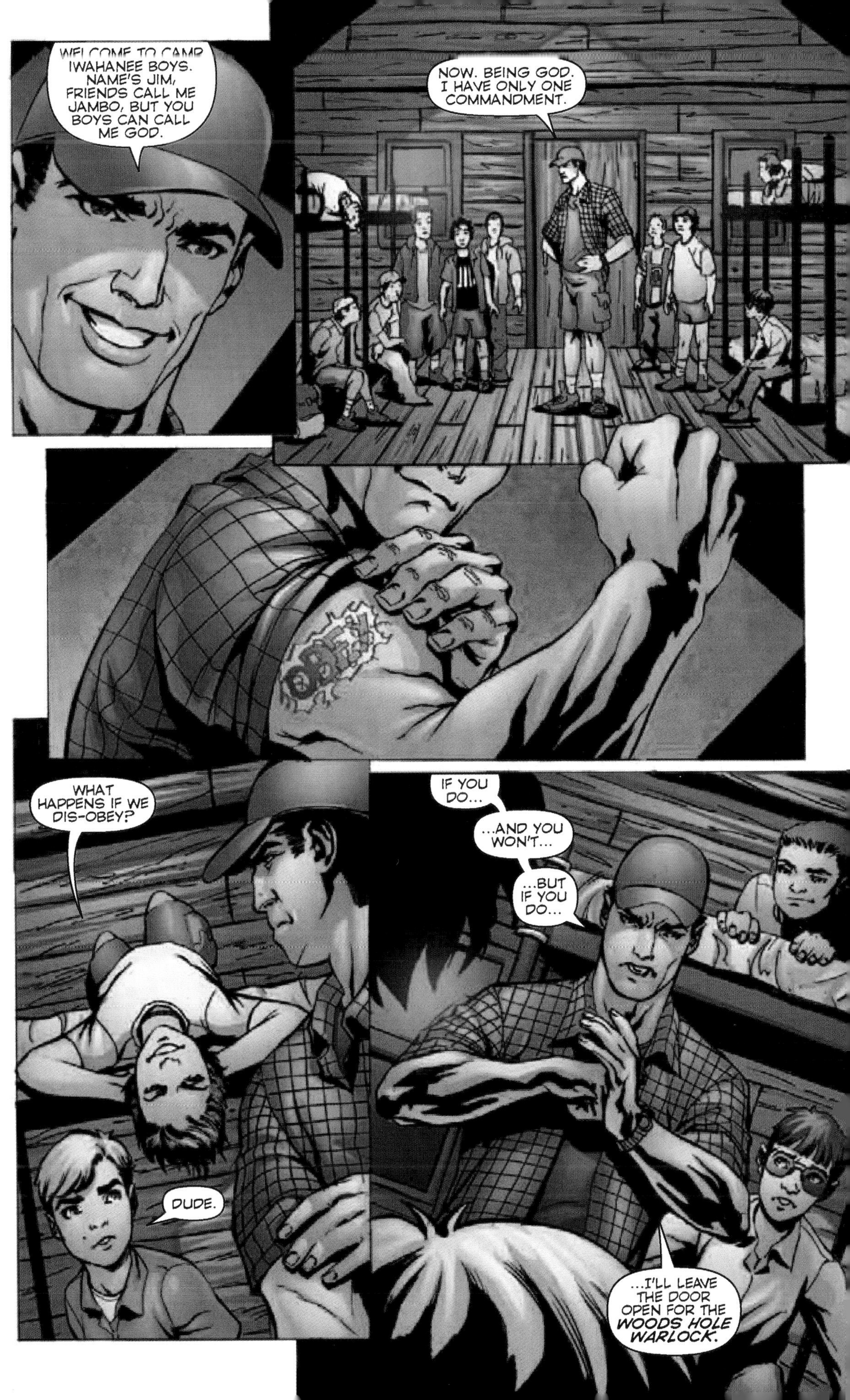
WELCOME TO CAMP IWAHANEE BOYS. NAME'S JIM, FRIENDS CALL ME JAMBO, BUT YOU BOYS CAN CALL ME GOD.
NOW. BEING GOD. I HAVE ONLY ONE COMMANDMENT.
WHAT HAPPENS IF WE DIS-OBEY?
DUDE.
IF YOU DO...
...AND YOU WON'T...
...BUT IF YOU DO...
...I'LL LEAVE THE DOOR OPEN FOR THE *WOODS HOLE WARLOCK*.

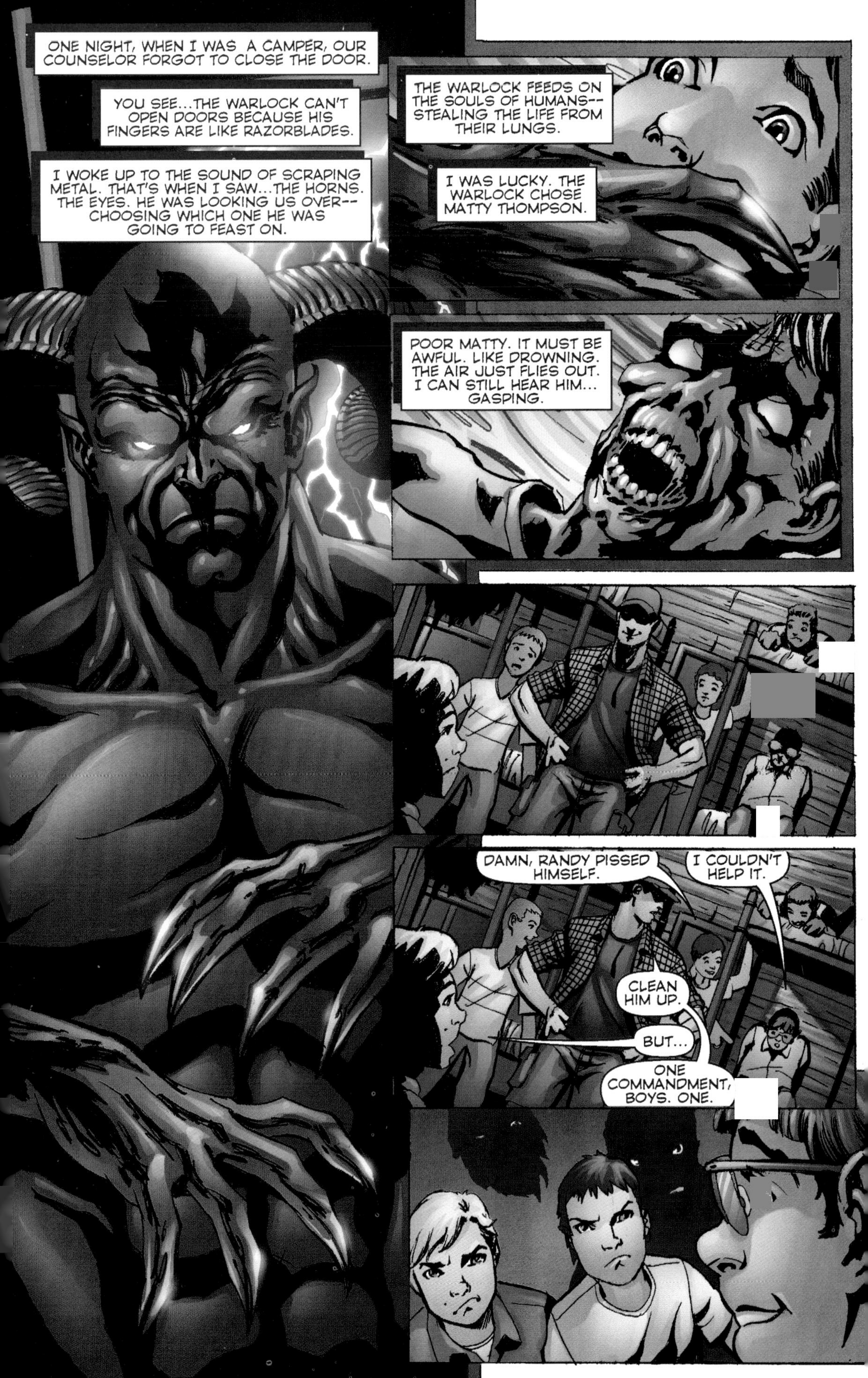
ONE NIGHT, WHEN I WAS A CAMPER, OUR COUNSELOR FORGOT TO CLOSE THE DOOR.
YOU SEE...THE WARLOCK CAN'T OPEN DOORS BECAUSE HIS FINGERS ARE LIKE RAZORBLADES.
I WOKE UP TO THE SOUND OF SCRAPING METAL. THAT'S WHEN I SAW...THE HORNS. THE EYES. HE WAS LOOKING US OVER--CHOOSING WHICH ONE HE WAS GOING TO FEAST ON.
THE WARLOCK FEEDS ON THE SOULS OF HUMANS--STEALING THE LIFE FROM THEIR LUNGS.
I WAS LUCKY. THE WARLOCK CHOSE MATTY THOMPSON.
POOR MATTY. IT MUST BE AWFUL. LIKE DROWNING. THE AIR JUST FLIES OUT. I CAN STILL HEAR HIM... GASPING.
DAMN, RANDY PISSED HIMSELF.
I COULDN'T HELP IT.
CLEAN HIM UP.
BUT...
ONE COMMANDMENT, BOYS. ONE.

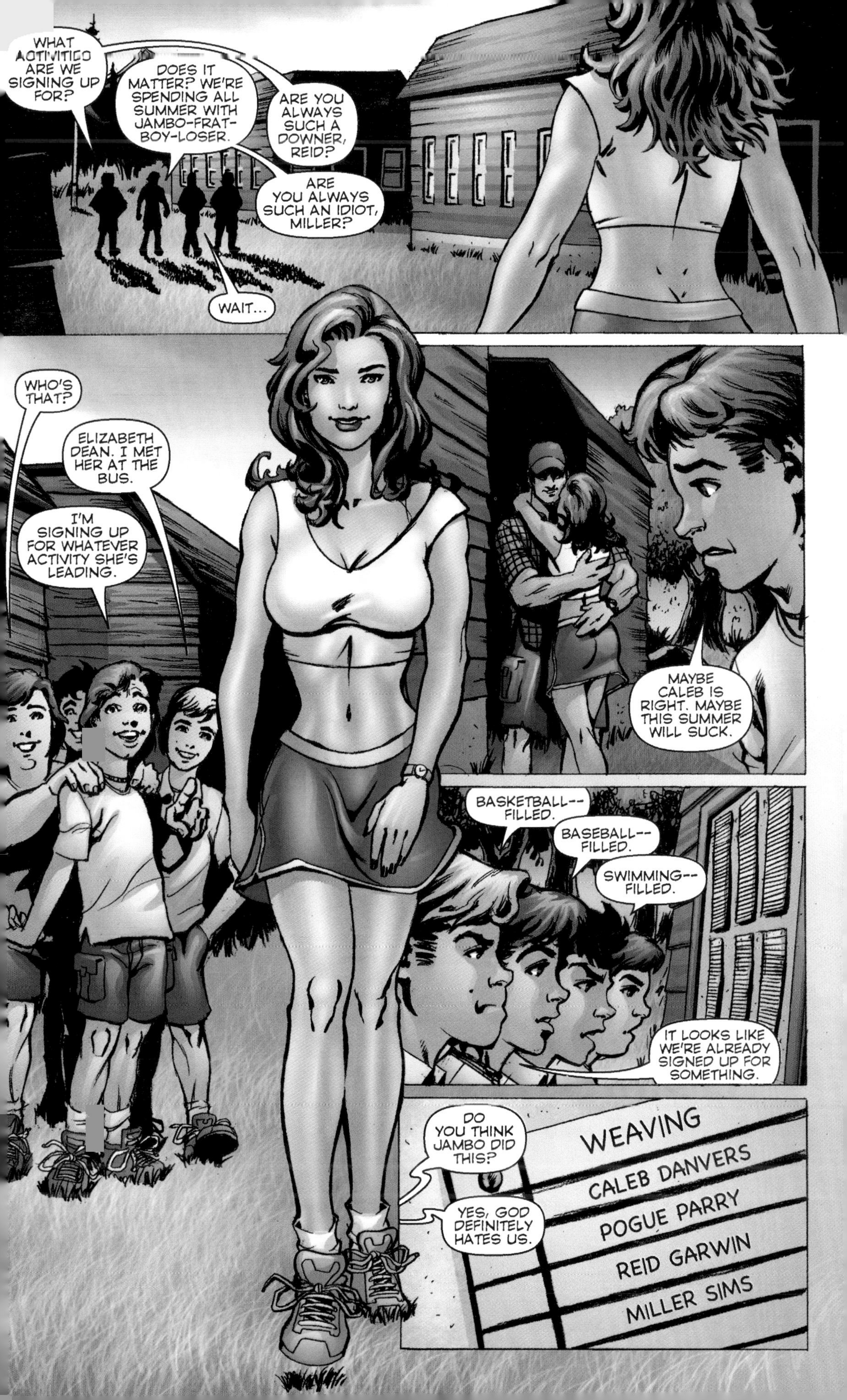
WHAT ACTIVITIES ARE WE SIGNING UP FOR?
DOES IT MATTER? WE'RE SPENDING ALL SUMMER WITH JAMBO-FRAT-BOY-LOSER.
ARE YOU ALWAYS SUCH A DOWNER, REID?
ARE YOU ALWAYS SUCH AN IDIOT, MILLER?
WAIT...
WHO'S THAT?
ELIZABETH DEAN. I MET HER AT THE BUS.
I'M SIGNING UP FOR WHATEVER ACTIVITY SHE'S LEADING.
MAYBE CALEB IS RIGHT. MAYBE THIS SUMMER WILL SUCK.
BASKETBALL-- FILLED.
BASEBALL-- FILLED.
SWIMMING-- FILLED.
IT LOOKS LIKE WE'RE ALREADY SIGNED UP FOR SOMETHING.
DO YOU THINK JAMBO DID THIS?
YES, GOD DEFINITELY HATES US.
WEAVING
CALEB DANVERS
POGUE PARRY
REID GARWIN
MILLER SIMS

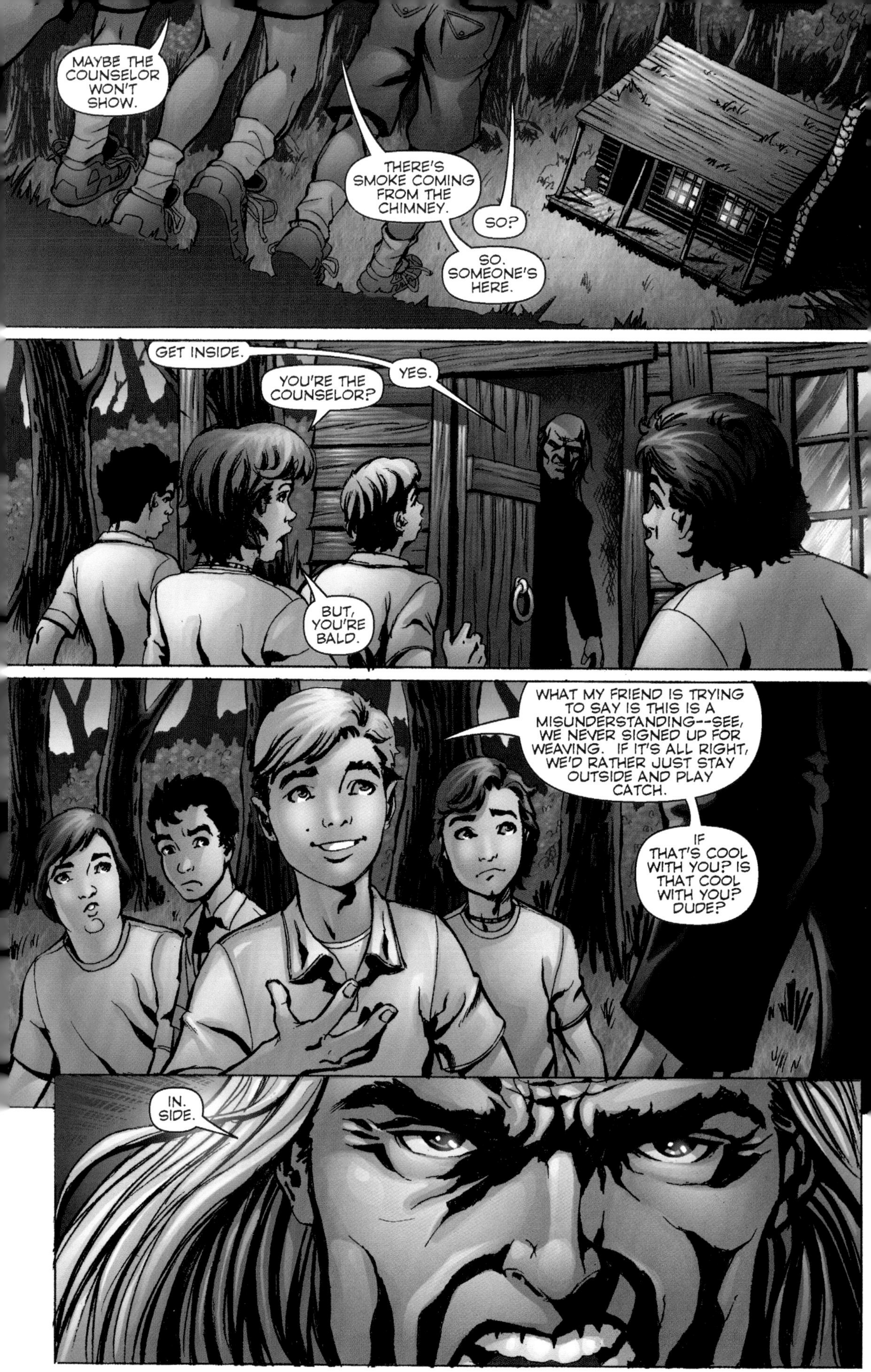
MAYBE THE COUNSELOR WON'T SHOW.
THERE'S SMOKE COMING FROM THE CHIMNEY.
SO?
SO. SOMEONE'S HERE.
GET INSIDE.
YOU'RE THE COUNSELOR?
YES.
BUT, YOU'RE BALD.
WHAT MY FRIEND IS TRYING TO SAY IS THIS IS A MISUNDERSTANDING--SEE, WE NEVER SIGNED UP FOR WEAVING. IF IT'S ALL RIGHT, WE'D RATHER JUST STAY OUTSIDE AND PLAY CATCH.
IF THAT'S COOL WITH YOU? IS THAT COOL WITH YOU? DUDE?
IN. SIDE.

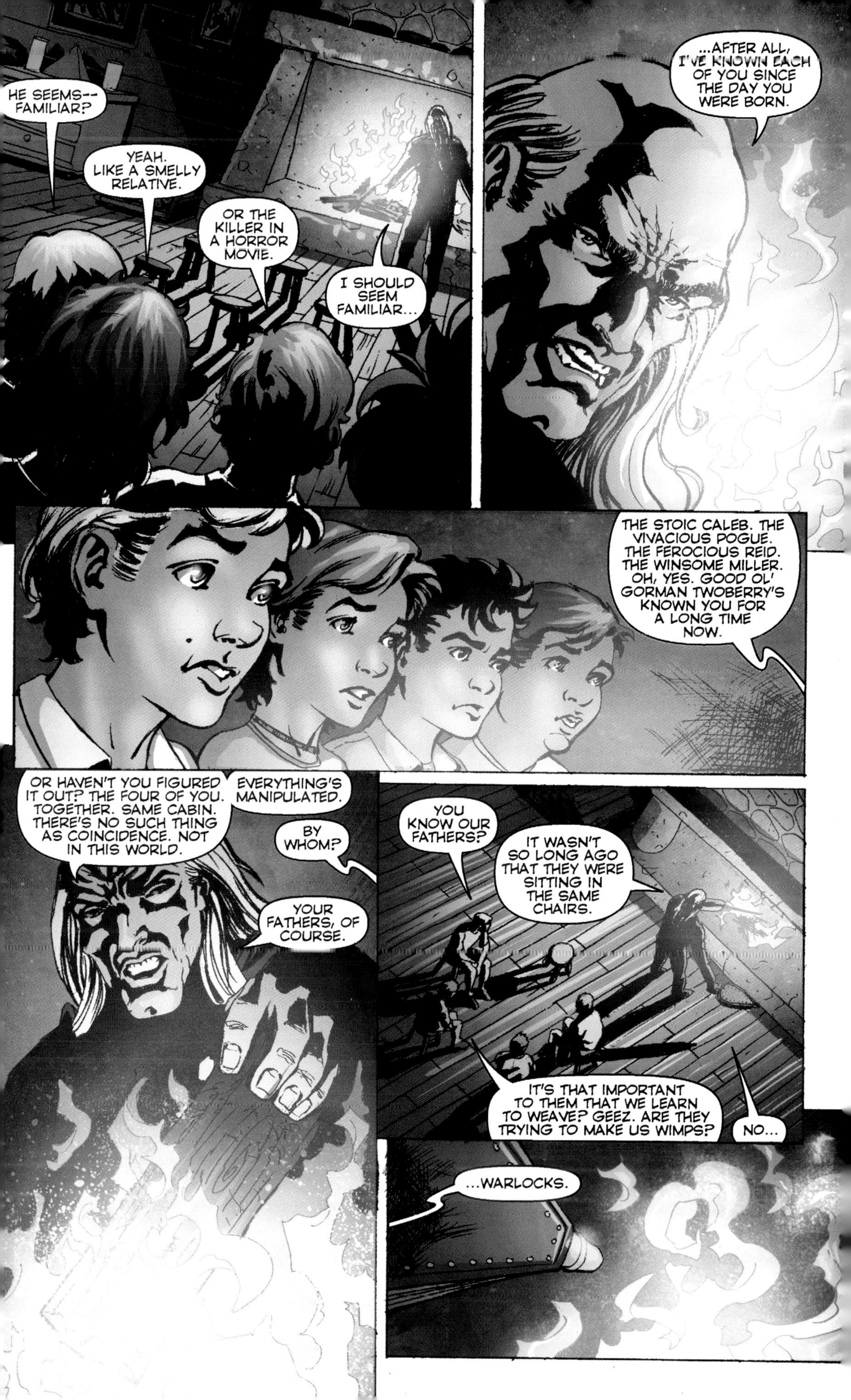
HE SEEMS-- FAMILIAR?
YEAH. LIKE A SMELLY RELATIVE.
OR THE KILLER IN A HORROR MOVIE.
I SHOULD SEEM FAMILIAR...
...AFTER ALL, I'VE KNOWN EACH OF YOU SINCE THE DAY YOU WERE BORN.
THE STOIC CALEB. THE VIVACIOUS POGUE. THE FEROCIOUS REID. THE WINSOME MILLER. OH, YES. GOOD OL' GORMAN TWOBERRY'S KNOWN YOU FOR A LONG TIME NOW.
OR HAVEN'T YOU FIGURED IT OUT? THE FOUR OF YOU. TOGETHER. SAME CABIN. THERE'S NO SUCH THING AS COINCIDENCE. NOT IN THIS WORLD.
EVERYTHING'S MANIPULATED.
BY WHOM?
YOUR FATHERS, OF COURSE.
YOU KNOW OUR FATHERS?
IT WASN'T SO LONG AGO THAT THEY WERE SITTING IN THE SAME CHAIRS.
IT'S THAT IMPORTANT TO THEM THAT WE LEARN TO WEAVE? GEEZ. ARE THEY TRYING TO MAKE US WIMPS?
NO...
...WARLOCKS.

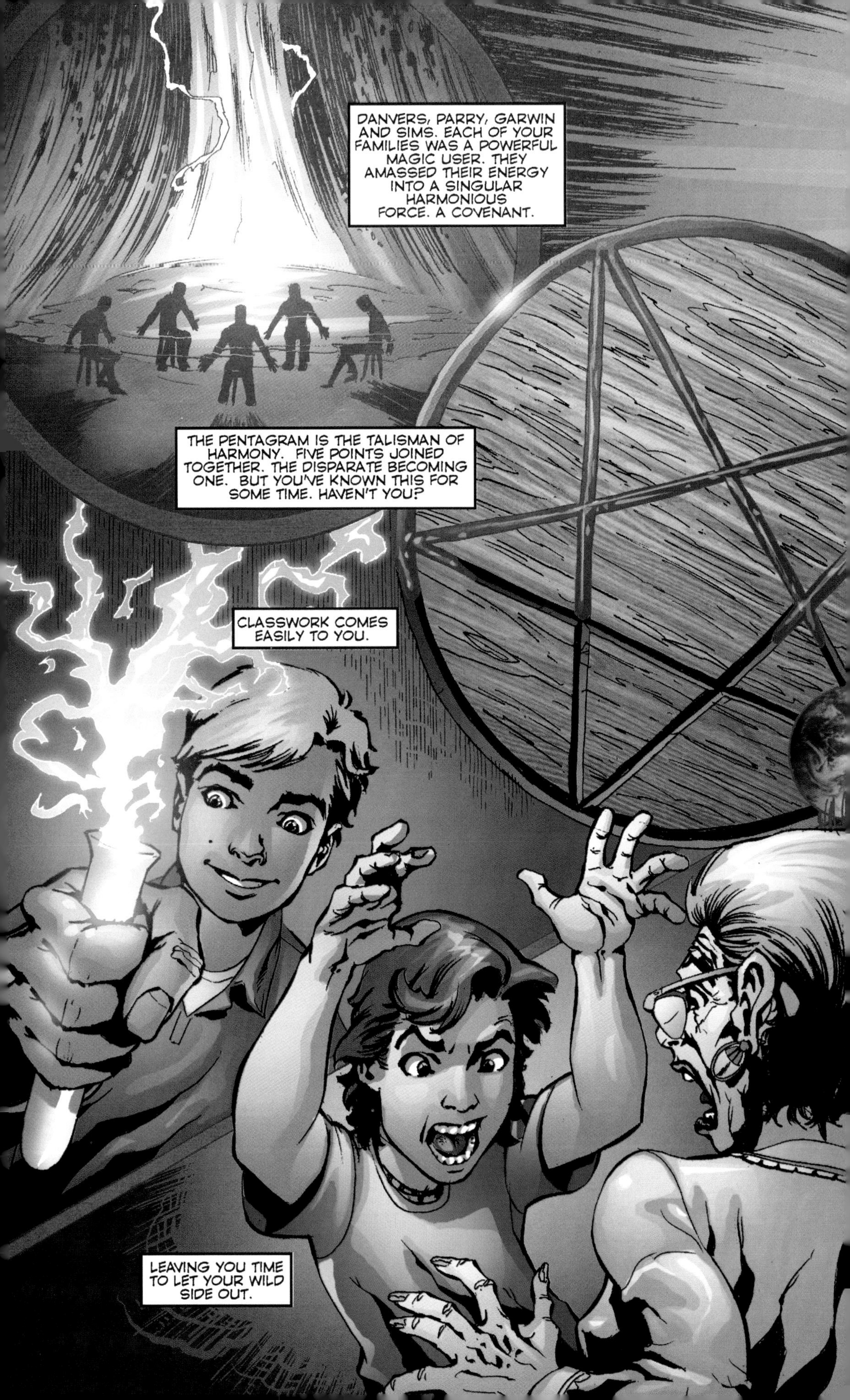
DANVERS, PARRY, GARWIN AND SIMS. EACH OF YOUR FAMILIES WAS A POWERFUL MAGIC USER. THEY AMASSED THEIR ENERGY INTO A SINGULAR HARMONIOUS FORCE. A COVENANT.
THE PENTAGRAM IS THE TALISMAN OF HARMONY. FIVE POINTS JOINED TOGETHER. THE DISPARATE BECOMING ONE. BUT YOU'VE KNOWN THIS FOR SOME TIME. HAVEN'T YOU?
CLASSWORK COMES EASILY TO YOU.
LEAVING YOU TIME TO LET YOUR WILD SIDE OUT.

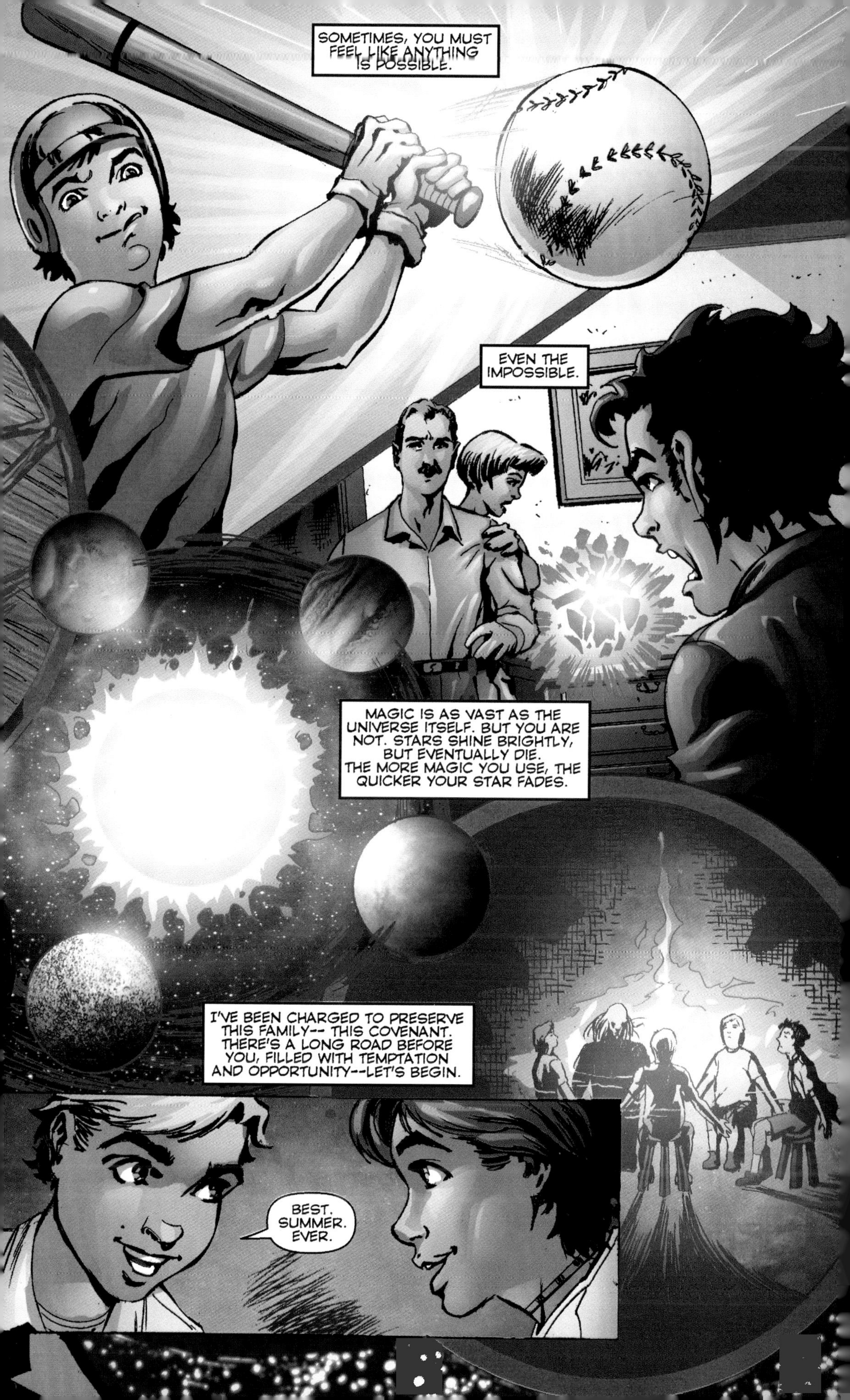
SOMETIMES, YOU MUST FEEL LIKE ANYTHING IS POSSIBLE.
EVEN THE IMPOSSIBLE.
MAGIC IS AS VAST AS THE UNIVERSE ITSELF. BUT YOU ARE NOT. STARS SHINE BRIGHTLY, BUT EVENTUALLY DIE. THE MORE MAGIC YOU USE, THE QUICKER YOUR STAR FADES.
I'VE BEEN CHARGED TO PRESERVE THIS FAMILY-- THIS COVENANT. THERE'S A LONG ROAD BEFORE YOU, FILLED WITH TEMPTATION AND OPPORTUNITY--LET'S BEGIN.
BEST. SUMMER. EVER.

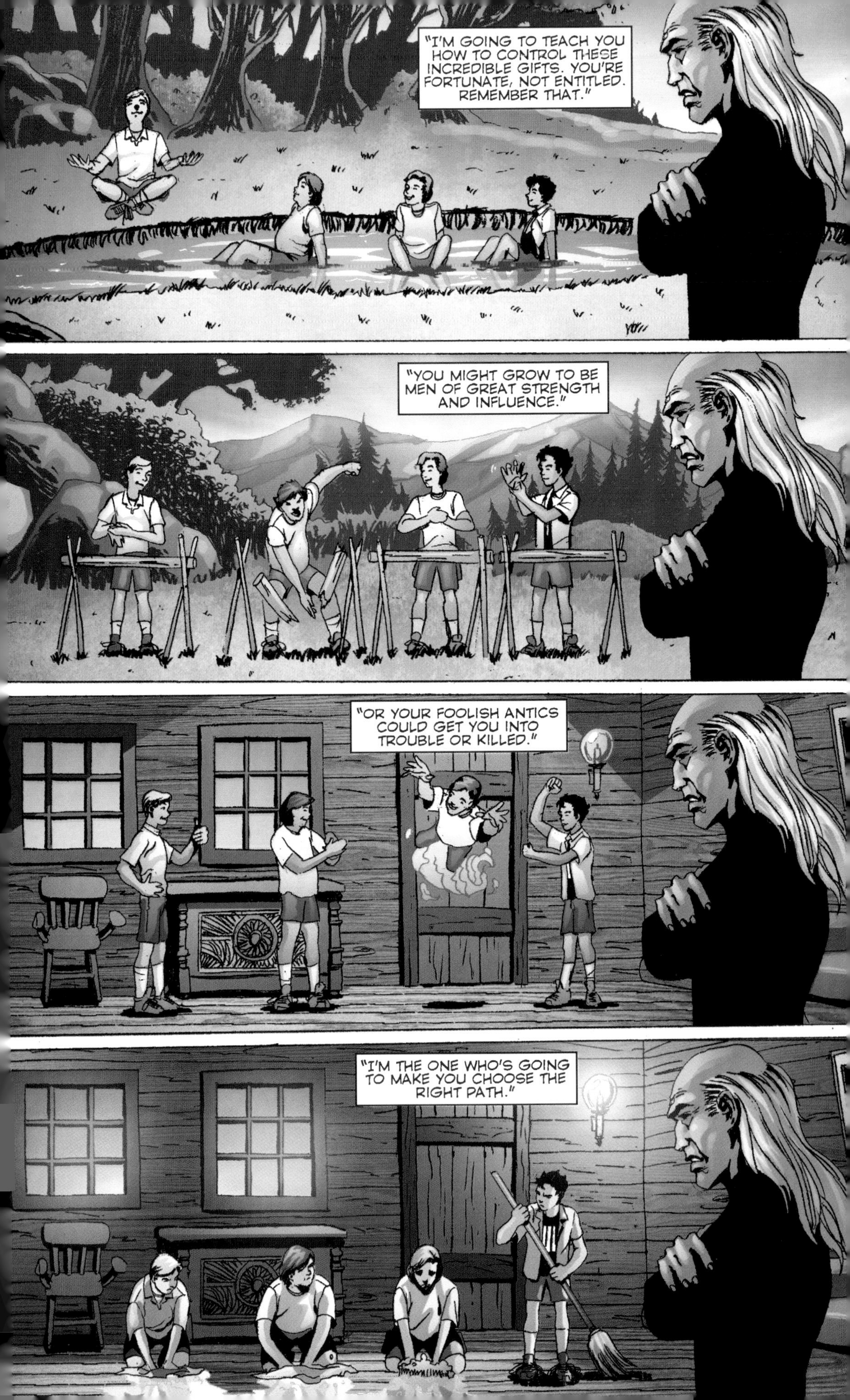
"I'M GOING TO TEACH YOU HOW TO CONTROL THESE INCREDIBLE GIFTS. YOU'RE FORTUNATE, NOT ENTITLED. REMEMBER THAT."
"YOU MIGHT GROW TO BE MEN OF GREAT STRENGTH AND INFLUENCE."
"OR YOUR FOOLISH ANTICS COULD GET YOU INTO TROUBLE OR KILLED."
"I'M THE ONE WHO'S GOING TO MAKE YOU CHOOSE THE RIGHT PATH."

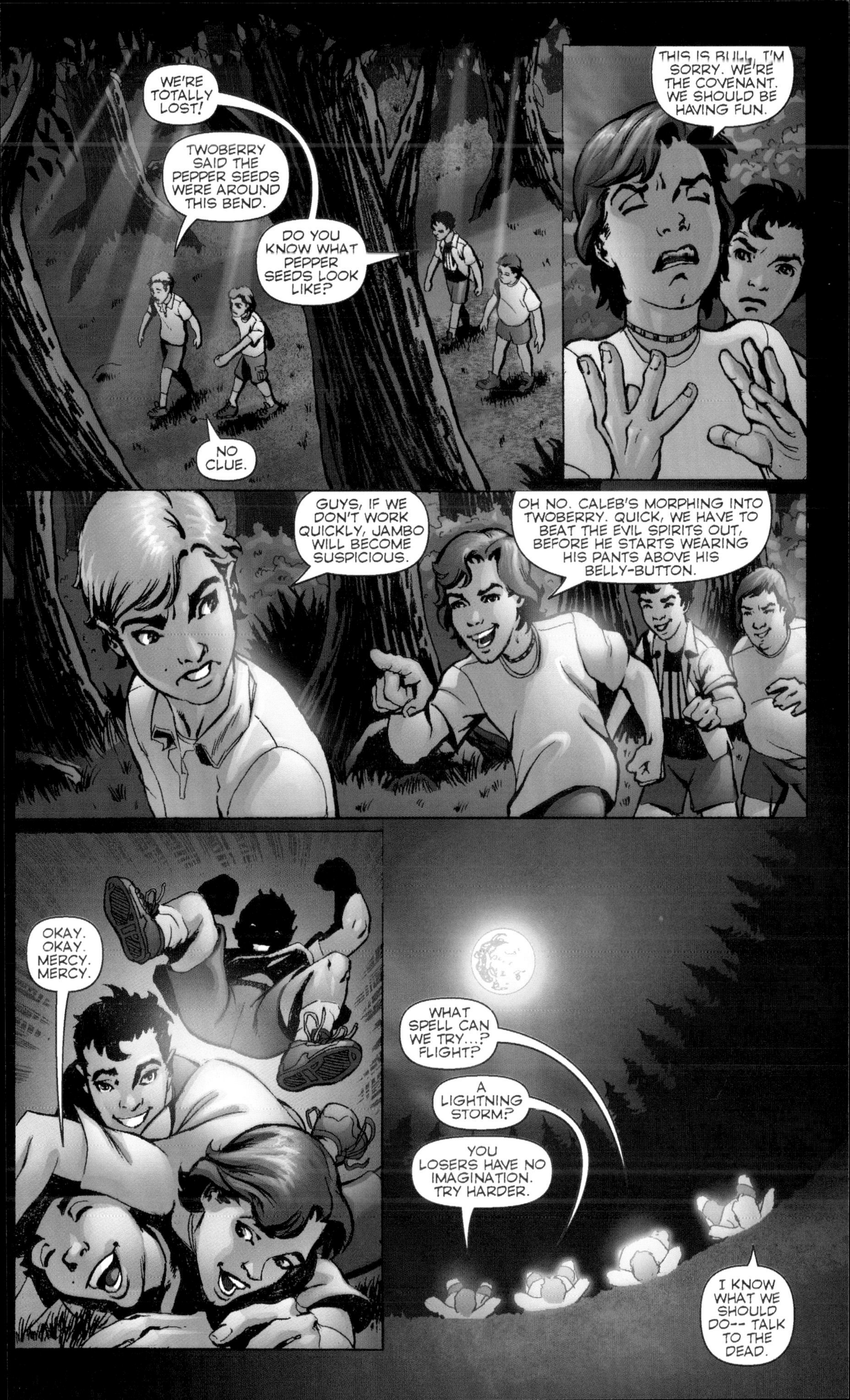
WE'RE TOTALLY LOST!
TWOBERRY SAID THE PEPPER SEEDS WERE AROUND THIS BEND.
DO YOU KNOW WHAT PEPPER SEEDS LOOK LIKE?
NO CLUE.
THIS IS BULL, I'M SORRY. WE'RE THE COVENANT. WE SHOULD BE HAVING FUN.
GUYS, IF WE DON'T WORK QUICKLY, JAMBO WILL BECOME SUSPICIOUS.
OH NO. CALEB'S MORPHING INTO TWOBERRY. QUICK, WE HAVE TO BEAT THE EVIL SPIRITS OUT, BEFORE HE STARTS WEARING HIS PANTS ABOVE HIS BELLY-BUTTON.
OKAY. OKAY. MERCY. MERCY.
WHAT SPELL CAN WE TRY...? FLIGHT?
A LIGHTNING STORM?
YOU LOSERS HAVE NO IMAGINATION. TRY HARDER.
I KNOW WHAT WE SHOULD DO-- TALK TO THE DEAD.

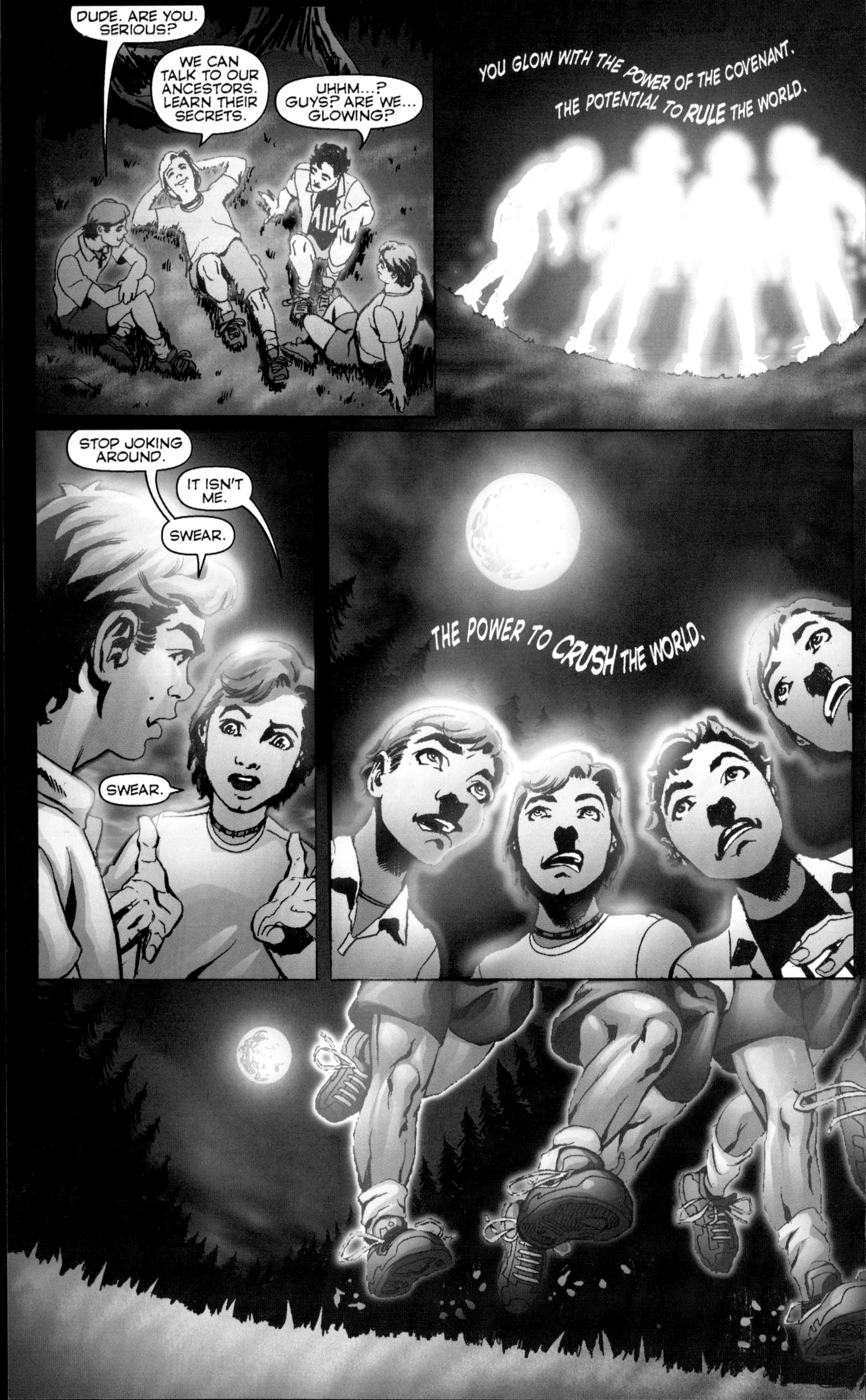
DUDE. ARE YOU. SERIOUS?
WE CAN TALK TO OUR ANCESTORS. LEARN THEIR SECRETS.
UHHM...? GUYS? ARE WE... GLOWING?
YOU GLOW WITH THE POWER OF THE COVENANT.
THE POTENTIAL TO RULE THE WORLD.
STOP JOKING AROUND.
IT ISN'T ME.
SWEAR.
SWEAR.
THE POWER TO CRUSH THE WORLD.

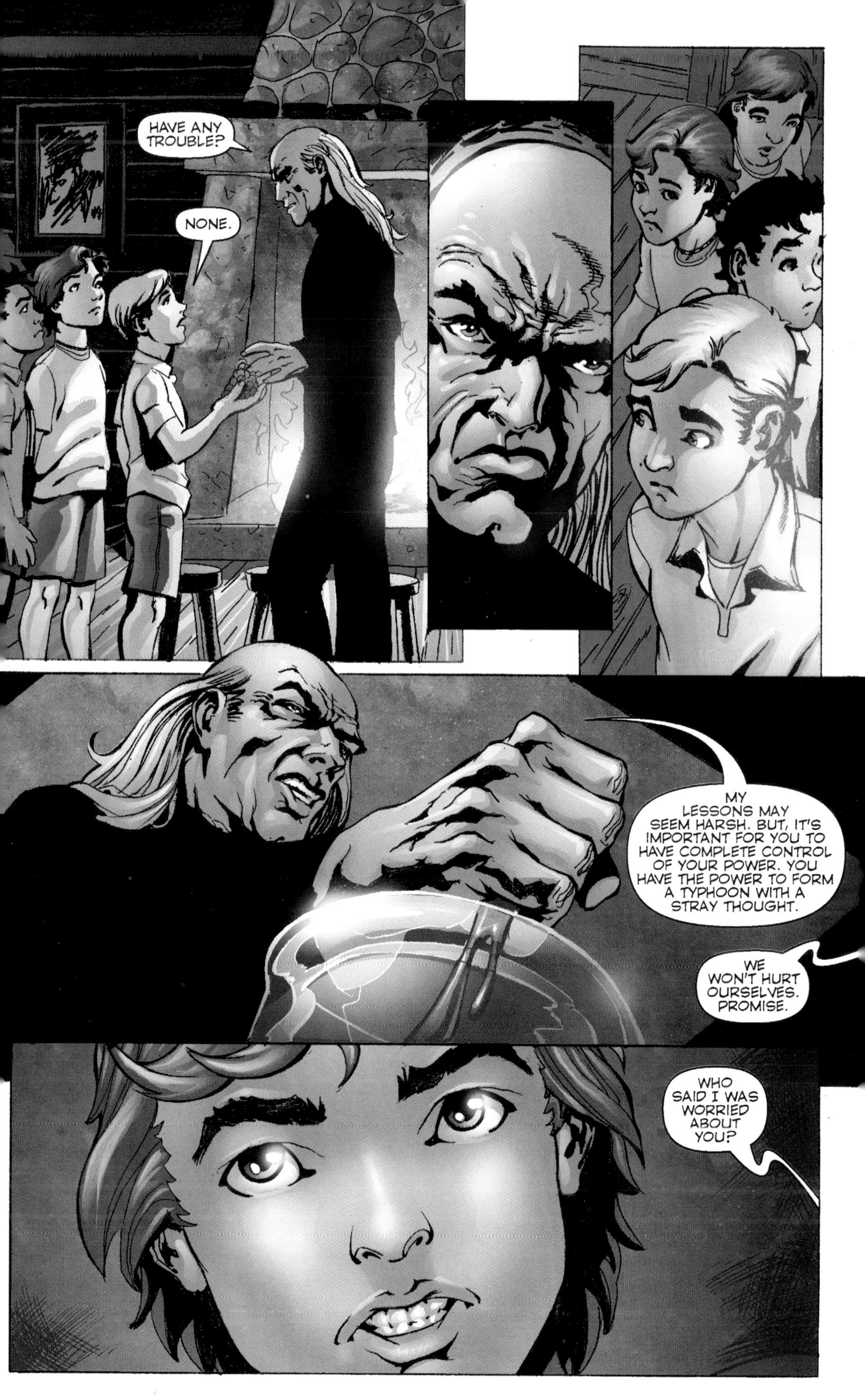
HAVE ANY TROUBLE?
NONE.
MY LESSONS MAY SEEM HARSH. BUT, IT'S IMPORTANT FOR YOU TO HAVE COMPLETE CONTROL OF YOUR POWER. YOU HAVE THE POWER TO FORM A TYPHOON WITH A STRAY THOUGHT.
WE WON'T HURT OURSELVES. PROMISE.
WHO SAID I WAS WORRIED ABOUT YOU?

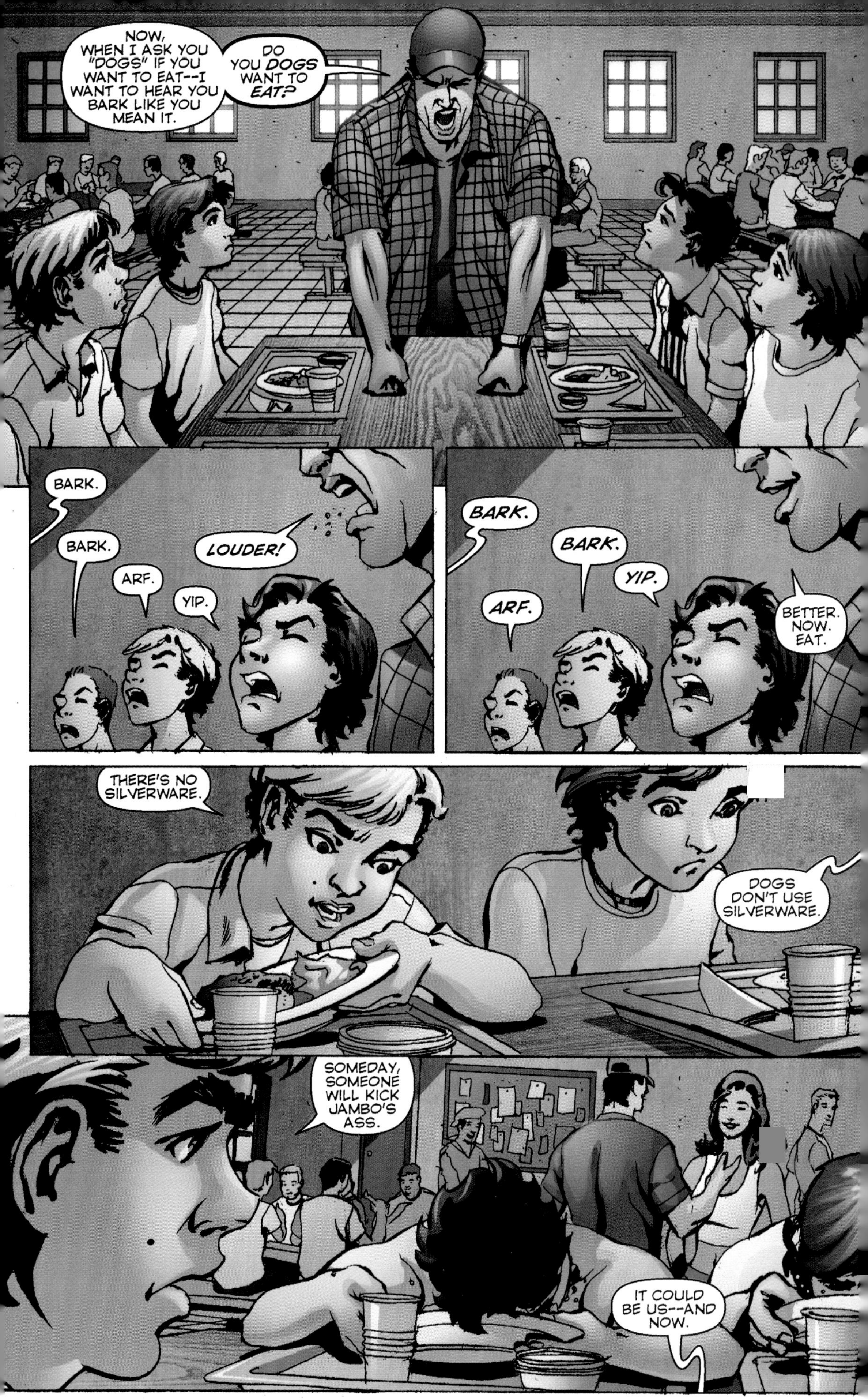
NOW, WHEN I ASK YOU "DOGS" IF YOU WANT TO EAT--I WANT TO HEAR YOU BARK LIKE YOU MEAN IT.
DO YOU DOGS WANT TO EAT?
BARK.
BARK.
ARF.
YIP.
LOUDER!
BARK.
BARK.
ARF.
YIP.
BETTER. NOW. EAT.
THERE'S NO SILVERWARE.
DOGS DON'T USE SILVERWARE.
SOMEDAY, SOMEONE WILL KICK JAMBO'S ASS.
IT COULD BE US--AND NOW.

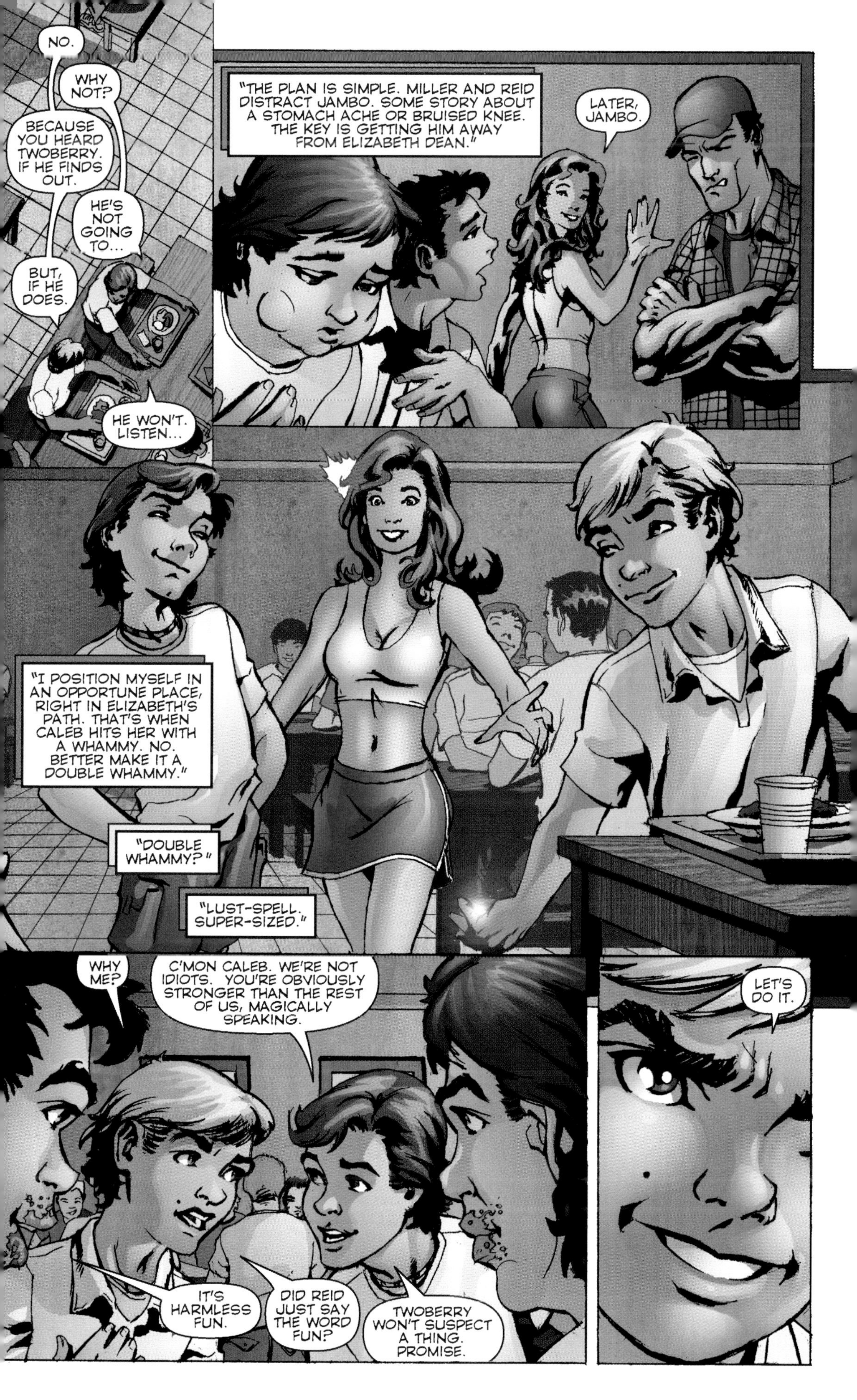
NO.
WHY NOT?
BECAUSE YOU HEARD TWOBERRY. IF HE FINDS OUT.
HE'S NOT GOING TO...
BUT, IF HE DOES.
HE WON'T. LISTEN...
"THE PLAN IS SIMPLE. MILLER AND REID DISTRACT JAMBO. SOME STORY ABOUT A STOMACH ACHE OR BRUISED KNEE. THE KEY IS GETTING HIM AWAY FROM ELIZABETH DEAN."
LATER, JAMBO.
"I POSITION MYSELF IN AN OPPORTUNE PLACE, RIGHT IN ELIZABETH'S PATH. THAT'S WHEN CALEB HITS HER WITH A WHAMMY. NO. BETTER MAKE IT A DOUBLE WHAMMY."
"DOUBLE WHAMMY?"
"LUST-SPELL. SUPER-SIZED."
WHY ME?
C'MON CALEB. WE'RE NOT IDIOTS. YOU'RE OBVIOUSLY STRONGER THAN THE REST OF US, MAGICALLY SPEAKING.
IT'S HARMLESS FUN.
DID REID JUST SAY THE WORD FUN?
TWOBERRY WON'T SUSPECT A THING. PROMISE.
LET'S DO IT.

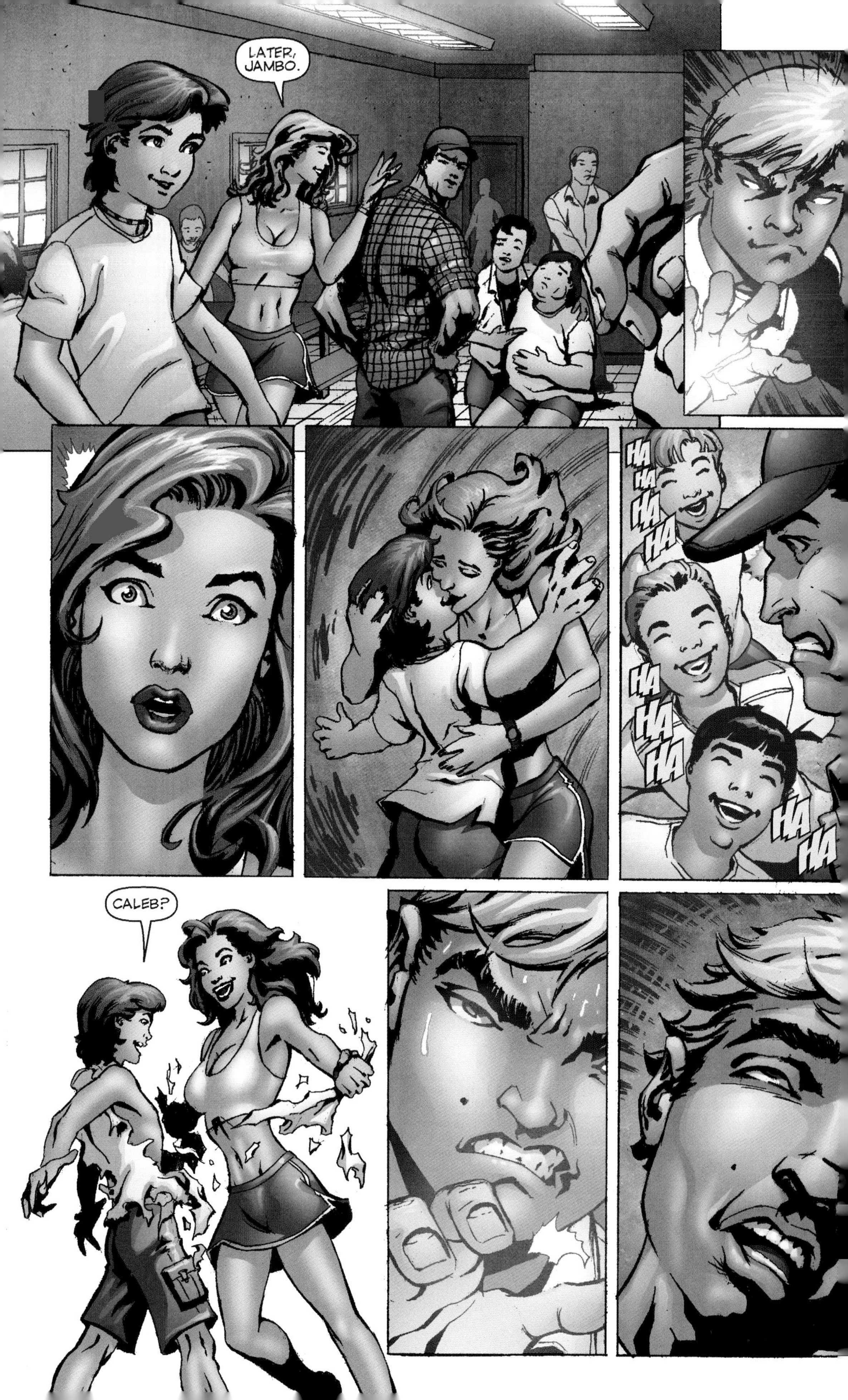
LATER, JAMBO.
HA HA HA HA
HA HA HA
HA HA
CALEB?

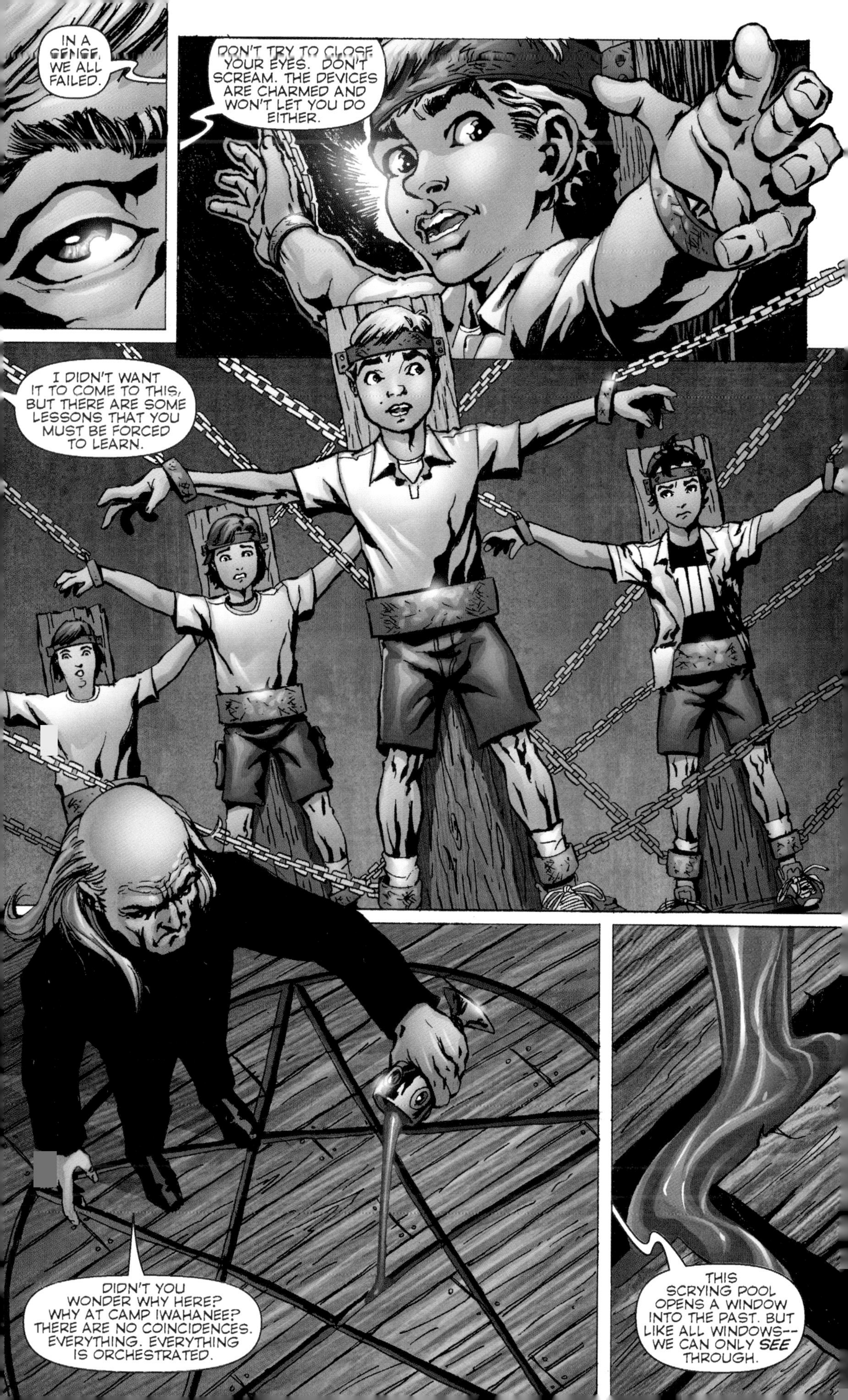
IN A SENSE, WE ALL FAILED.
DON'T TRY TO CLOSE YOUR EYES. DON'T SCREAM. THE DEVICES ARE CHARMED AND WON'T LET YOU DO EITHER.
I DIDN'T WANT IT TO COME TO THIS, BUT THERE ARE SOME LESSONS THAT YOU MUST BE FORCED TO LEARN.
DIDN'T YOU WONDER WHY HERE? WHY AT CAMP IWAHANEE? THERE ARE NO COINCIDENCES. EVERYTHING. EVERYTHING IS ORCHESTRATED.
THIS SCRYING POOL OPENS A WINDOW INTO THE PAST. BUT LIKE ALL WINDOWS-- WE CAN ONLY SEE THROUGH.

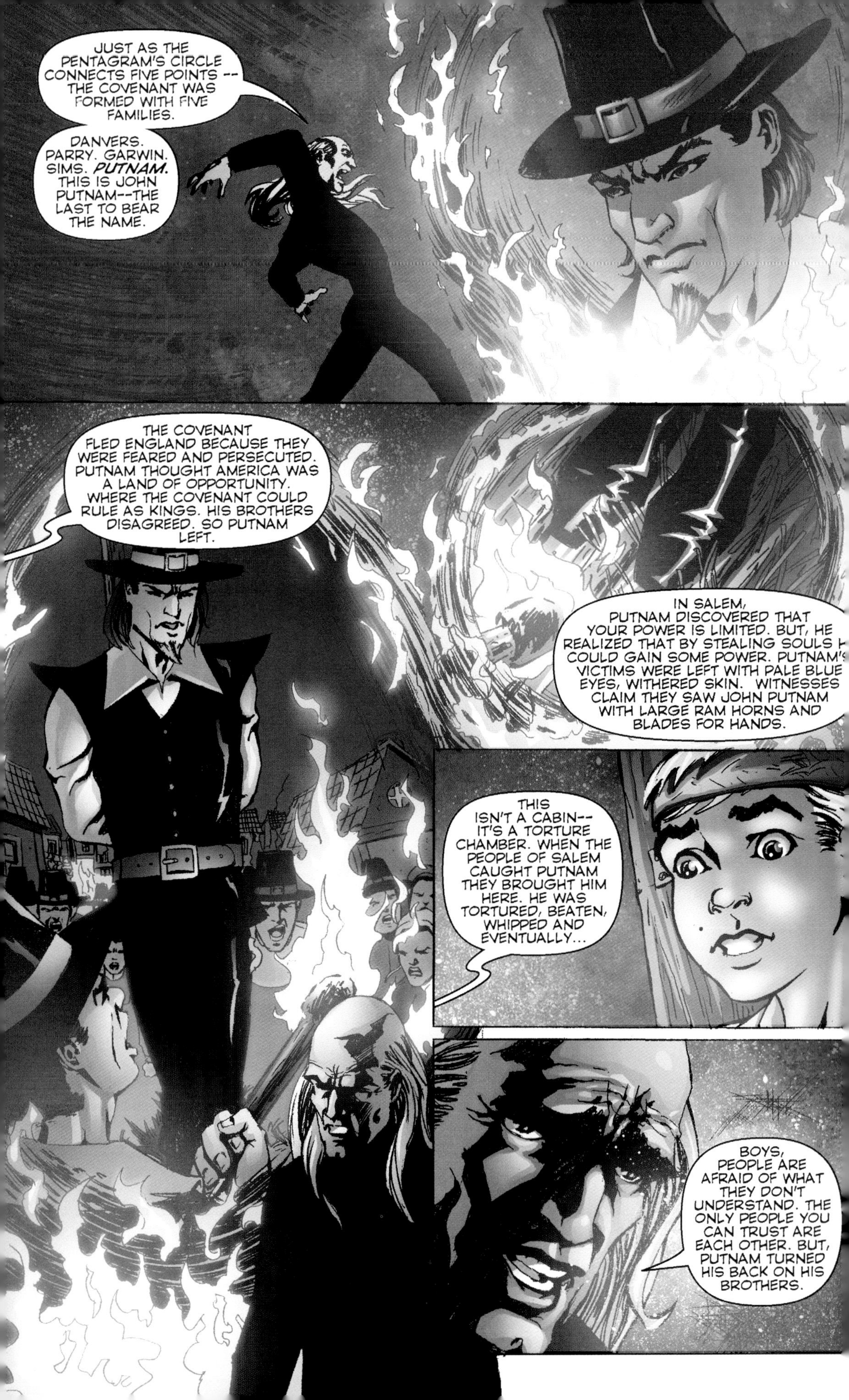
JUST AS THE PENTAGRAM'S CIRCLE CONNECTS FIVE POINTS -- THE COVENANT WAS FORMED WITH FIVE FAMILIES.
DANVERS. PARRY. GARWIN. SIMS. *PUTNAM.* THIS IS JOHN PUTNAM--THE LAST TO BEAR THE NAME.
THE COVENANT FLED ENGLAND BECAUSE THEY WERE FEARED AND PERSECUTED. PUTNAM THOUGHT AMERICA WAS A LAND OF OPPORTUNITY. WHERE THE COVENANT COULD RULE AS KINGS. HIS BROTHERS DISAGREED. SO PUTNAM LEFT.
IN SALEM, PUTNAM DISCOVERED THAT YOUR POWER IS LIMITED. BUT, HE REALIZED THAT BY STEALING SOULS HE COULD GAIN SOME POWER. PUTNAM'S VICTIMS WERE LEFT WITH PALE BLUE EYES, WITHERED SKIN. WITNESSES CLAIM THEY SAW JOHN PUTNAM WITH LARGE RAM HORNS AND BLADES FOR HANDS.
THIS ISN'T A CABIN-- IT'S A TORTURE CHAMBER. WHEN THE PEOPLE OF SALEM CAUGHT PUTNAM THEY BROUGHT HIM HERE. HE WAS TORTURED, BEATEN, WHIPPED AND EVENTUALLY...
BOYS, PEOPLE ARE AFRAID OF WHAT THEY DON'T UNDERSTAND. THE ONLY PEOPLE YOU CAN TRUST ARE EACH OTHER. BUT, PUTNAM TURNED HIS BACK ON HIS BROTHERS.

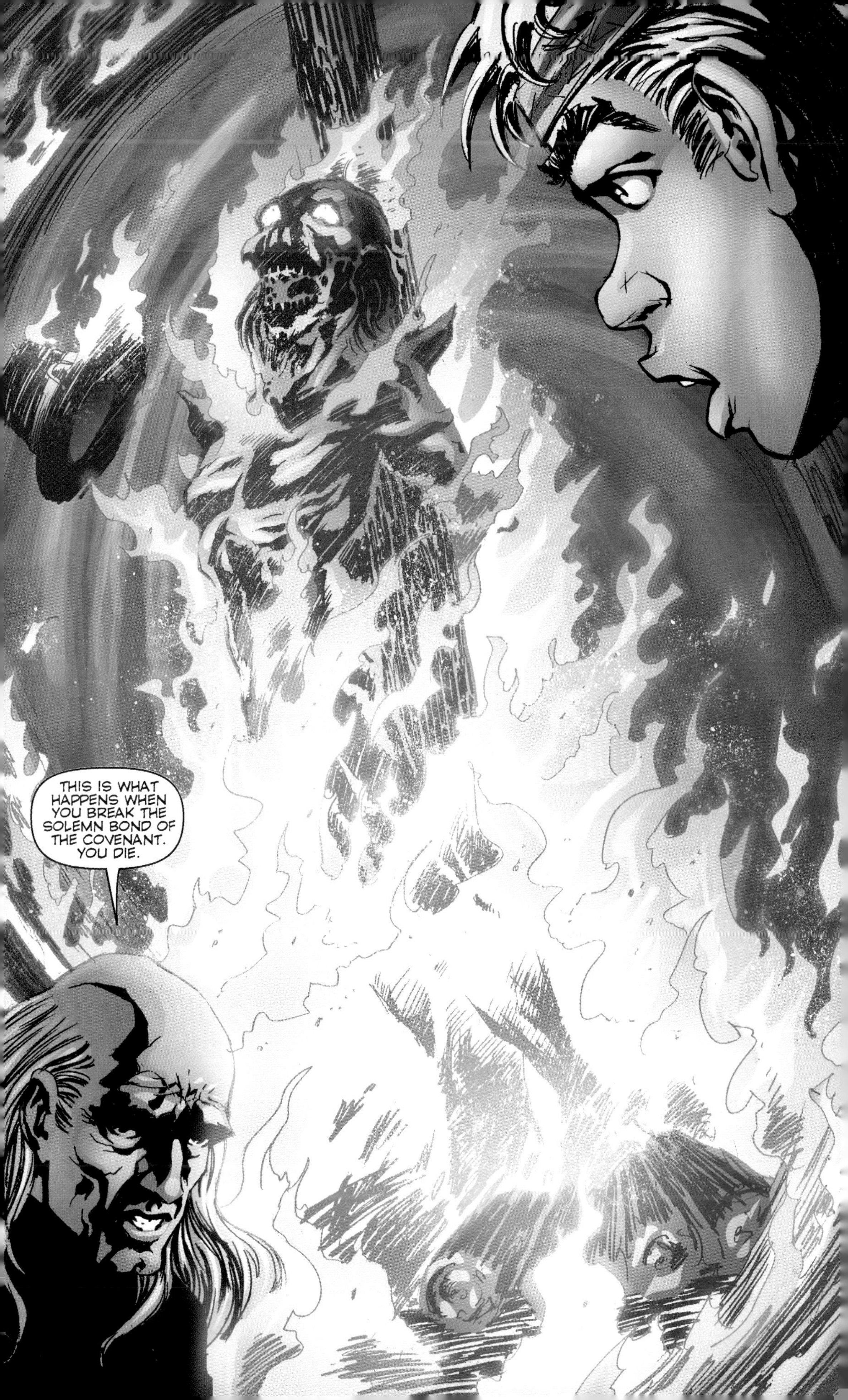
THIS IS WHAT HAPPENS WHEN YOU BREAK THE SOLEMN BOND OF THE COVENANT. YOU DIE.

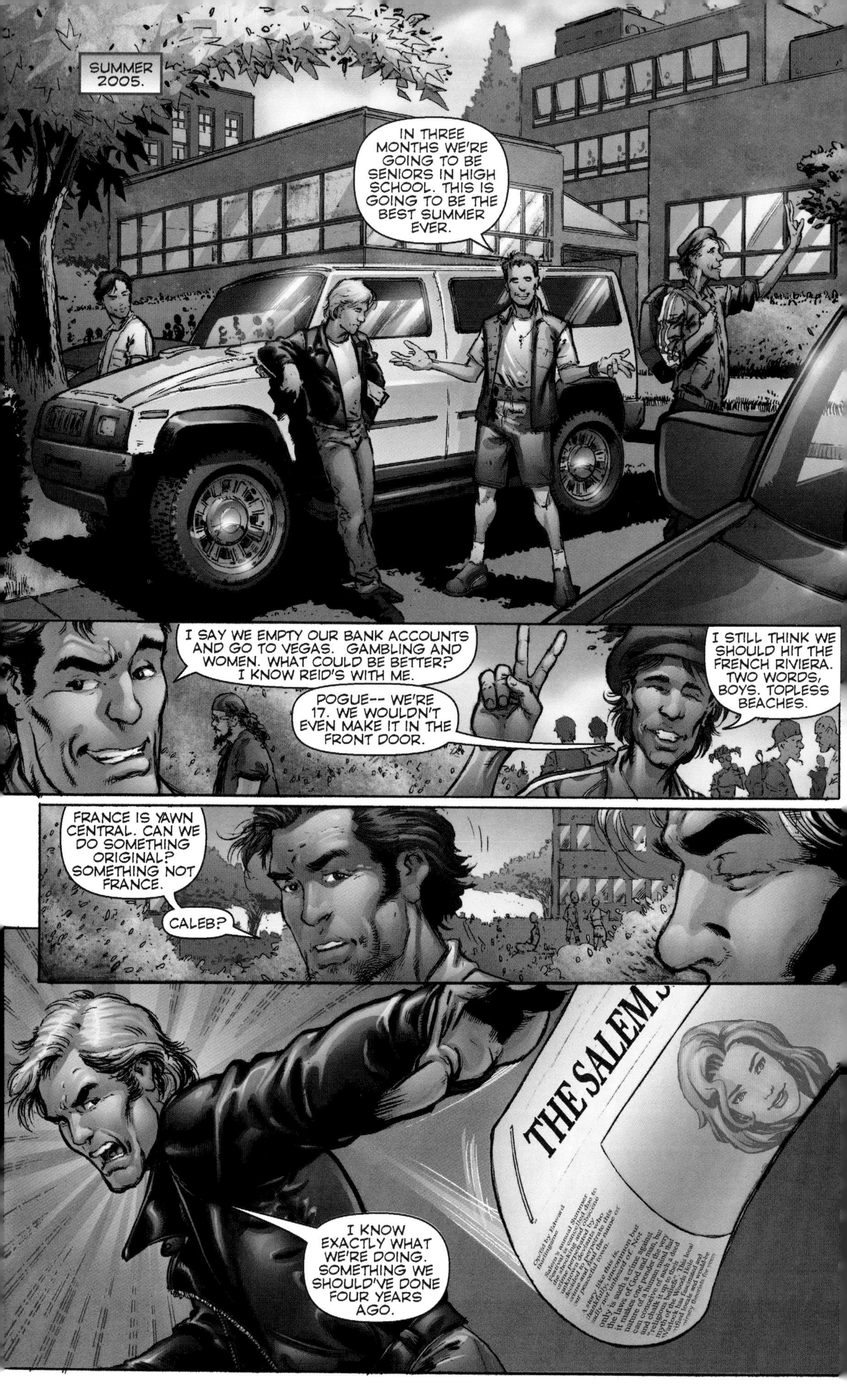
SUMMER 2005.
IN THREE MONTHS WE'RE GOING TO BE SENIORS IN HIGH SCHOOL. THIS IS GOING TO BE THE BEST SUMMER EVER.
I SAY WE EMPTY OUR BANK ACCOUNTS AND GO TO VEGAS. GAMBLING AND WOMEN. WHAT COULD BE BETTER? I KNOW REID'S WITH ME.
POGUE-- WE'RE 17. WE WOULDN'T EVEN MAKE IT IN THE FRONT DOOR.
I STILL THINK WE SHOULD HIT THE FRENCH RIVIERA. TWO WORDS, BOYS. TOPLESS BEACHES.
FRANCE IS YAWN CENTRAL. CAN WE DO SOMETHING ORIGINAL? SOMETHING NOT FRANCE.
CALEB?
THE SALEM
I KNOW EXACTLY WHAT WE'RE DOING. SOMETHING WE SHOULD'VE DONE FOUR YEARS AGO.

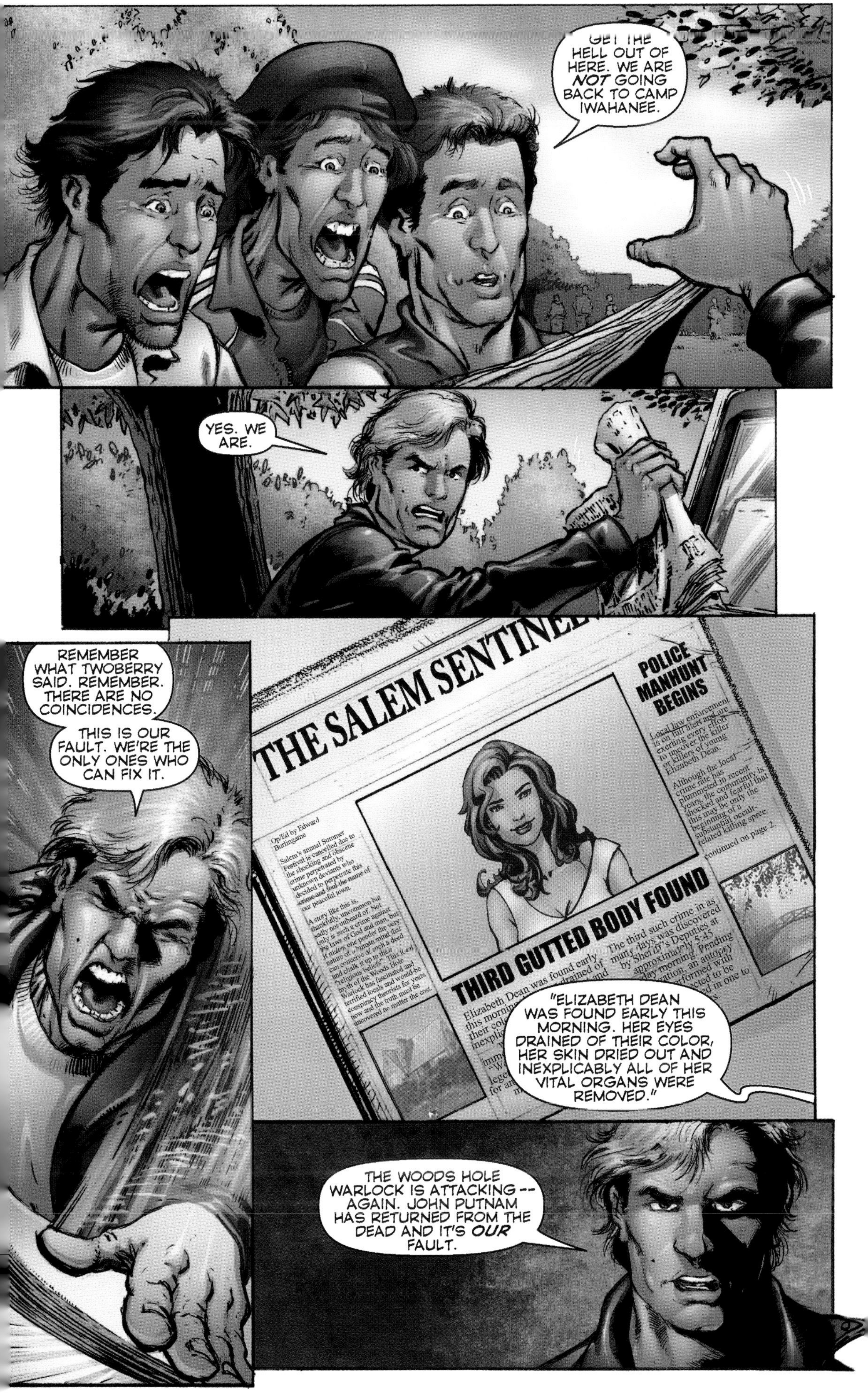
GET THE HELL OUT OF HERE. WE ARE *NOT* GOING BACK TO CAMP IWAHANEE.
YES. WE ARE.
REMEMBER WHAT TWOBERRY SAID. REMEMBER. THERE ARE NO COINCIDENCES.
THIS IS OUR FAULT. WE'RE THE ONLY ONES WHO CAN FIX IT.
THE SALEM SENTINE
POLICE MANHUNT BEGINS
THIRD GUTTED BODY FOUND
"ELIZABETH DEAN WAS FOUND EARLY THIS MORNING. HER EYES DRAINED OF THEIR COLOR, HER SKIN DRIED OUT AND INEXPLICABLY ALL OF HER VITAL ORGANS WERE REMOVED."
THE WOODS HOLE WARLOCK IS ATTACKING -- AGAIN. JOHN PUTNAM HAS RETURNED FROM THE DEAD AND IT'S *OUR* FAULT.

Art by:

**Tyler Kirkham**

**Matt "Batt" Banning**

and **Brian Buccellato**

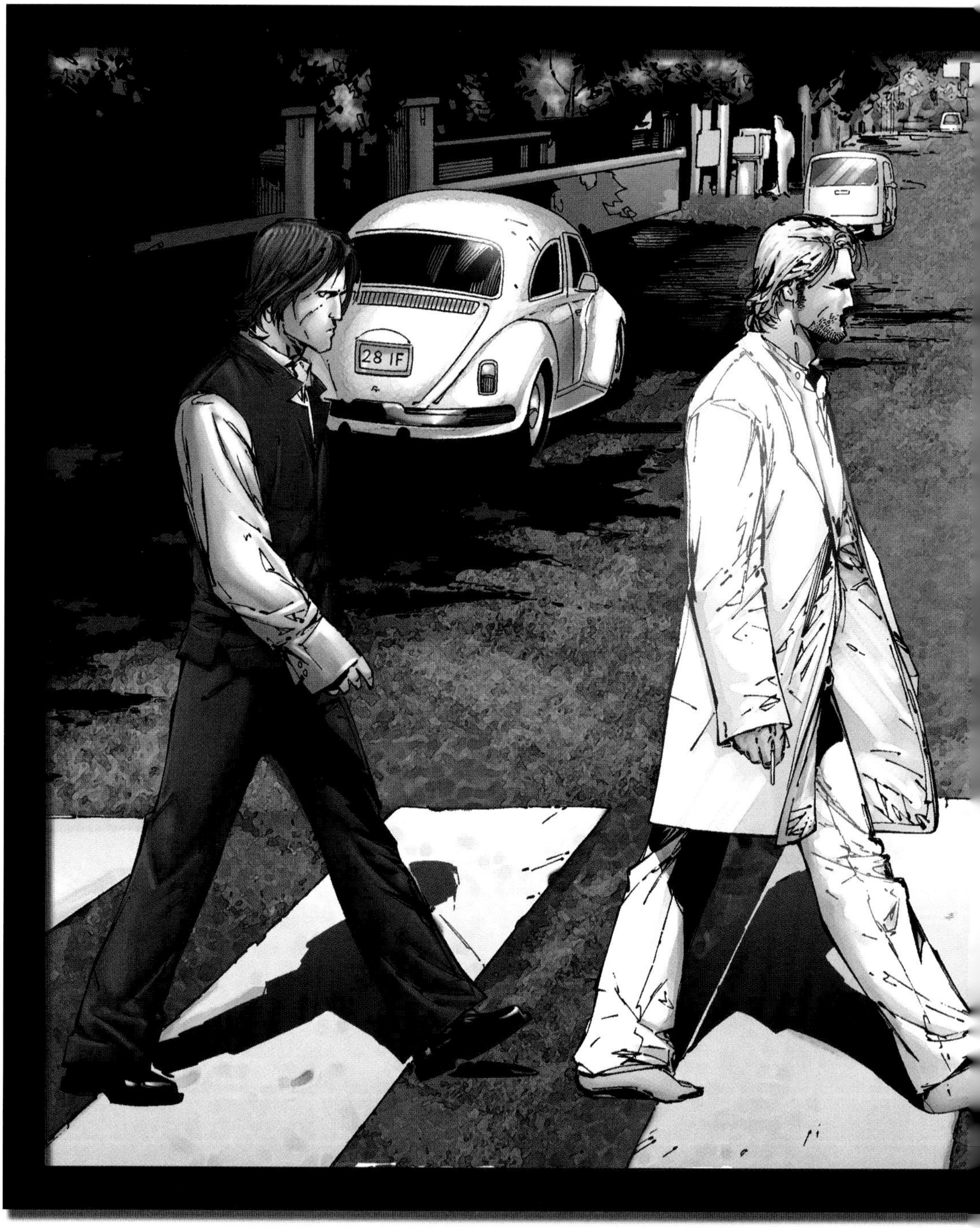

28 IF

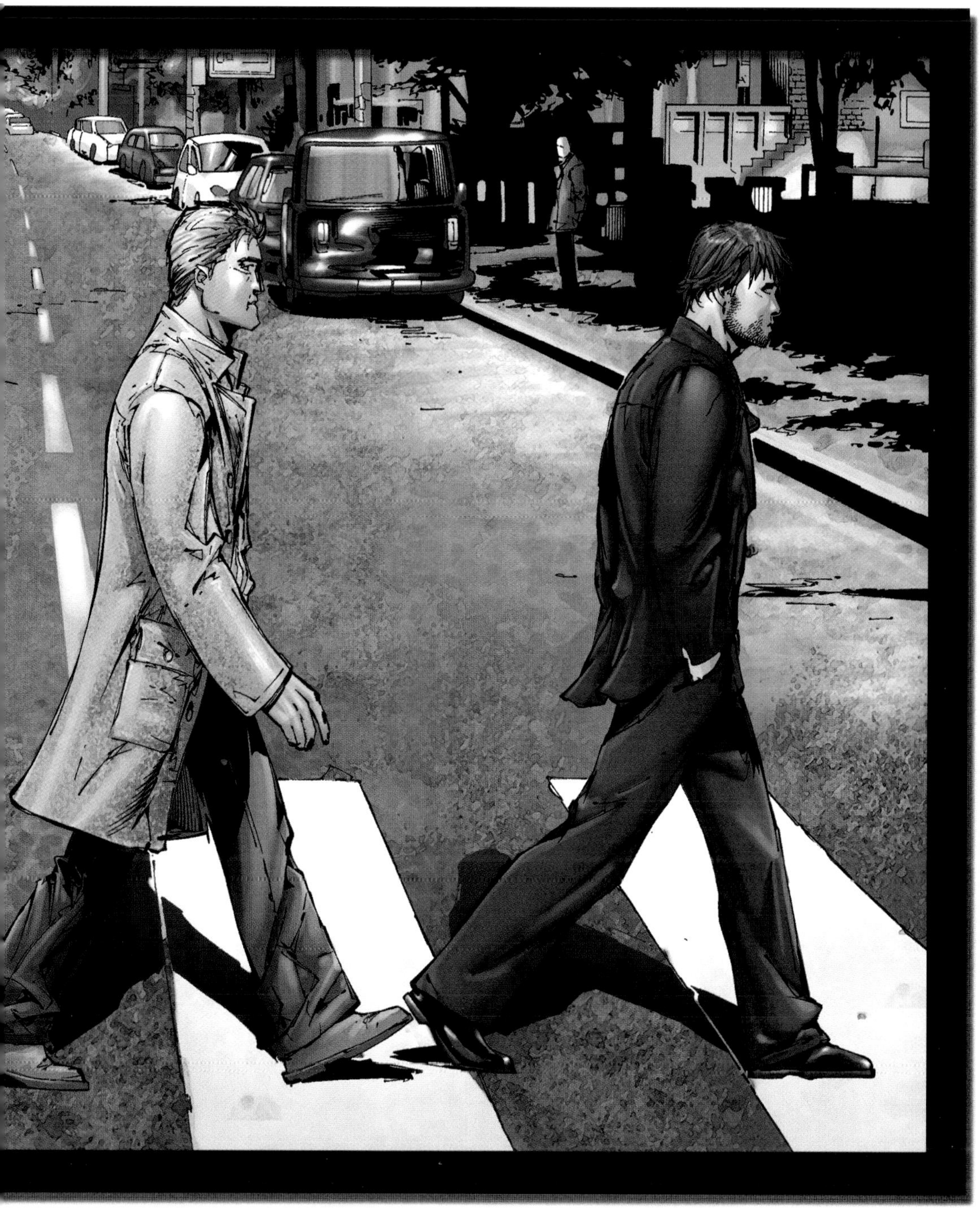

# CHAPTER 2

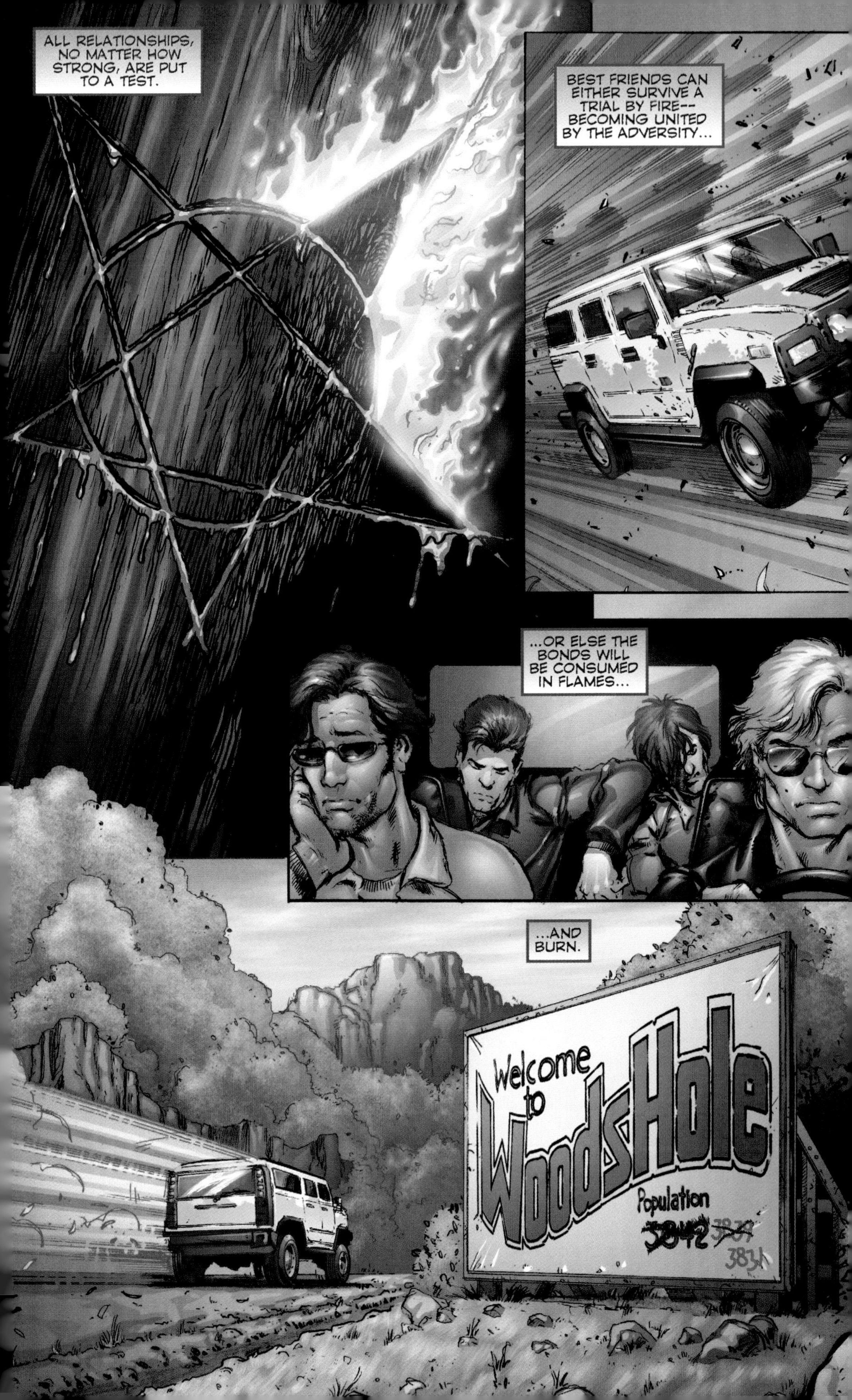
ALL RELATIONSHIPS, NO MATTER HOW STRONG, ARE PUT TO A TEST.
BEST FRIENDS CAN EITHER SURVIVE A TRIAL BY FIRE-- BECOMING UNITED BY THE ADVERSITY...
...OR ELSE THE BONDS WILL BE CONSUMED IN FLAMES...
...AND BURN.
Welcome to WoodsHole
Population
3842 3839
3831

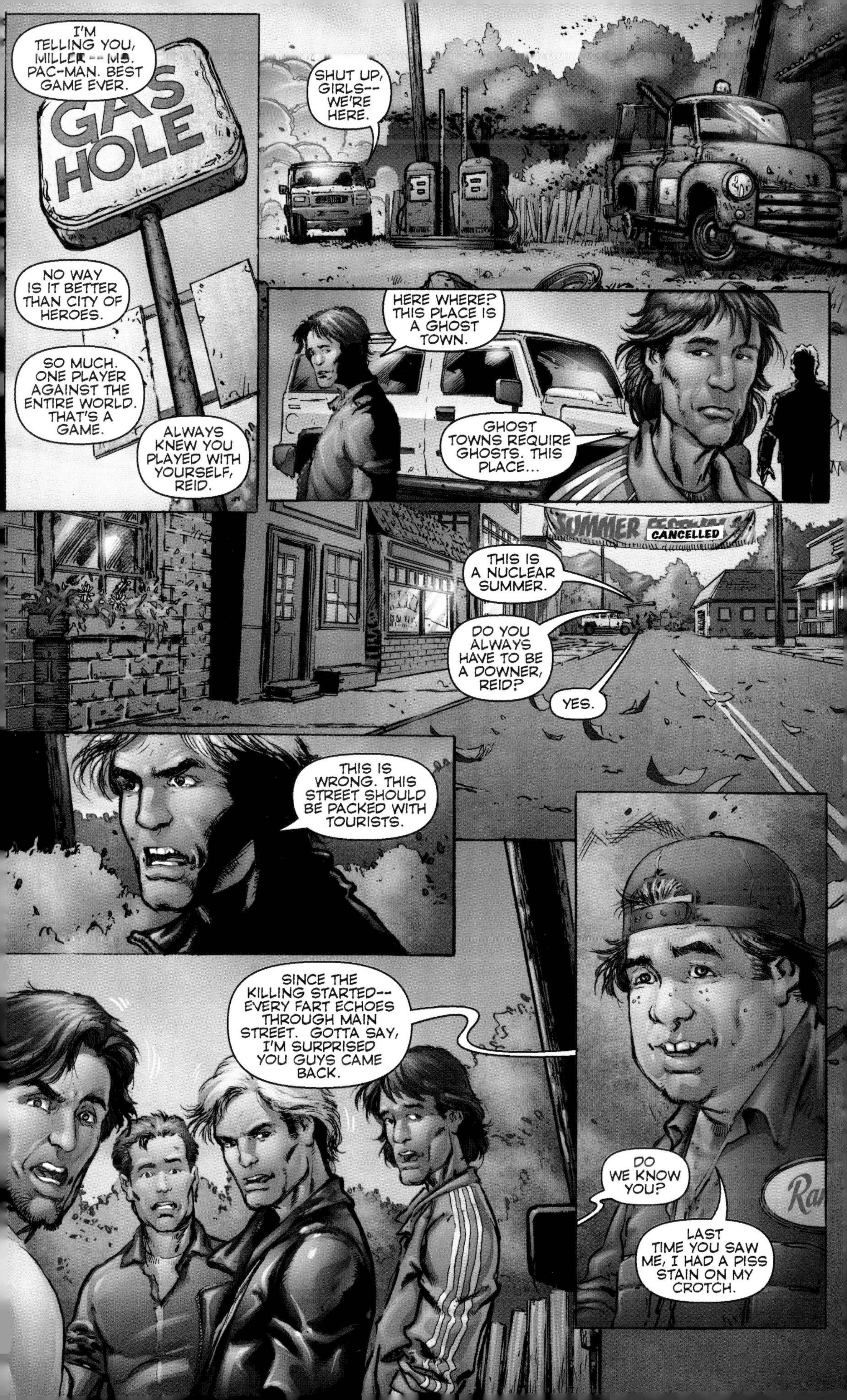
I'M TELLING YOU, MILLER--MS. PAC-MAN. BEST GAME EVER.
GAS HOLE
SHUT UP, GIRLS--WE'RE HERE.
NO WAY IS IT BETTER THAN CITY OF HEROES.
SO MUCH. ONE PLAYER AGAINST THE ENTIRE WORLD. THAT'S A GAME.
ALWAYS KNEW YOU PLAYED WITH YOURSELF, REID.
HERE WHERE? THIS PLACE IS A GHOST TOWN.
GHOST TOWNS REQUIRE GHOSTS. THIS PLACE...
SUMMER
CANCELLED
THIS IS A NUCLEAR SUMMER.
DO YOU ALWAYS HAVE TO BE A DOWNER, REID?
YES.
THIS IS WRONG. THIS STREET SHOULD BE PACKED WITH TOURISTS.
SINCE THE KILLING STARTED--EVERY FART ECHOES THROUGH MAIN STREET. GOTTA SAY, I'M SURPRISED YOU GUYS CAME BACK.
DO WE KNOW YOU?
LAST TIME YOU SAW ME, I HAD A PISS STAIN ON MY CROTCH.

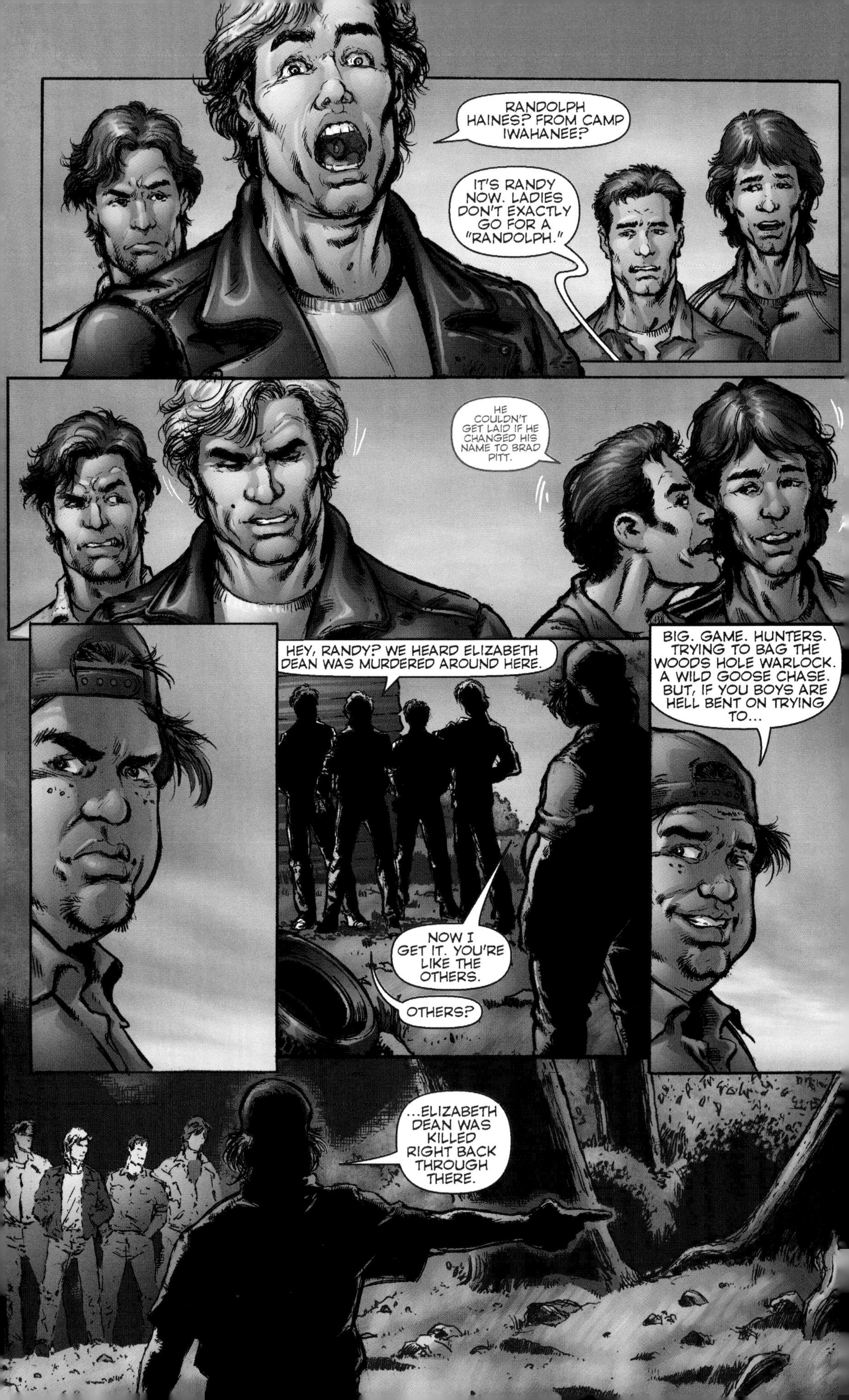
RANDOLPH HAINES? FROM CAMP IWAHANEE?
IT'S RANDY NOW. LADIES DON'T EXACTLY GO FOR A "RANDOLPH."
HE COULDN'T GET LAID IF HE CHANGED HIS NAME TO BRAD PITT.
HEY, RANDY? WE HEARD ELIZABETH DEAN WAS MURDERED AROUND HERE.
NOW I GET IT. YOU'RE LIKE THE OTHERS.
OTHERS?
BIG. GAME. HUNTERS. TRYING TO BAG THE WOODS HOLE WARLOCK. A WILD GOOSE CHASE. BUT, IF YOU BOYS ARE HELL BENT ON TRYING TO...
...ELIZABETH DEAN WAS KILLED RIGHT BACK THROUGH THERE.

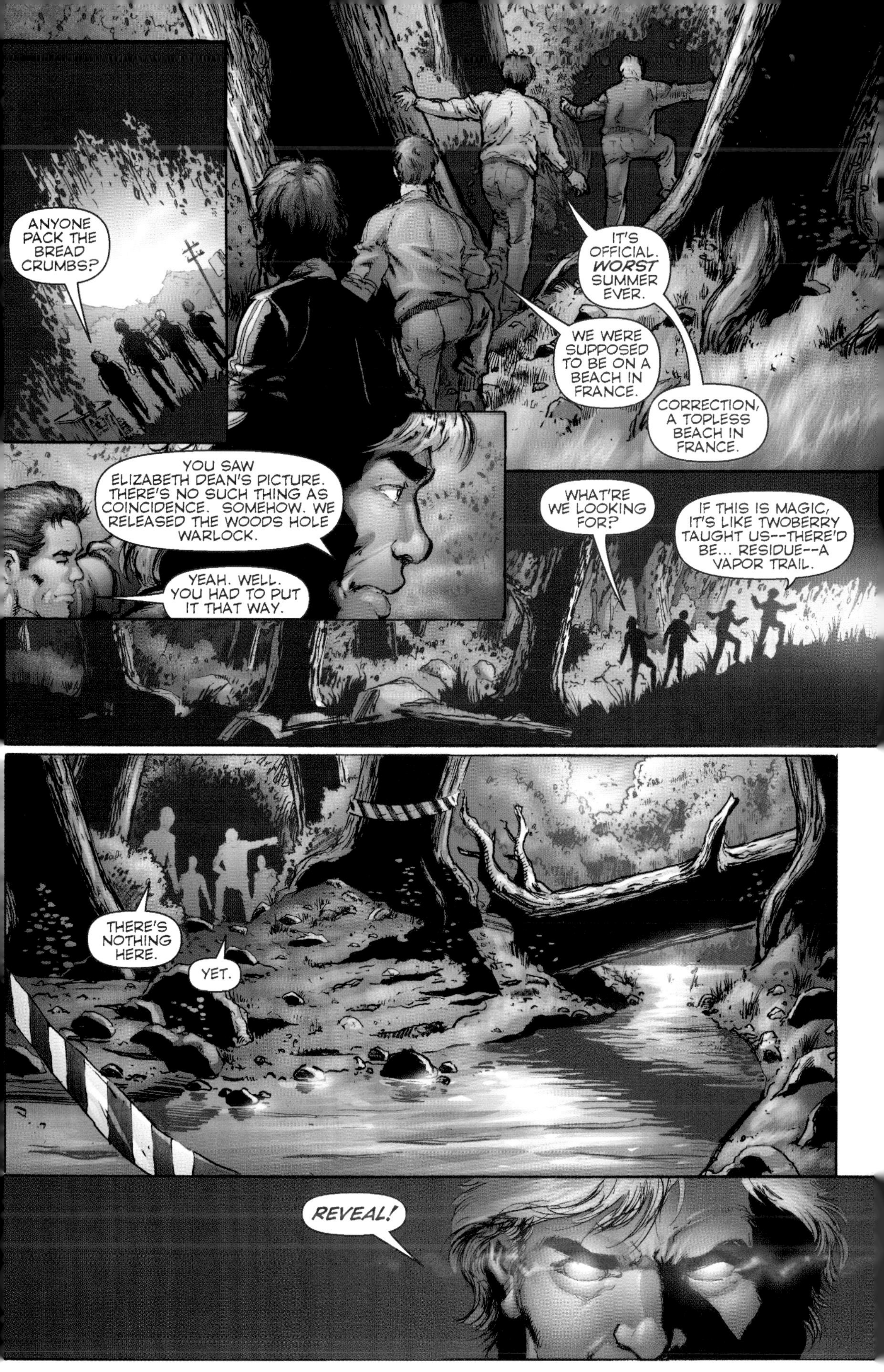
ANYONE PACK THE BREAD CRUMBS?
IT'S OFFICIAL. WORST SUMMER EVER.
WE WERE SUPPOSED TO BE ON A BEACH IN FRANCE.
CORRECTION, A TOPLESS BEACH IN FRANCE.
YOU SAW ELIZABETH DEAN'S PICTURE. THERE'S NO SUCH THING AS COINCIDENCE. SOMEHOW. WE RELEASED THE WOODS HOLE WARLOCK.
YEAH. WELL. YOU HAD TO PUT IT THAT WAY.
WHAT'RE WE LOOKING FOR?
IF THIS IS MAGIC, IT'S LIKE TWOBERRY TAUGHT US--THERE'D BE... RESIDUE--A VAPOR TRAIL.
THERE'S NOTHING HERE.
YET.
REVEAL!

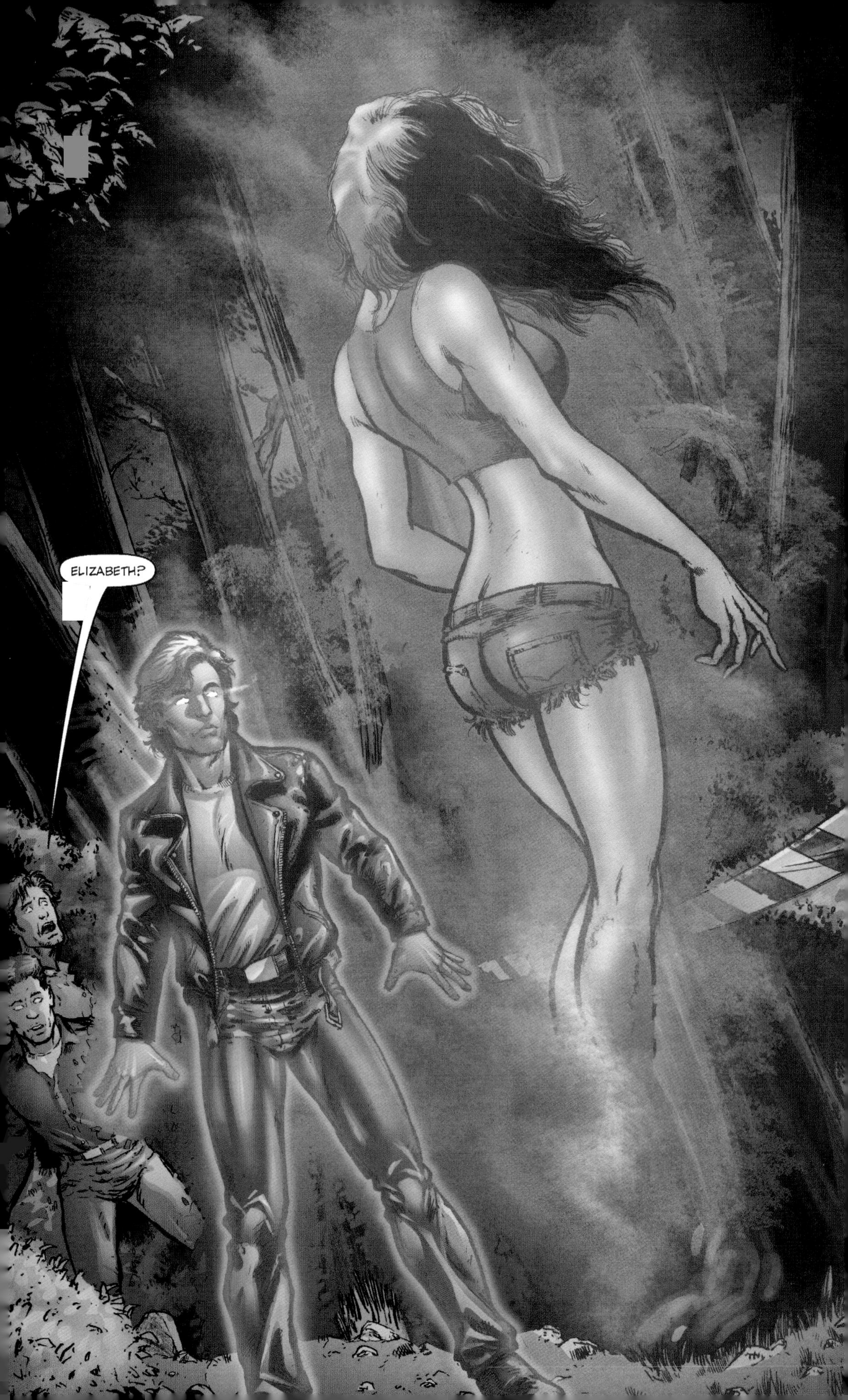
ELIZABETH?

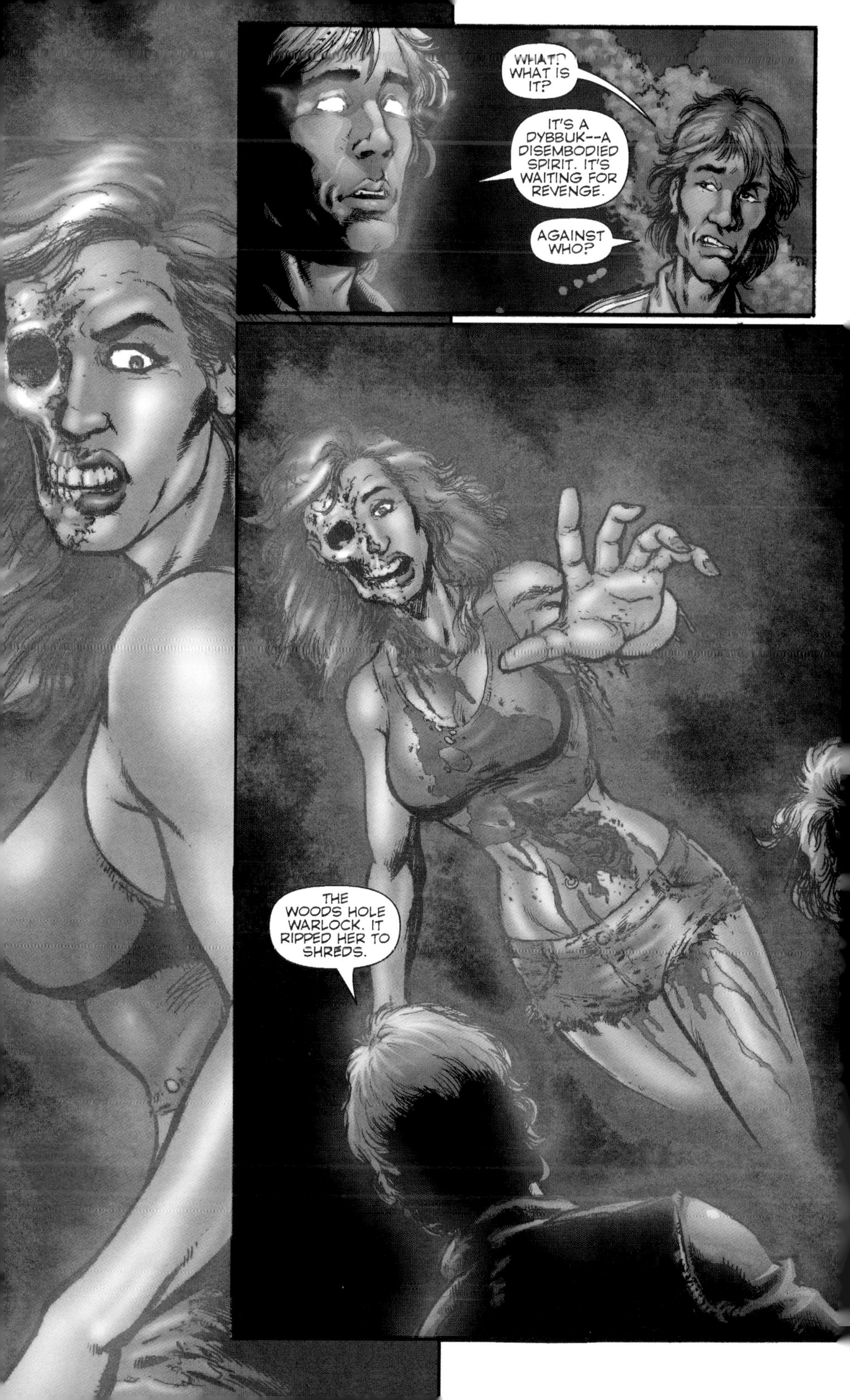
WHAT? WHAT IS IT?
IT'S A DYBBUK--A DISEMBODIED SPIRIT. IT'S WAITING FOR REVENGE.
AGAINST WHO?
THE WOODS HOLE WARLOCK. IT RIPPED HER TO SHREDS.

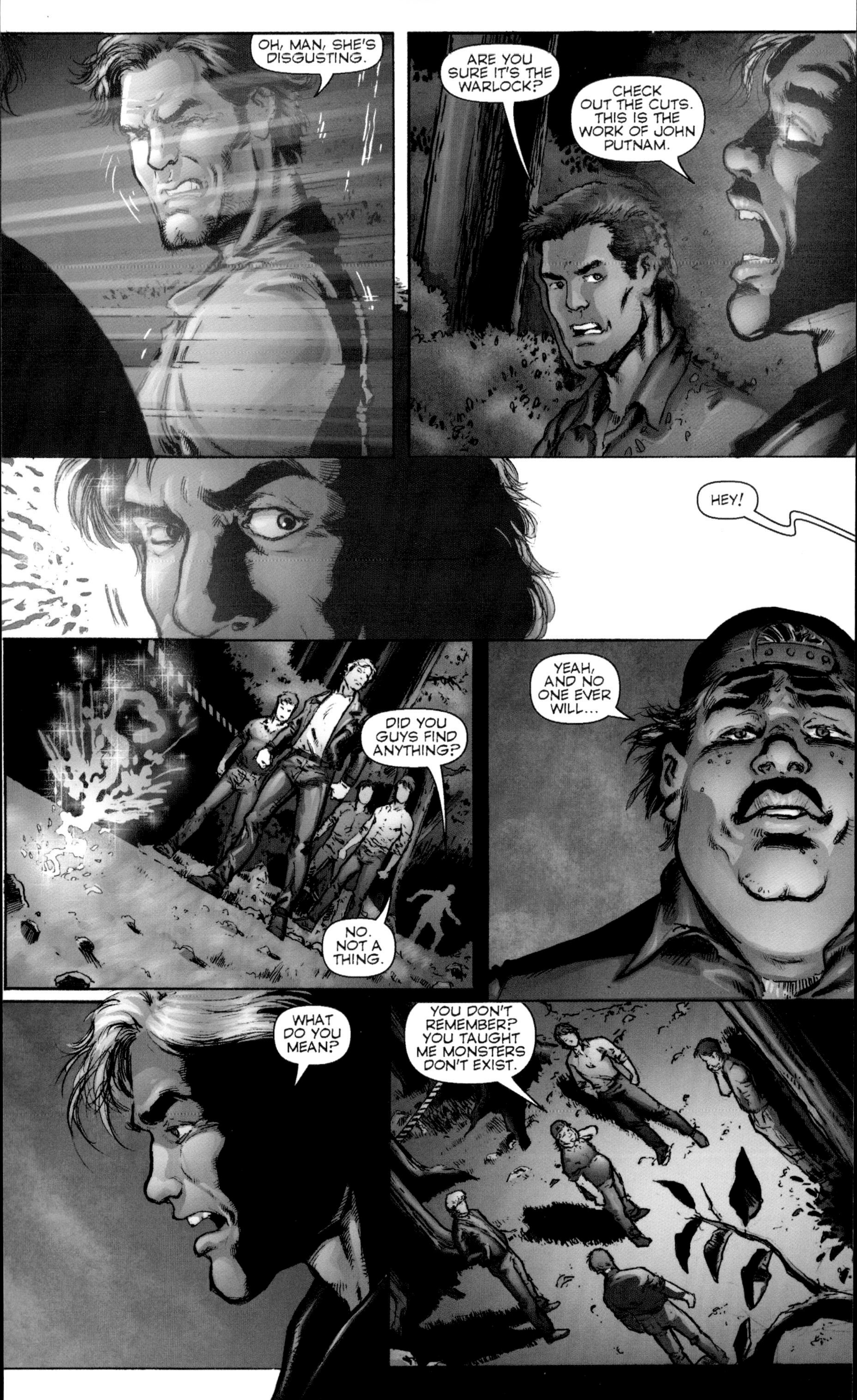
OH, MAN, SHE'S DISGUSTING.
ARE YOU SURE IT'S THE WARLOCK?
CHECK OUT THE CUTS. THIS IS THE WORK OF JOHN PUTNAM.
HEY!
DID YOU GUYS FIND ANYTHING?
NO. NOT A THING.
YEAH, AND NO ONE EVER WILL...
WHAT DO YOU MEAN?
YOU DON'T REMEMBER? YOU TAUGHT ME MONSTERS DON'T EXIST.

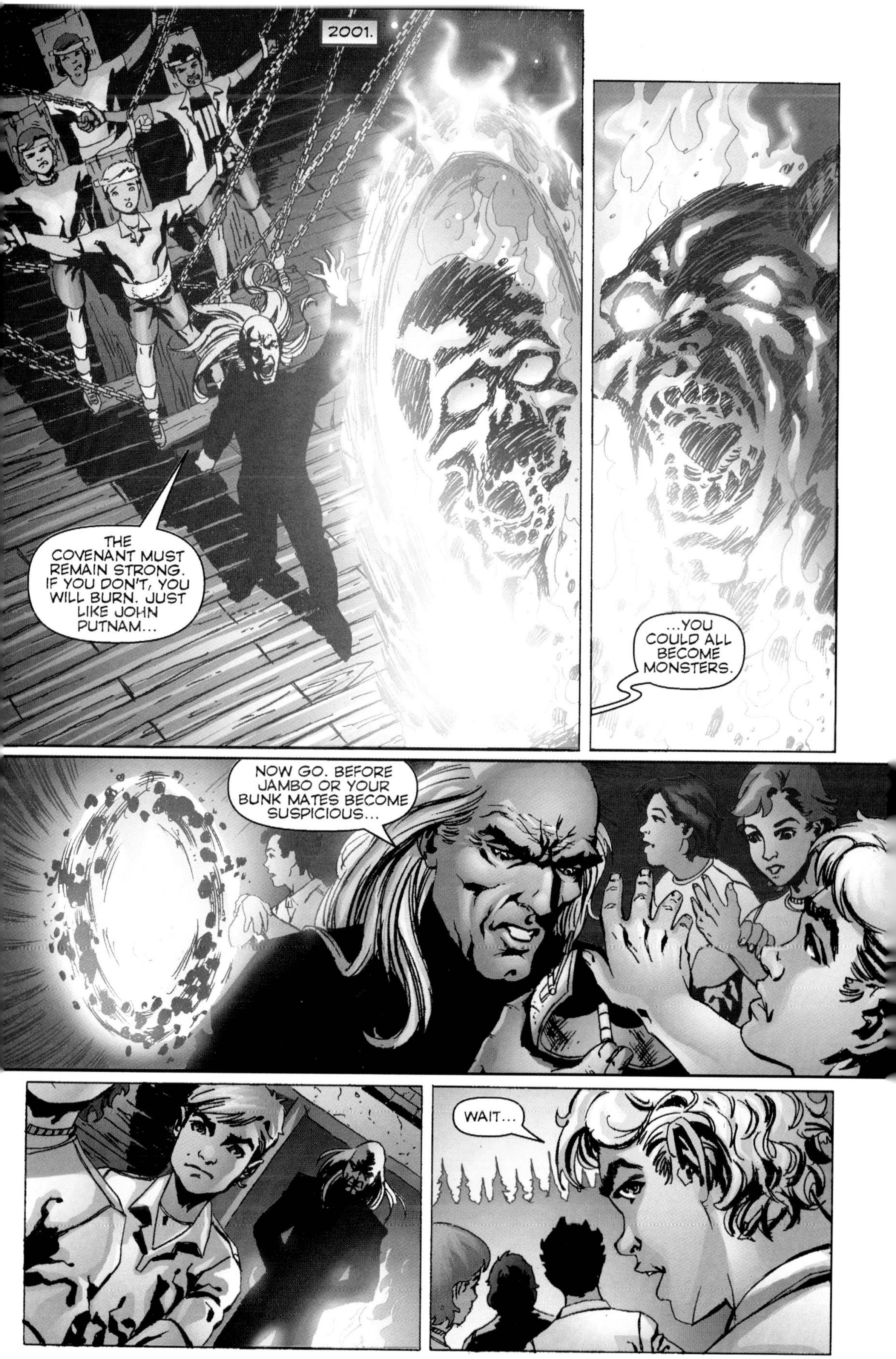
2001.
THE COVENANT MUST REMAIN STRONG. IF YOU DON'T, YOU WILL BURN. JUST LIKE JOHN PUTNAM...
...YOU COULD ALL BECOME MONSTERS.
NOW GO. BEFORE JAMBO OR YOUR BUNK MATES BECOME SUSPICIOUS...
WAIT...

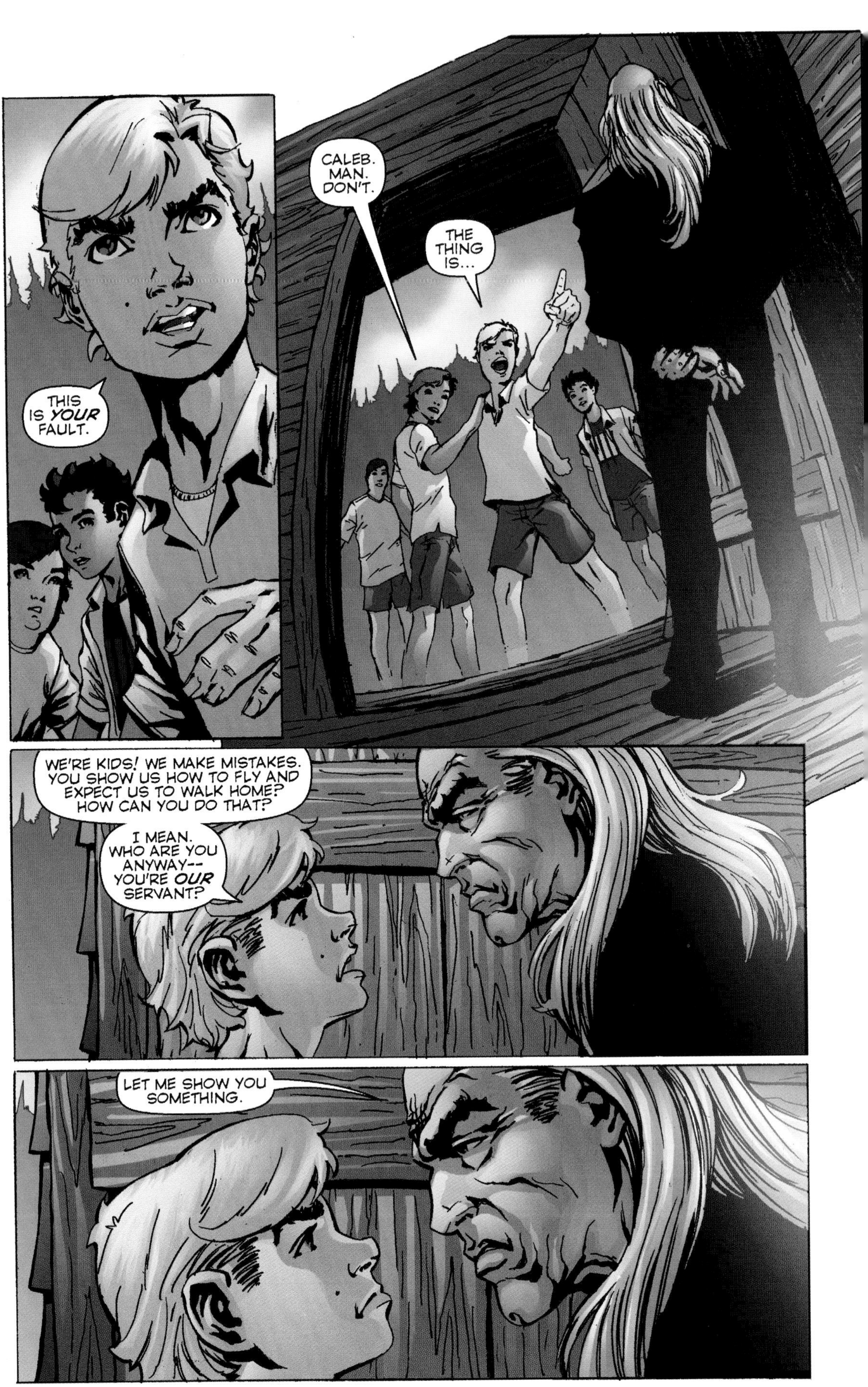
THIS IS *YOUR* FAULT.
CALEB. MAN. DON'T.
THE THING IS...
WE'RE KIDS! WE MAKE MISTAKES. YOU SHOW US HOW TO FLY AND EXPECT US TO WALK HOME? HOW CAN YOU DO THAT?
I MEAN. WHO ARE YOU ANYWAY-- YOU'RE *OUR* SERVANT?
LET ME SHOW YOU SOMETHING.

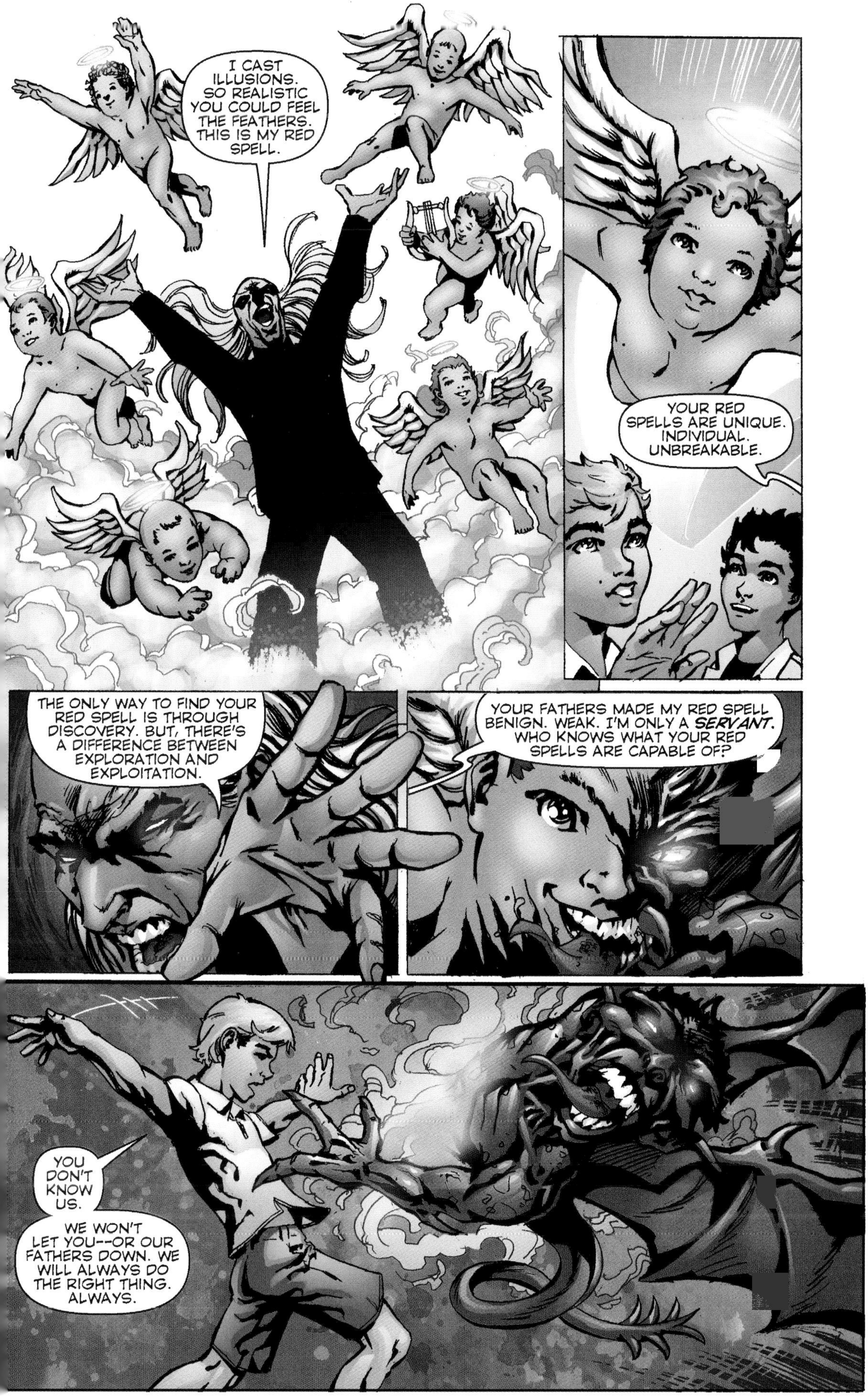
I CAST ILLUSIONS. SO REALISTIC YOU COULD FEEL THE FEATHERS. THIS IS MY RED SPELL.
YOUR RED SPELLS ARE UNIQUE. INDIVIDUAL. UNBREAKABLE.
THE ONLY WAY TO FIND YOUR RED SPELL IS THROUGH DISCOVERY. BUT, THERE'S A DIFFERENCE BETWEEN EXPLORATION AND EXPLOITATION.
YOUR FATHERS MADE MY RED SPELL BENIGN. WEAK. I'M ONLY A SERVANT. WHO KNOWS WHAT YOUR RED SPELLS ARE CAPABLE OF?
YOU DON'T KNOW US.
WE WON'T LET YOU--OR OUR FATHERS DOWN. WE WILL ALWAYS DO THE RIGHT THING. ALWAYS.

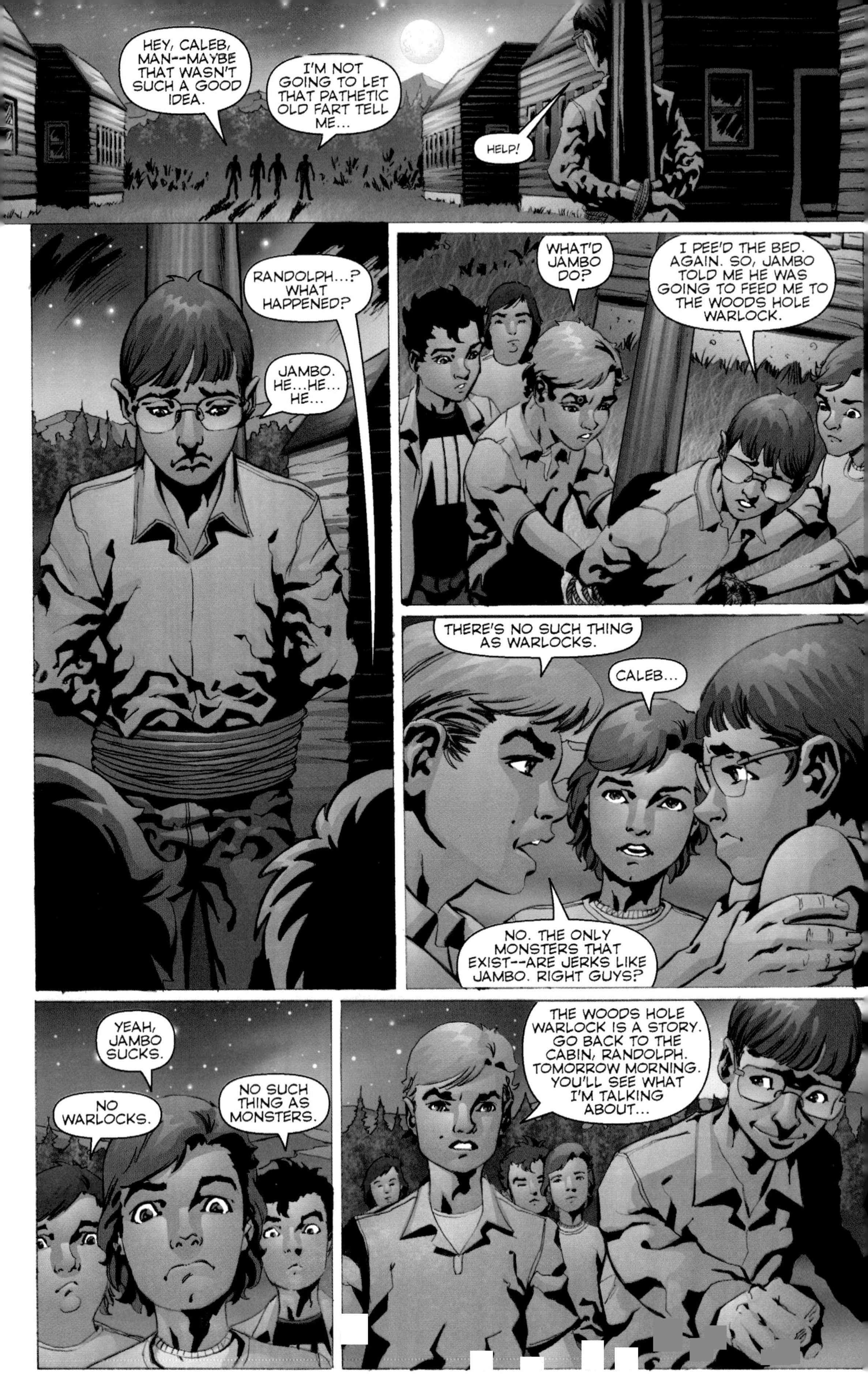
HEY, CALEB, MAN--MAYBE THAT WASN'T SUCH A GOOD IDEA.
I'M NOT GOING TO LET THAT PATHETIC OLD FART TELL ME...
HELP!
RANDOLPH...? WHAT HAPPENED?
JAMBO. HE...HE... HE...
WHAT'D JAMBO DO?
I PEE'D THE BED. AGAIN. SO, JAMBO TOLD ME HE WAS GOING TO FEED ME TO THE WOODS HOLE WARLOCK.
THERE'S NO SUCH THING AS WARLOCKS.
CALEB...
NO. THE ONLY MONSTERS THAT EXIST--ARE JERKS LIKE JAMBO. RIGHT GUYS?
YEAH, JAMBO SUCKS.
NO WARLOCKS.
NO SUCH THING AS MONSTERS.
THE WOODS HOLE WARLOCK IS A STORY. GO BACK TO THE CABIN, RANDOLPH. TOMORROW MORNING. YOU'LL SEE WHAT I'M TALKING ABOUT...

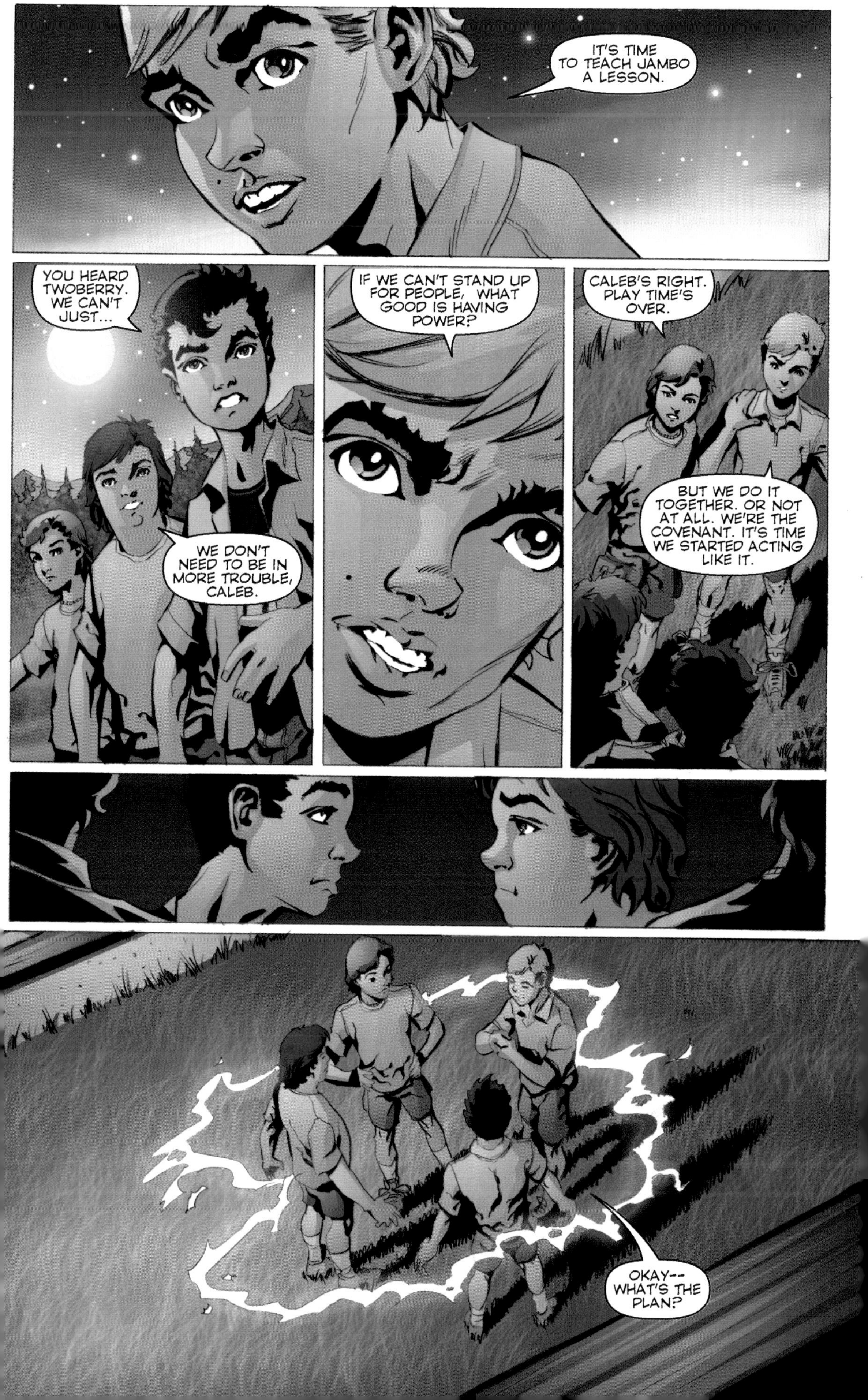
IT'S TIME TO TEACH JAMBO A LESSON.
YOU HEARD TWOBERRY. WE CAN'T JUST...
WE DON'T NEED TO BE IN MORE TROUBLE, CALEB.
IF WE CAN'T STAND UP FOR PEOPLE, WHAT GOOD IS HAVING POWER?
CALEB'S RIGHT. PLAY TIME'S OVER.
BUT WE DO IT TOGETHER. OR NOT AT ALL. WE'RE THE COVENANT. IT'S TIME WE STARTED ACTING LIKE IT.
OKAY-- WHAT'S THE PLAN?

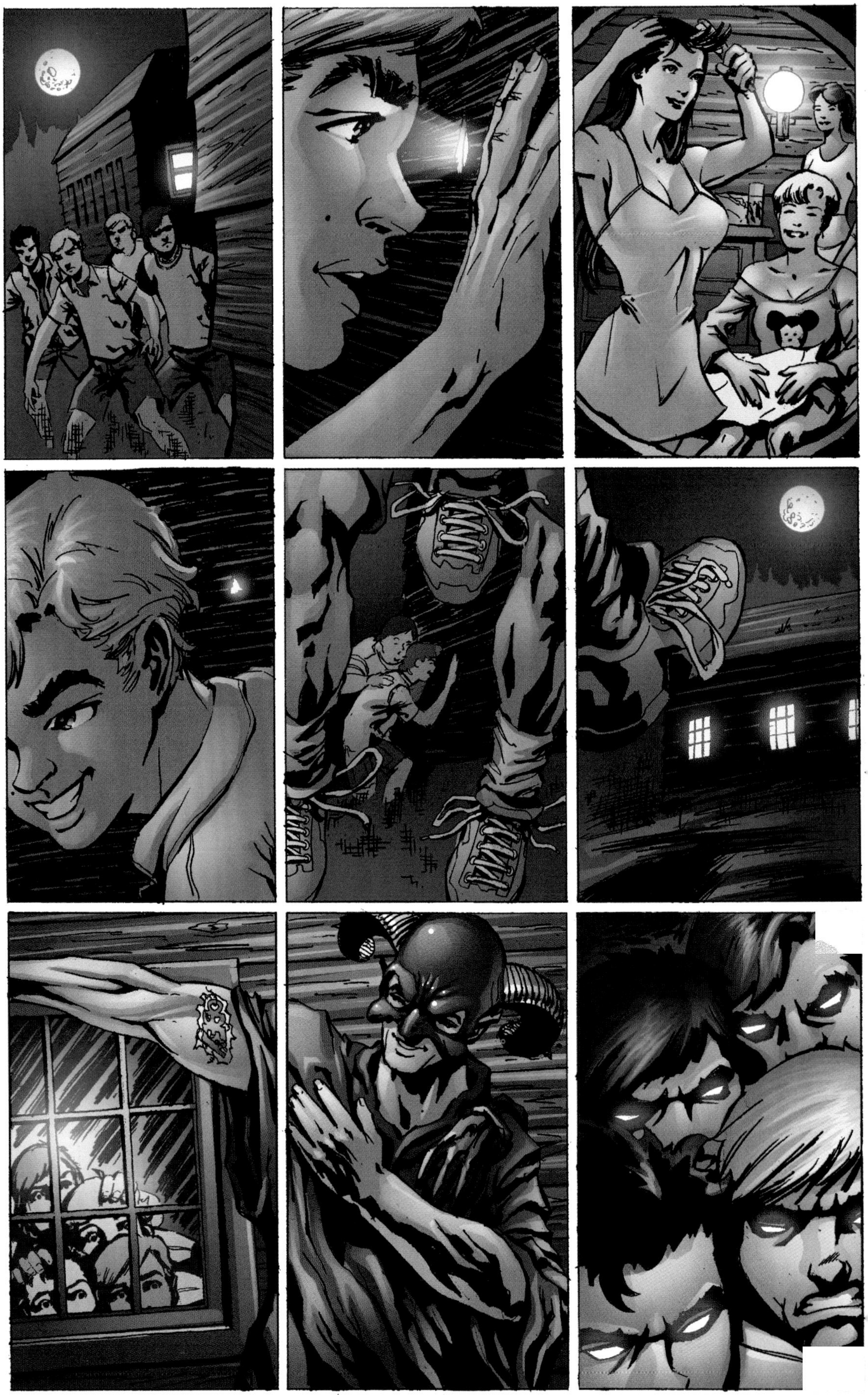

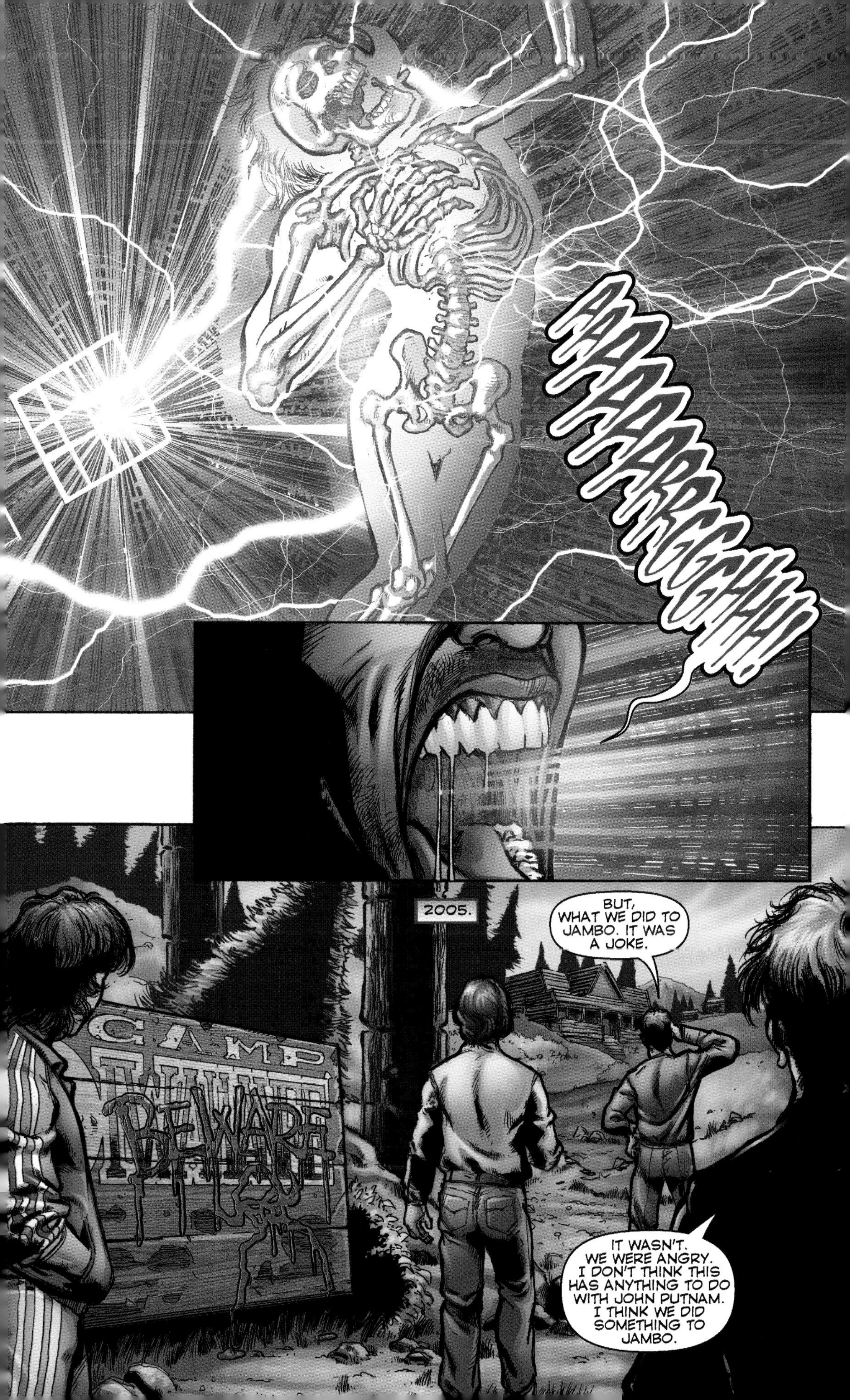
AAAARRGGHHH!
CAMP
BEWARE
2005.
BUT, WHAT WE DID TO JAMBO. IT WAS A JOKE.
IT WASN'T. WE WERE ANGRY. I DON'T THINK THIS HAS ANYTHING TO DO WITH JOHN PUTNAM. I THINK WE DID SOMETHING TO JAMBO.

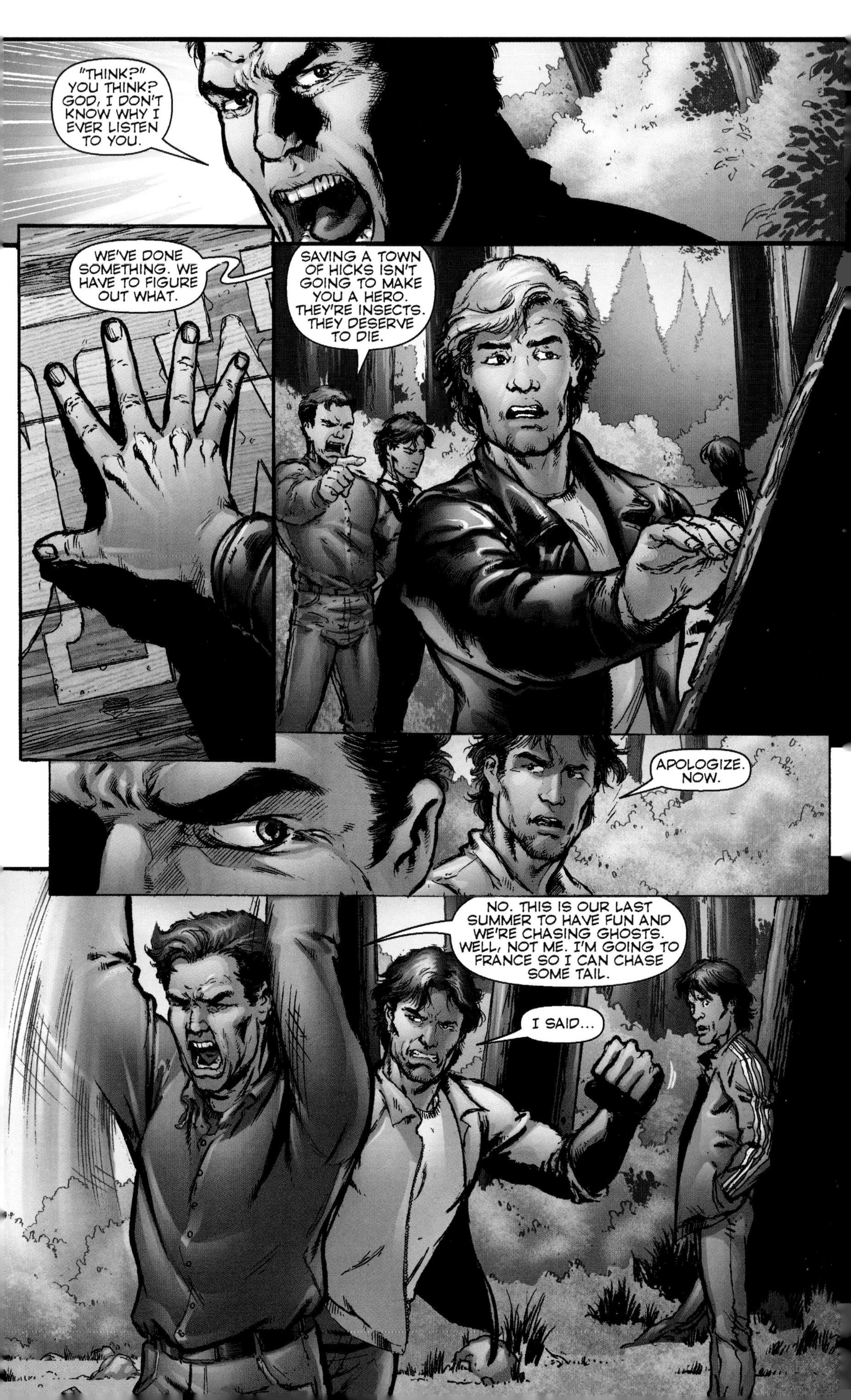
"THINK?" YOU THINK? GOD, I DON'T KNOW WHY I EVER LISTEN TO YOU.
WE'VE DONE SOMETHING. WE HAVE TO FIGURE OUT WHAT.
SAVING A TOWN OF HICKS ISN'T GOING TO MAKE YOU A HERO. THEY'RE INSECTS. THEY DESERVE TO DIE.
APOLOGIZE. NOW.
NO. THIS IS OUR LAST SUMMER TO HAVE FUN AND WE'RE CHASING GHOSTS. WELL, NOT ME. I'M GOING TO FRANCE SO I CAN CHASE SOME TAIL.
I SAID...

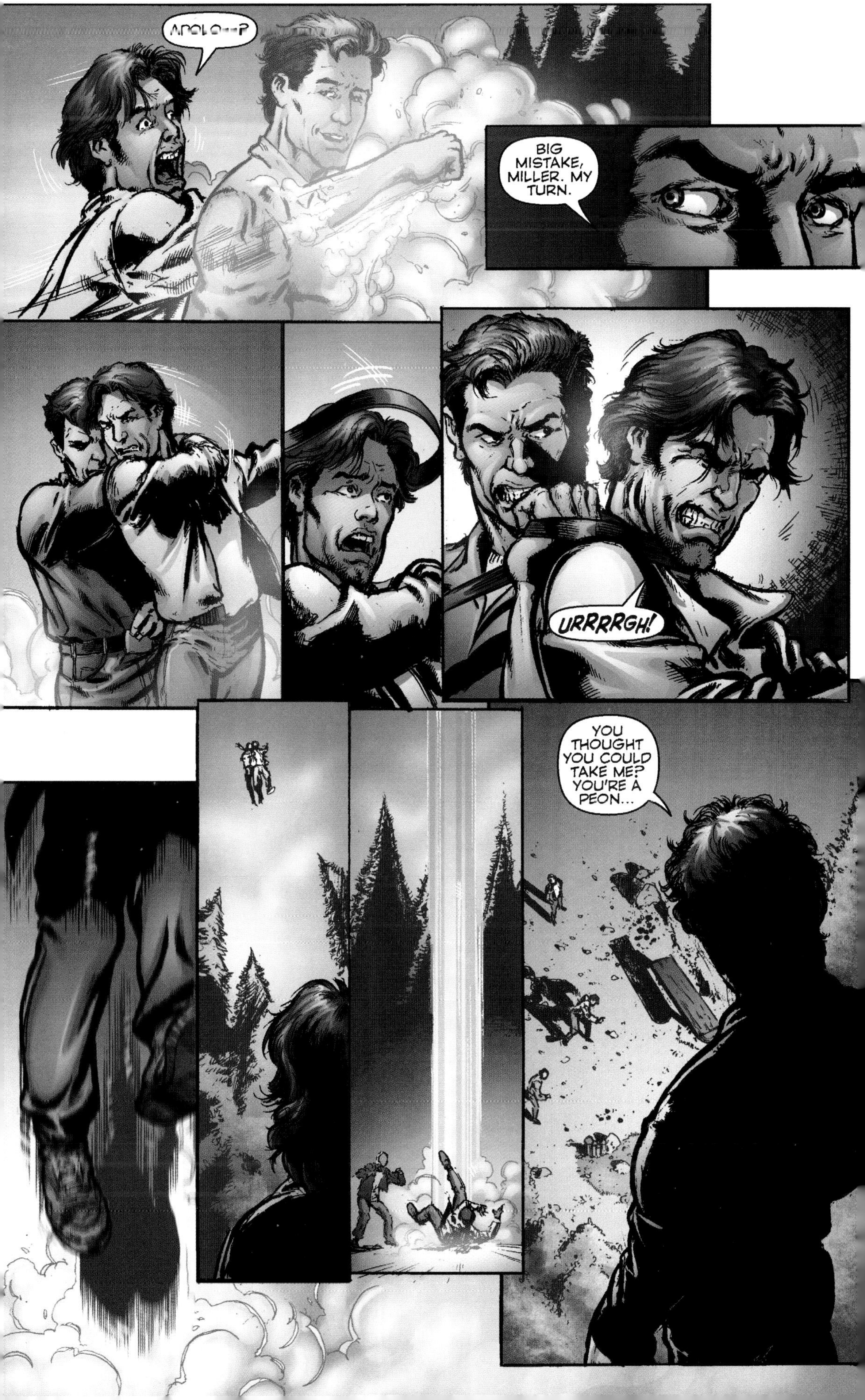
APOLO--?
BIG MISTAKE, MILLER. MY TURN.
URRRRGH!
YOU THOUGHT YOU COULD TAKE ME? YOU'RE A PEON...

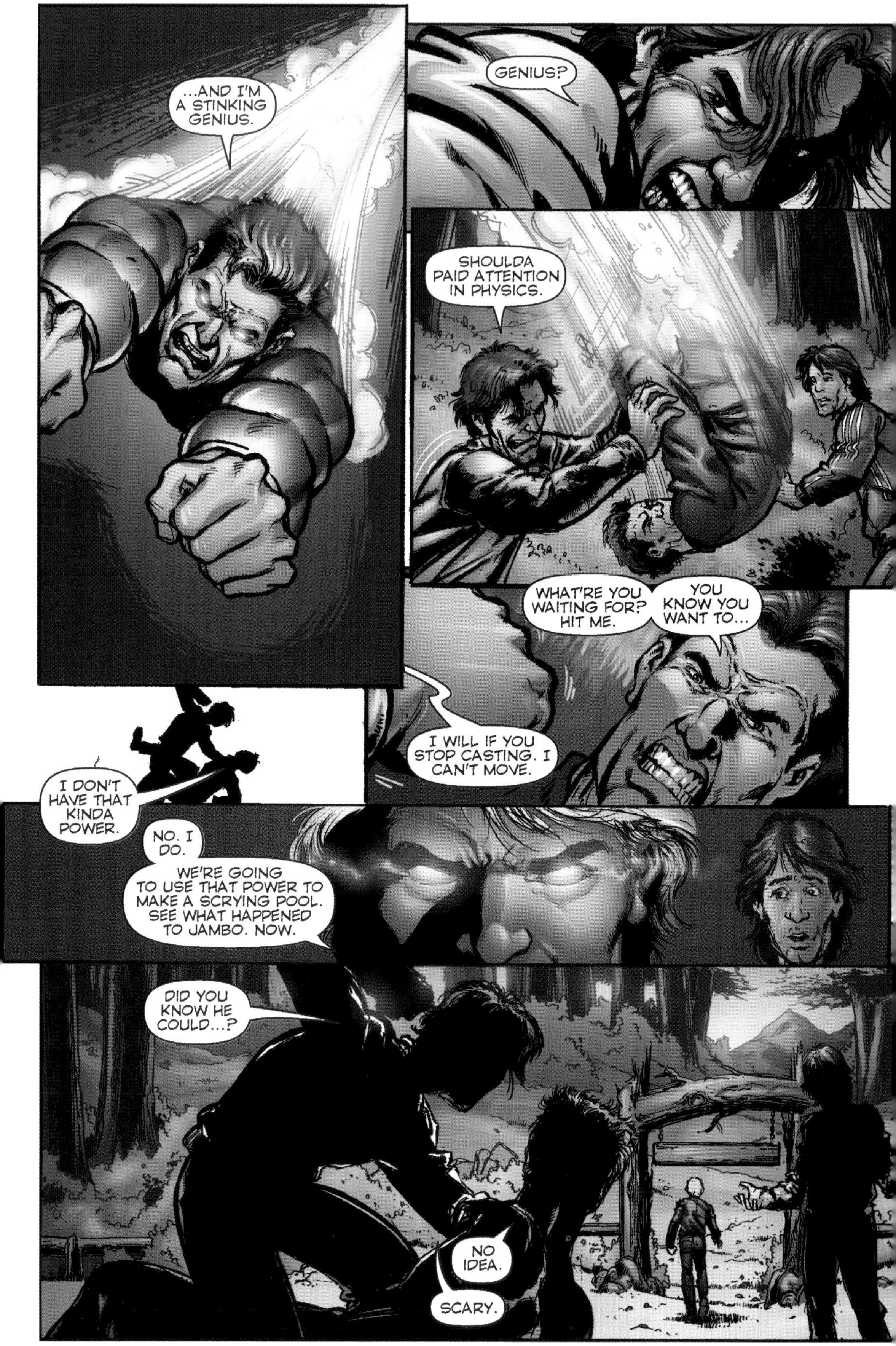
...AND I'M A STINKING GENIUS.
GENIUS?
SHOULDA PAID ATTENTION IN PHYSICS.
WHAT'RE YOU WAITING FOR? HIT ME.
YOU KNOW YOU WANT TO...
I WILL IF YOU STOP CASTING. I CAN'T MOVE.
I DON'T HAVE THAT KINDA POWER.
NO. I DO.
WE'RE GOING TO USE THAT POWER TO MAKE A SCRYING POOL. SEE WHAT HAPPENED TO JAMBO. NOW.
DID YOU KNOW HE COULD...?
NO IDEA.
SCARY.

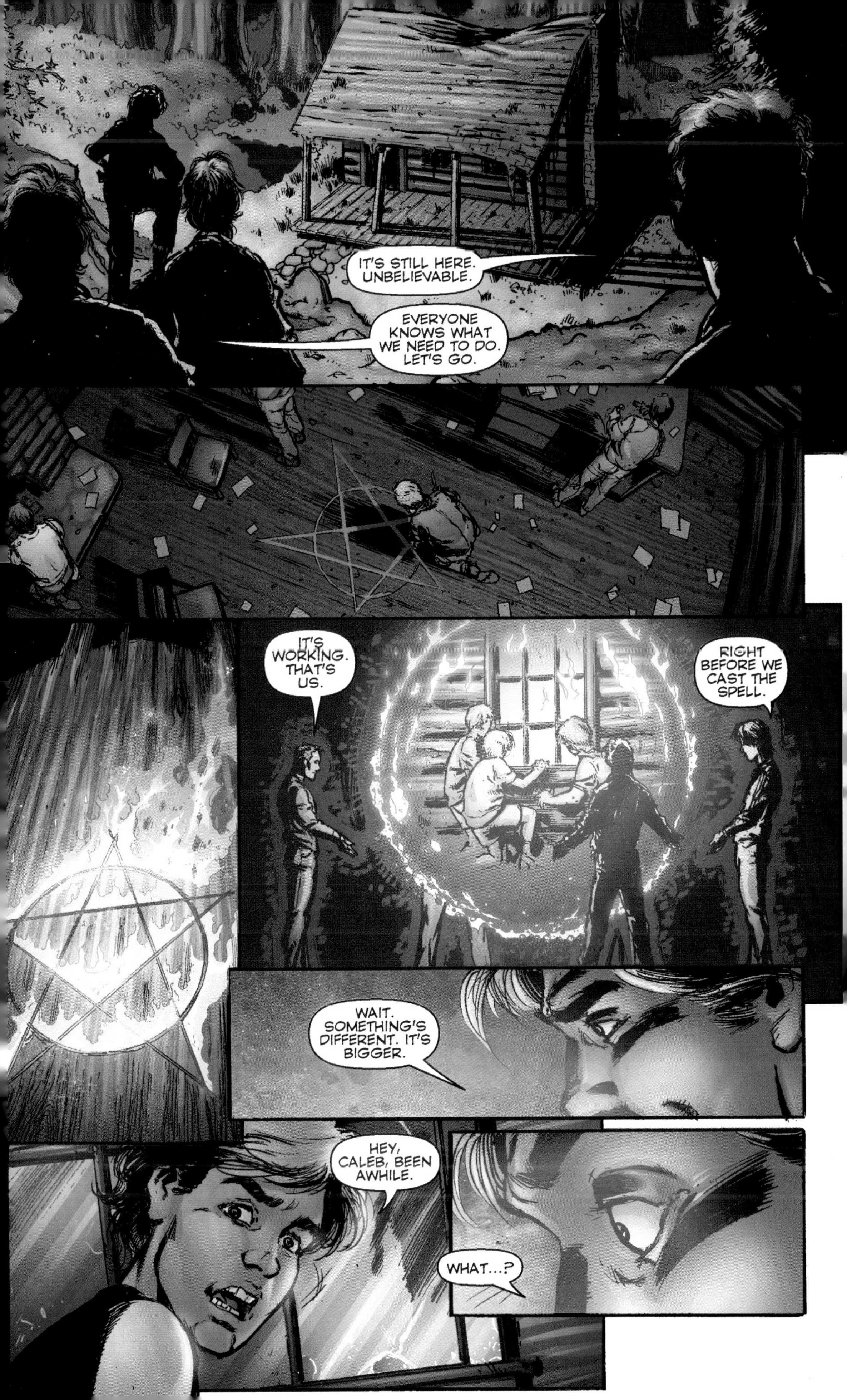
IT'S STILL HERE. UNBELIEVABLE.
EVERYONE KNOWS WHAT WE NEED TO DO. LET'S GO.
IT'S WORKING. THAT'S US.
RIGHT BEFORE WE CAST THE SPELL.
WAIT. SOMETHING'S DIFFERENT. IT'S BIGGER.
HEY, CALEB, BEEN AWHILE.
WHAT...?

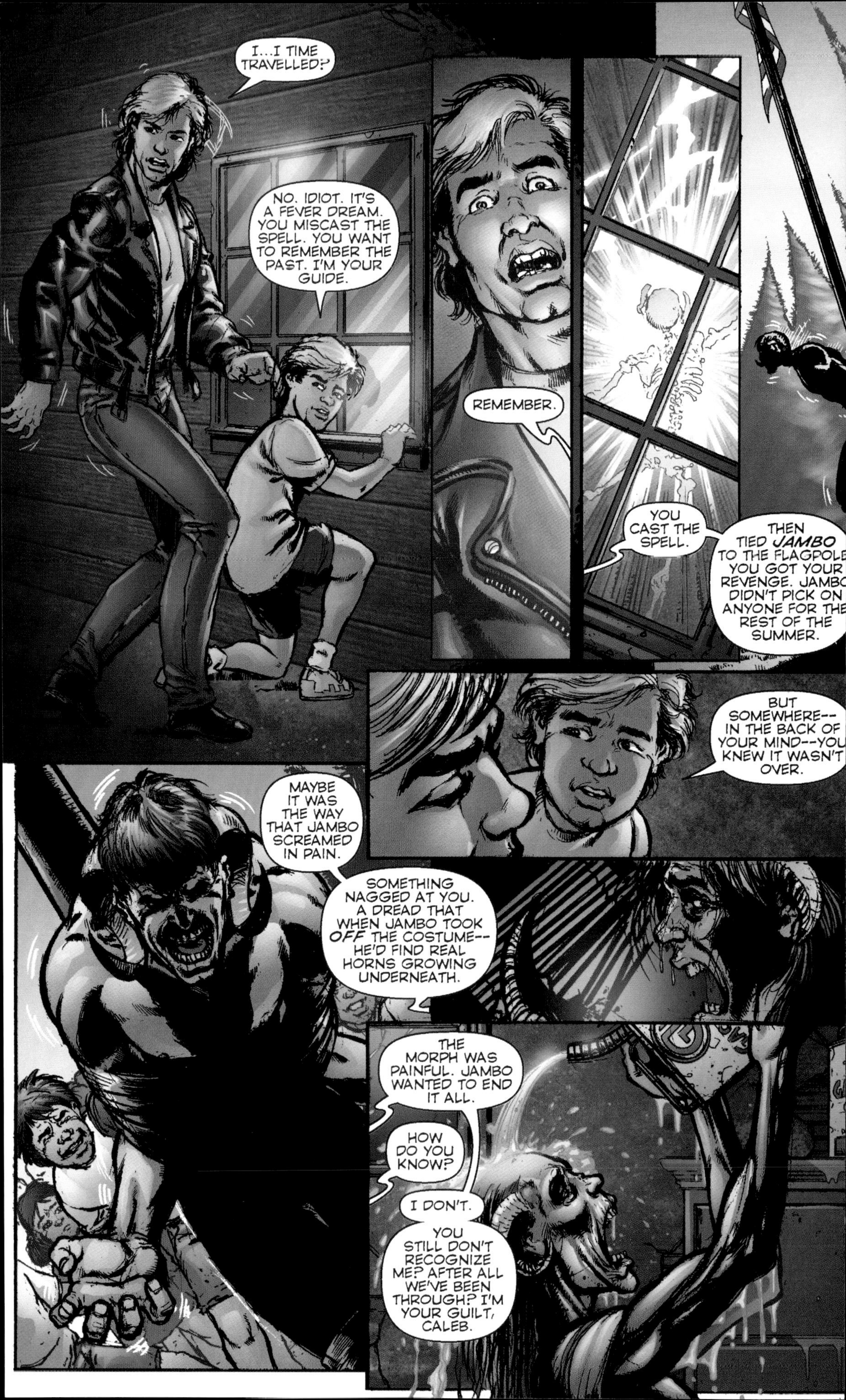
I...I TIME TRAVELLED?
NO. IDIOT. IT'S A FEVER DREAM. YOU MISCAST THE SPELL. YOU WANT TO REMEMBER THE PAST. I'M YOUR GUIDE.
REMEMBER.
YOU CAST THE SPELL.
THEN TIED *JAMBO* TO THE FLAGPOLE. YOU GOT YOUR REVENGE. JAMBO DIDN'T PICK ON ANYONE FOR THE REST OF THE SUMMER.
BUT SOMEWHERE-- IN THE BACK OF YOUR MIND--YOU KNEW IT WASN'T OVER.
MAYBE IT WAS THE WAY THAT JAMBO SCREAMED IN PAIN.
SOMETHING NAGGED AT YOU. A DREAD THAT WHEN JAMBO TOOK *OFF* THE COSTUME-- HE'D FIND REAL HORNS GROWING UNDERNEATH.
THE MORPH WAS PAINFUL. JAMBO WANTED TO END IT ALL.
HOW DO YOU KNOW?
I DON'T.
YOU STILL DON'T RECOGNIZE ME? AFTER ALL WE'VE BEEN THROUGH? I'M YOUR GUILT, CALEB.

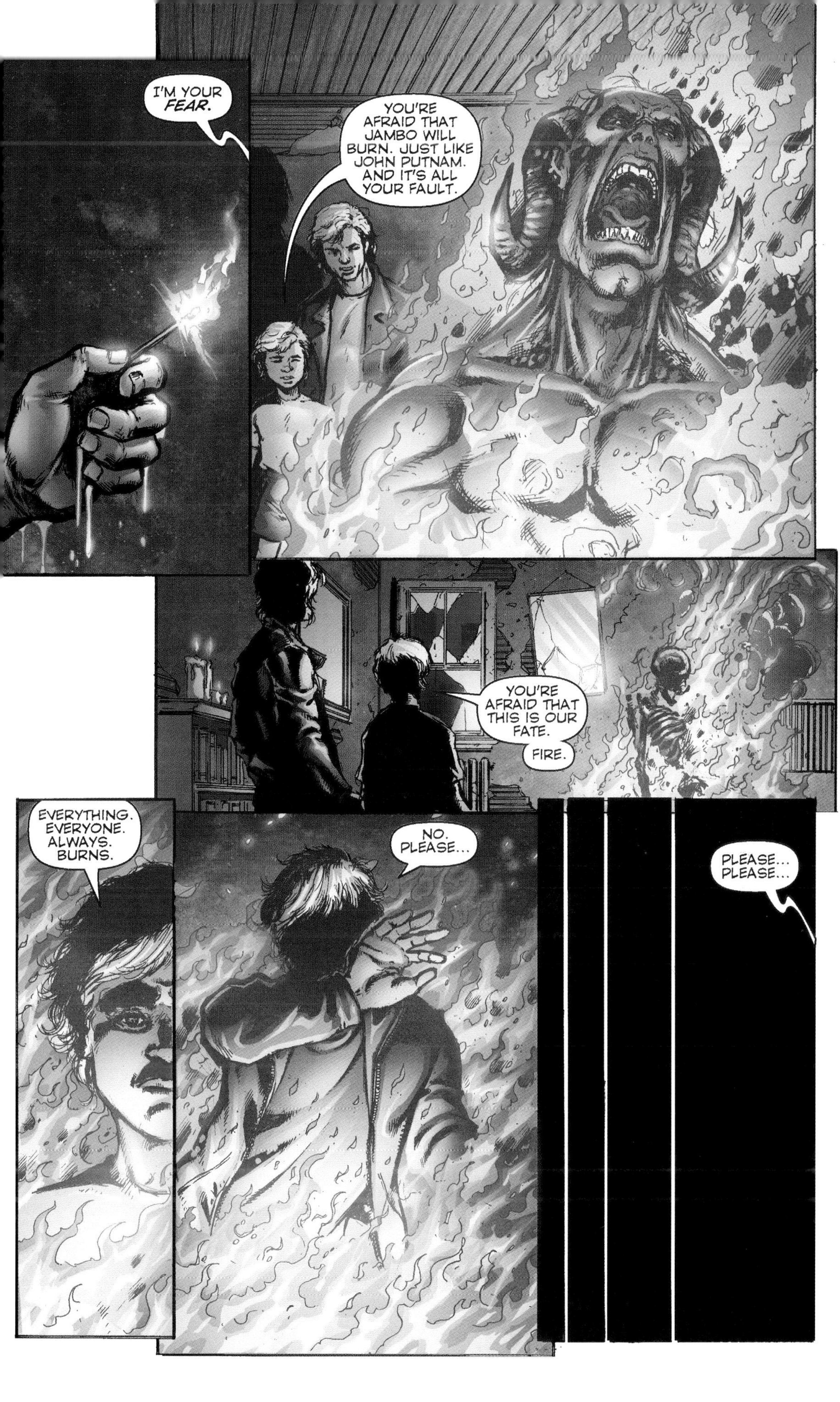
I'M YOUR *FEAR*.
YOU'RE AFRAID THAT JAMBO WILL BURN. JUST LIKE JOHN PUTNAM. AND IT'S ALL YOUR FAULT.
YOU'RE AFRAID THAT THIS IS OUR FATE.
FIRE.
EVERYTHING. EVERYONE. ALWAYS. BURNS.
NO. PLEASE...
PLEASE... PLEASE...

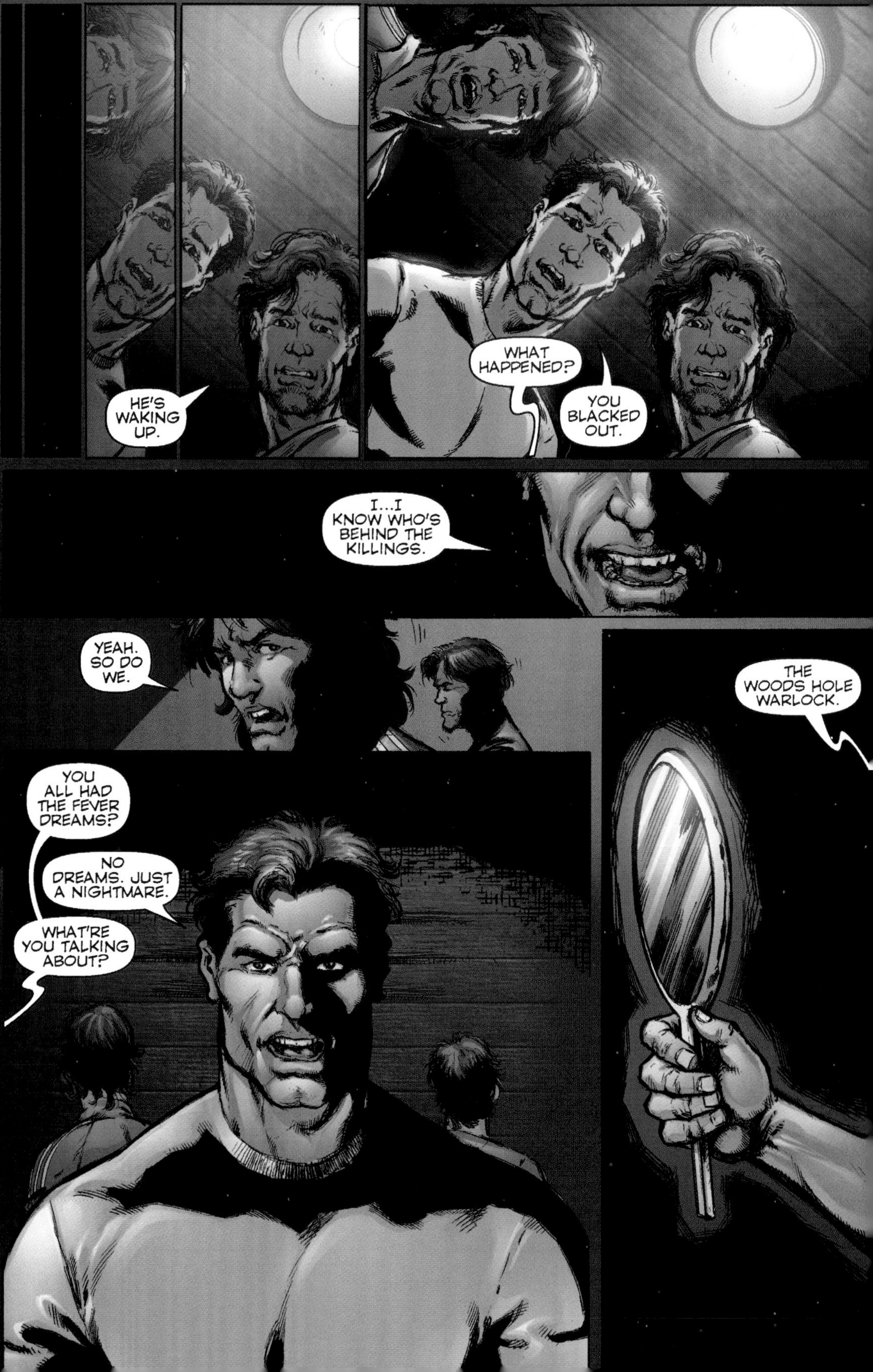
HE'S WAKING UP.
WHAT HAPPENED?
YOU BLACKED OUT.
I...I KNOW WHO'S BEHIND THE KILLINGS.
YEAH. SO DO WE.
THE WOODS HOLE WARLOCK.
YOU ALL HAD THE FEVER DREAMS?
NO DREAMS. JUST A NIGHTMARE.
WHAT'RE YOU TALKING ABOUT?

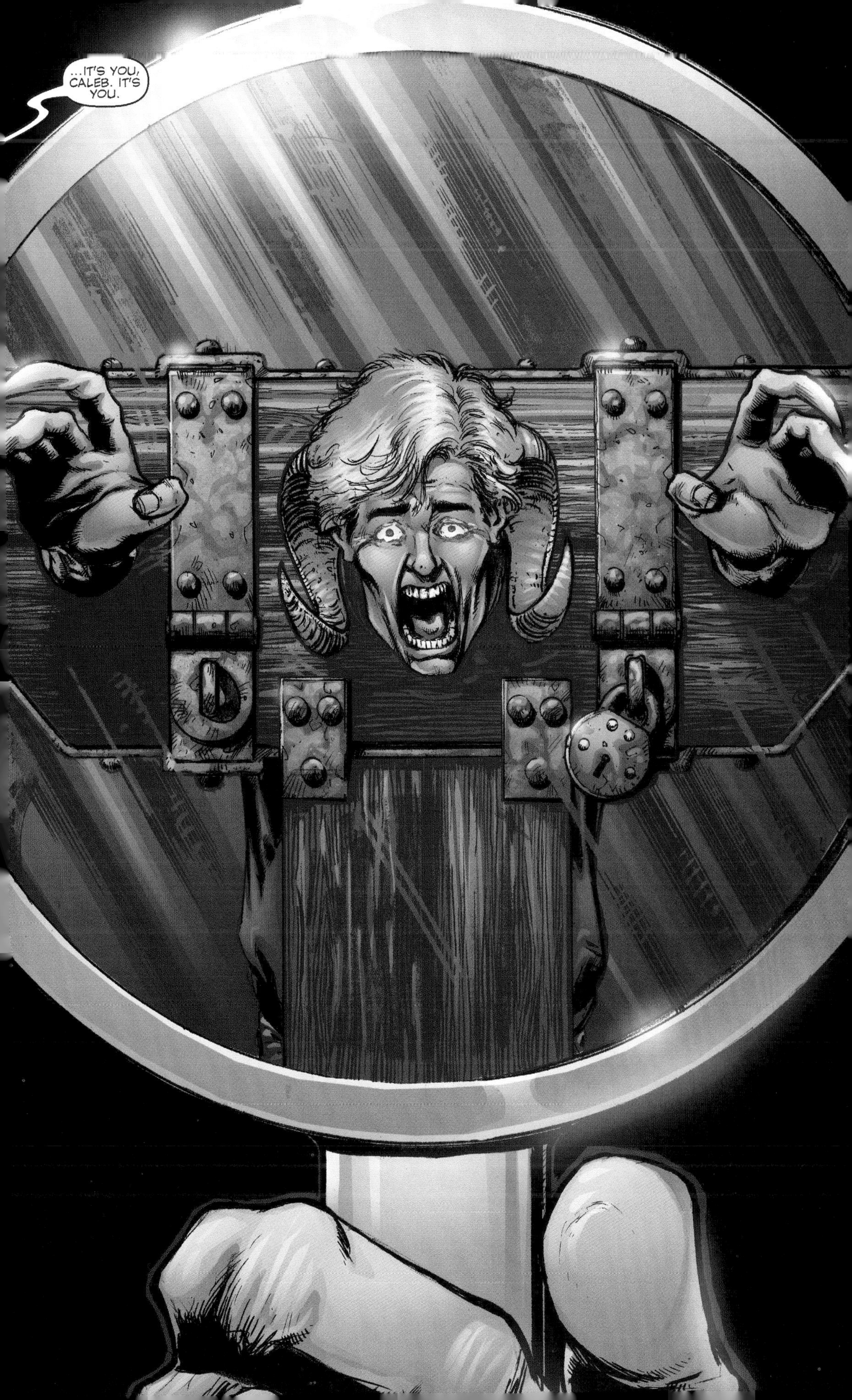
...IT'S YOU, CALEB. IT'S YOU.

ART BY: **RODOLFO MIGLIARI** AND **STEVE FIRCHOW**

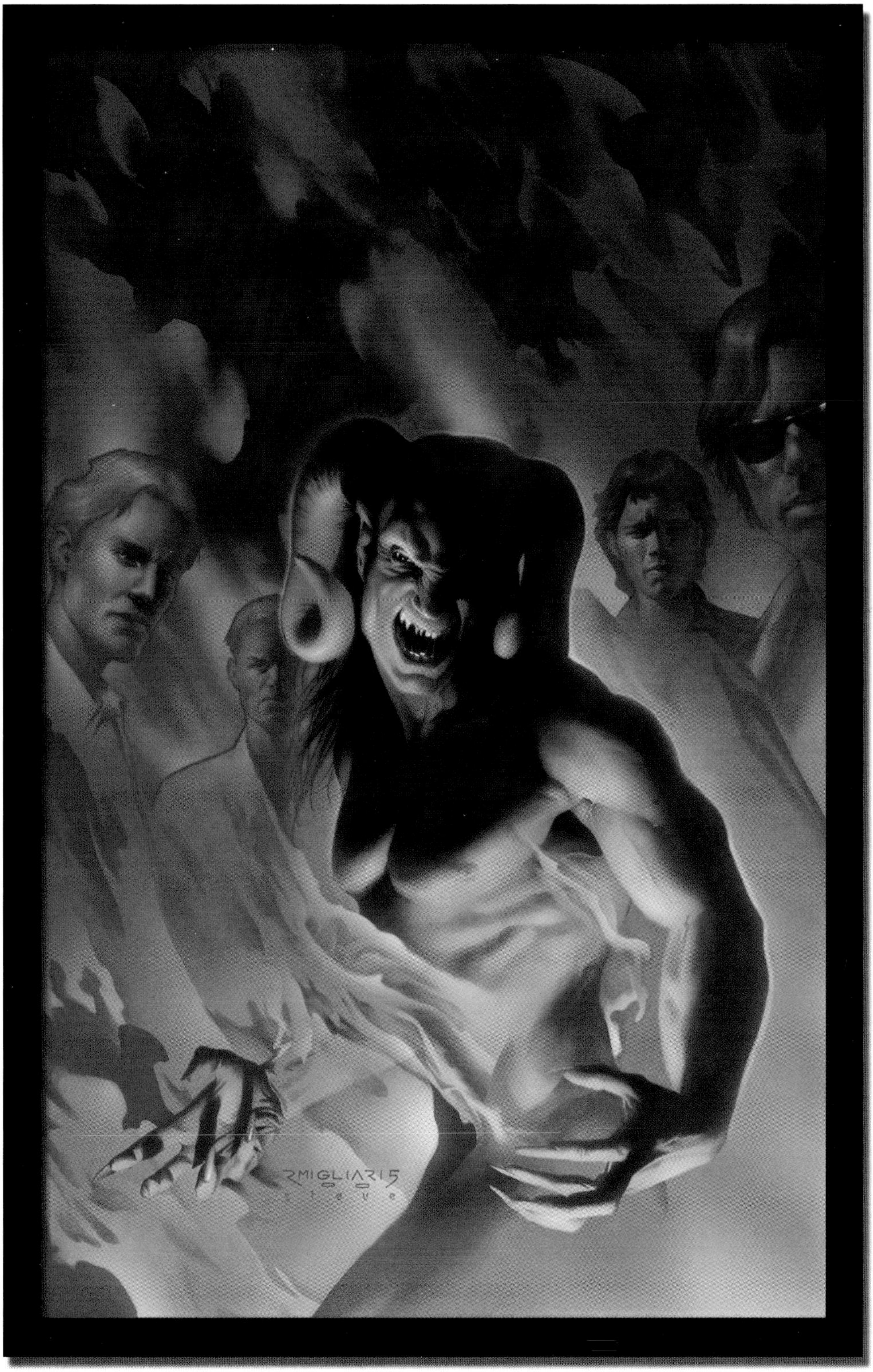

RMIGLIARI5
steve


# CHAPTER 3

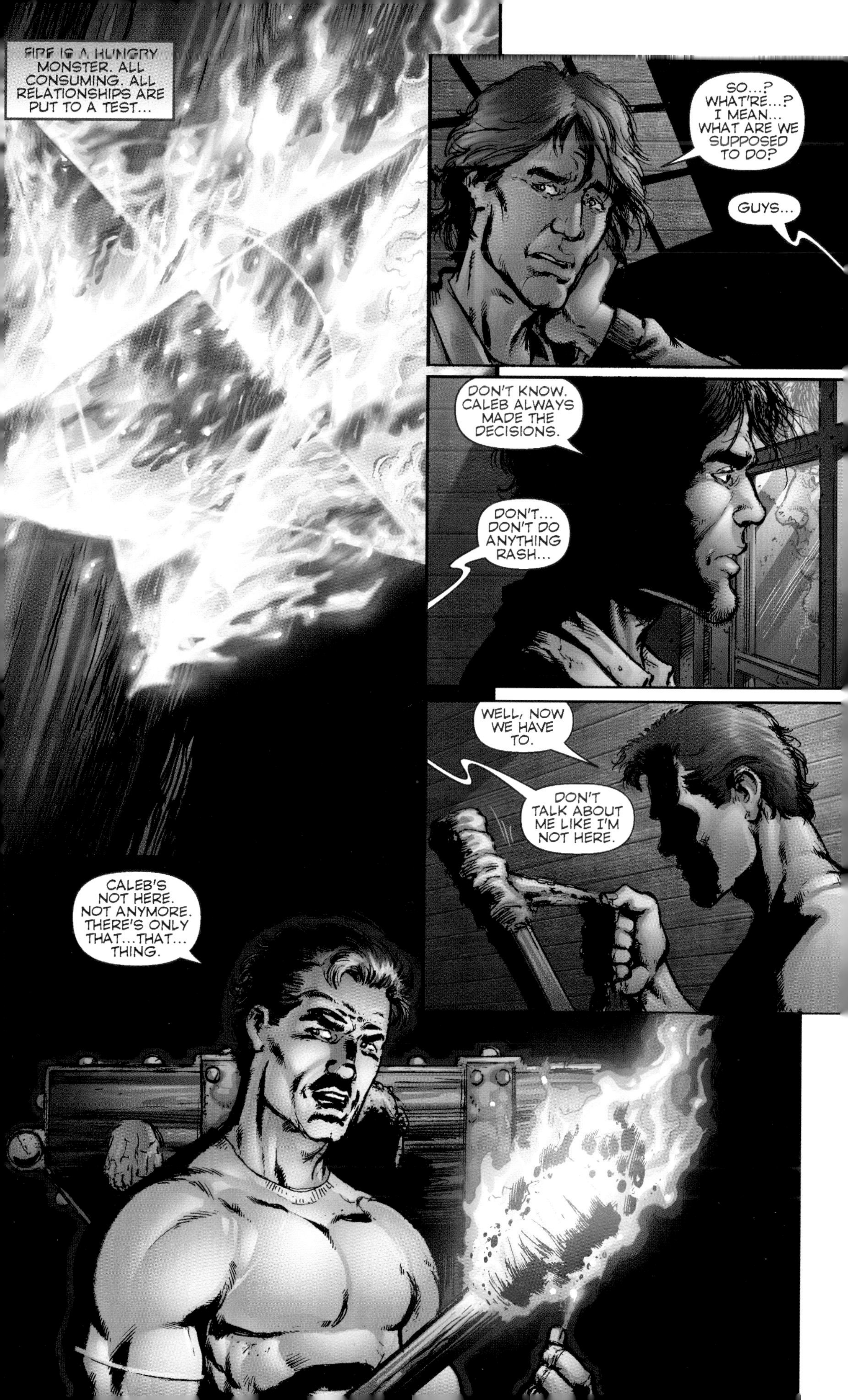
FIRE IS A HUNGRY MONSTER. ALL CONSUMING. ALL RELATIONSHIPS ARE PUT TO A TEST...
SO...? WHAT'RE...? I MEAN... WHAT ARE WE SUPPOSED TO DO?
GUYS...
DON'T KNOW. CALEB ALWAYS MADE THE DECISIONS.
DON'T... DON'T DO ANYTHING RASH...
WELL, NOW WE HAVE TO.
DON'T TALK ABOUT ME LIKE I'M NOT HERE.
CALEB'S NOT HERE. NOT ANYMORE. THERE'S ONLY THAT...THAT... THING.

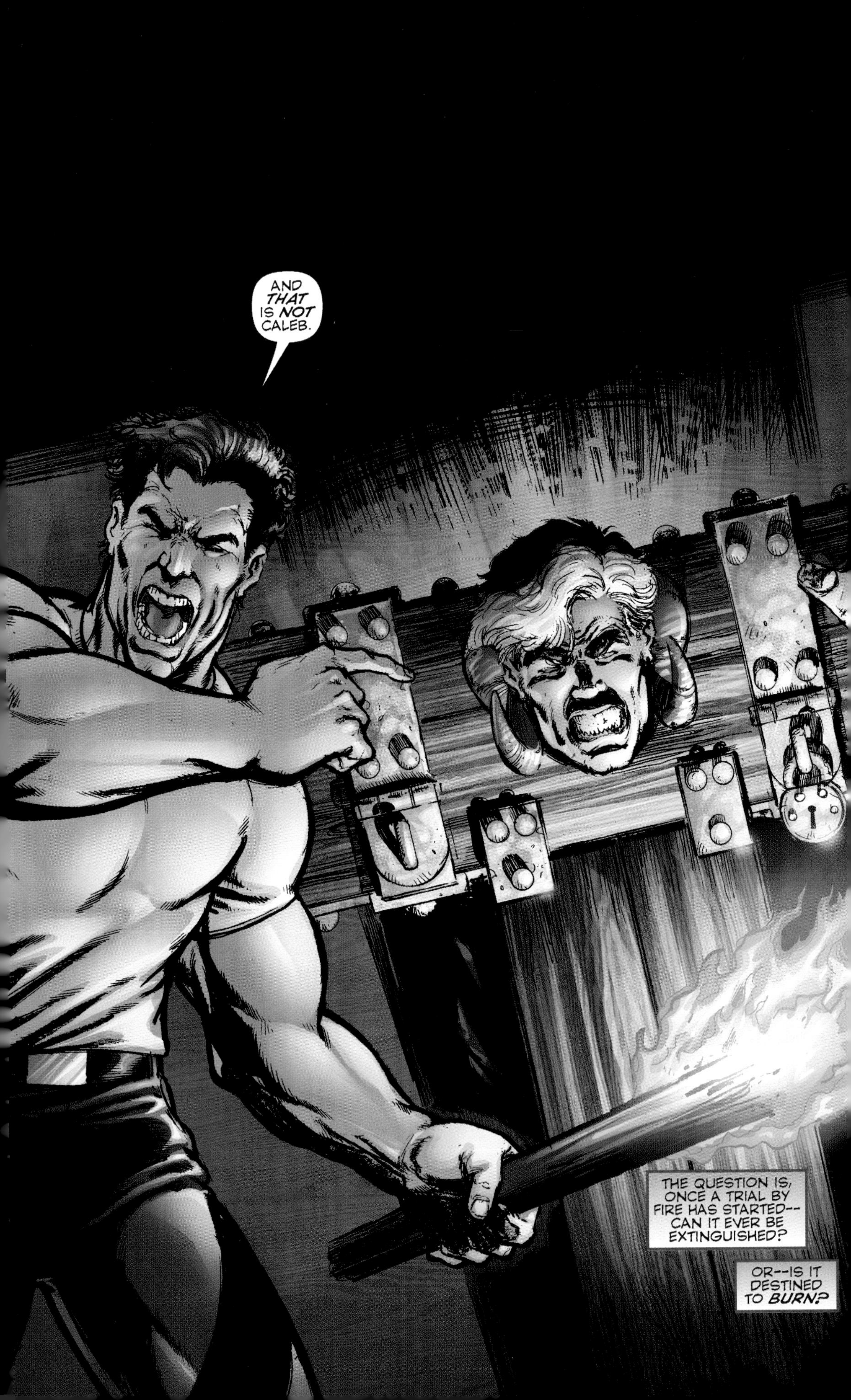
AND THAT IS NOT CALEB.
THE QUESTION IS, ONCE A TRIAL BY FIRE HAS STARTED-- CAN IT EVER BE EXTINGUISHED?
OR--IS IT DESTINED TO BURN?

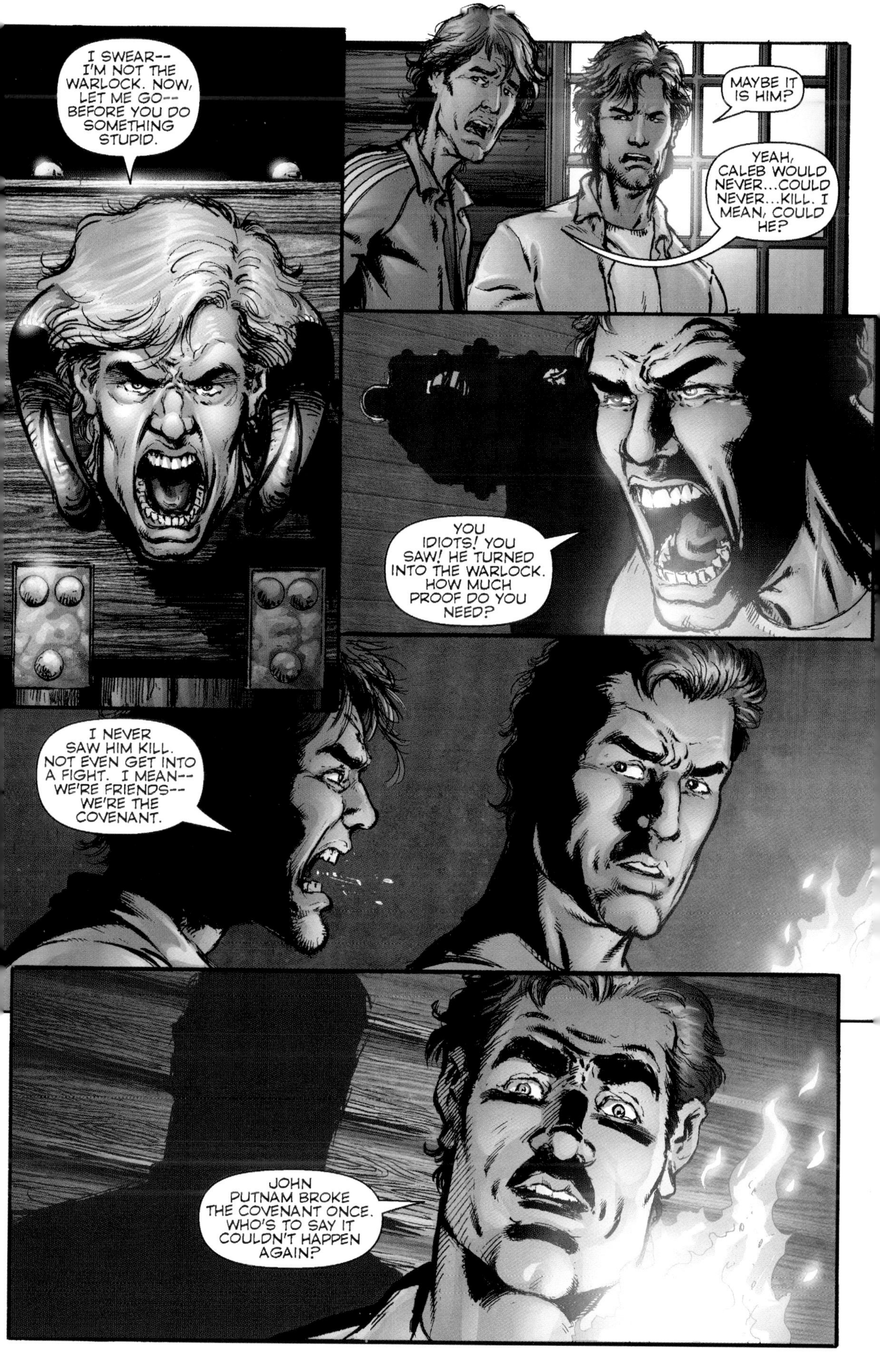
I SWEAR-- I'M NOT THE WARLOCK. NOW, LET ME GO-- BEFORE YOU DO SOMETHING STUPID.
MAYBE IT IS HIM?
YEAH, CALEB WOULD NEVER...COULD NEVER...KILL. I MEAN, COULD HE?
YOU IDIOTS! YOU SAW! HE TURNED INTO THE WARLOCK. HOW MUCH PROOF DO YOU NEED?
I NEVER SAW HIM KILL. NOT EVEN GET INTO A FIGHT. I MEAN-- WE'RE FRIENDS-- WE'RE THE COVENANT.
JOHN PUTNAM BROKE THE COVENANT ONCE. WHO'S TO SAY IT COULDN'T HAPPEN AGAIN?

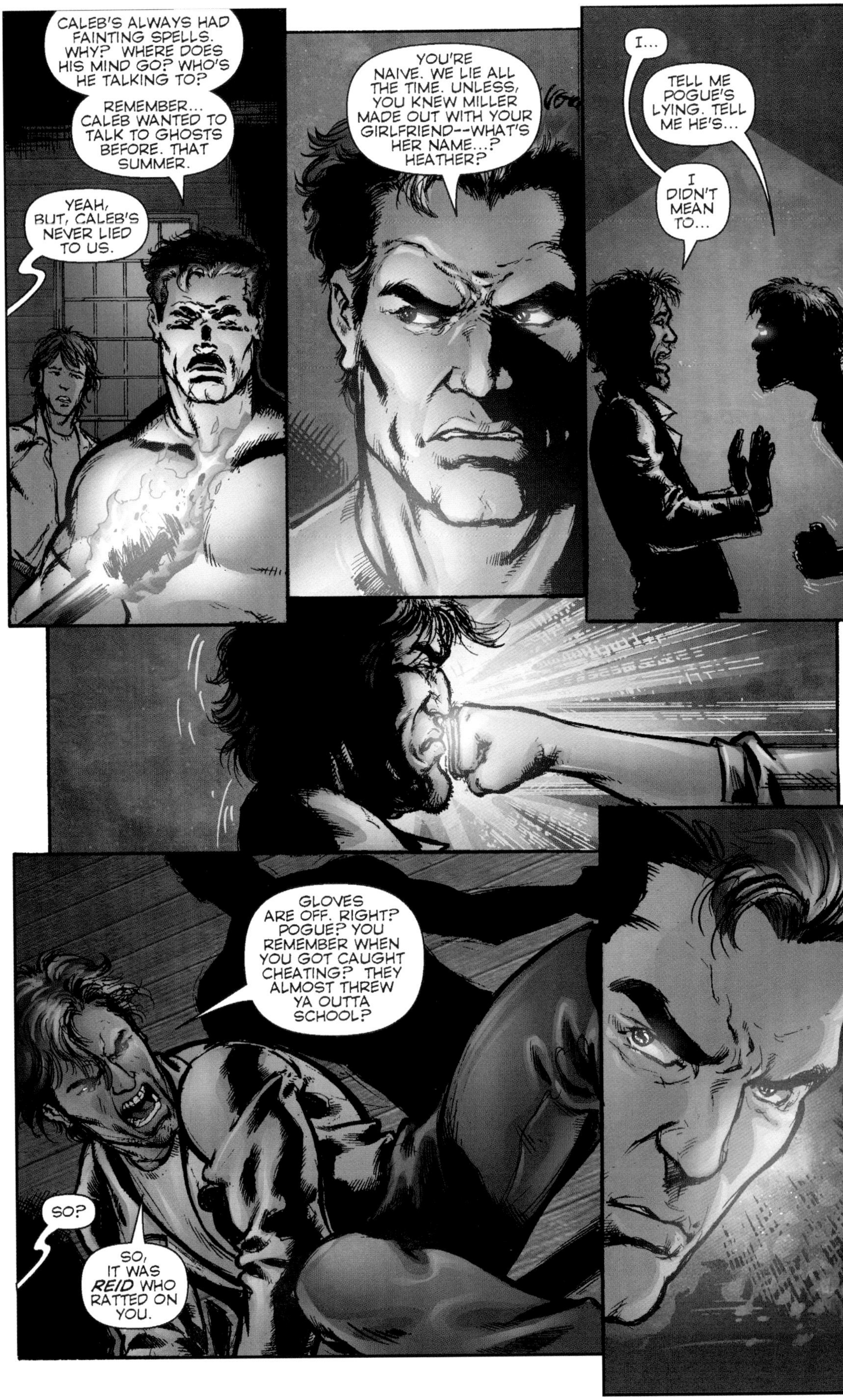
CALEB'S ALWAYS HAD FAINTING SPELLS. WHY? WHERE DOES HIS MIND GO? WHO'S HE TALKING TO?
REMEMBER... CALEB WANTED TO TALK TO GHOSTS BEFORE. THAT SUMMER.
YEAH, BUT, CALEB'S NEVER LIED TO US.
YOU'RE NAIVE. WE LIE ALL THE TIME. UNLESS, YOU KNEW MILLER MADE OUT WITH YOUR GIRLFRIEND--WHAT'S HER NAME...? HEATHER?
I...
TELL ME POGUE'S LYING. TELL ME HE'S...
I DIDN'T MEAN TO...
GLOVES ARE OFF. RIGHT? POGUE? YOU REMEMBER WHEN YOU GOT CAUGHT CHEATING? THEY ALMOST THREW YA OUTTA SCHOOL?
SO?
SO, IT WAS *REID* WHO RATTED ON YOU.

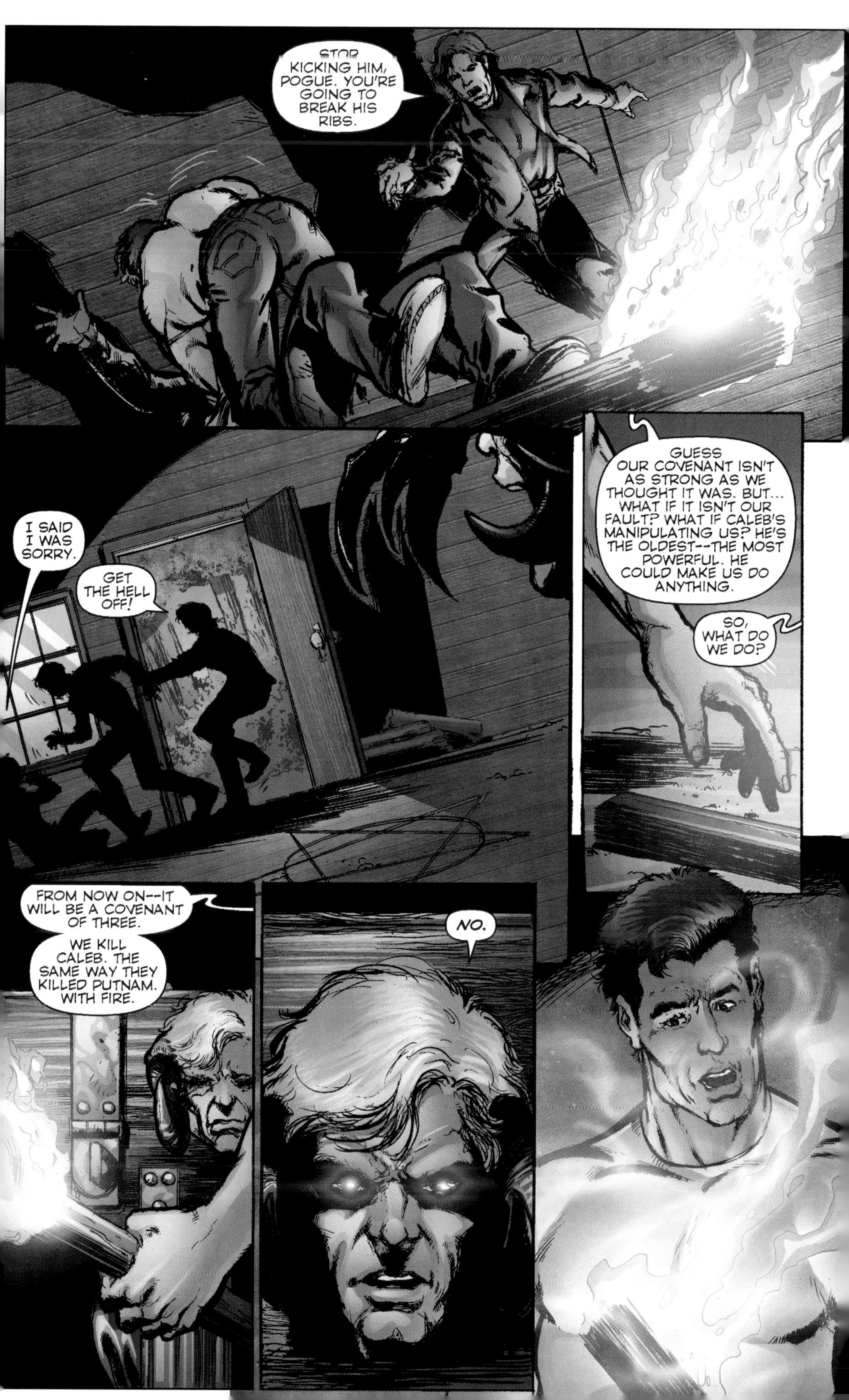
STOP KICKING HIM, POGUE. YOU'RE GOING TO BREAK HIS RIBS.
I SAID I WAS SORRY.
GET THE HELL OFF!
GUESS OUR COVENANT ISN'T AS STRONG AS WE THOUGHT IT WAS. BUT... WHAT IF IT ISN'T OUR FAULT? WHAT IF CALEB'S MANIPULATING US? HE'S THE OLDEST--THE MOST POWERFUL. HE COULD MAKE US DO ANYTHING.
SO, WHAT DO WE DO?
FROM NOW ON--IT WILL BE A COVENANT OF THREE.
WE KILL CALEB. THE SAME WAY THEY KILLED PUTNAM. WITH FIRE.
NO.

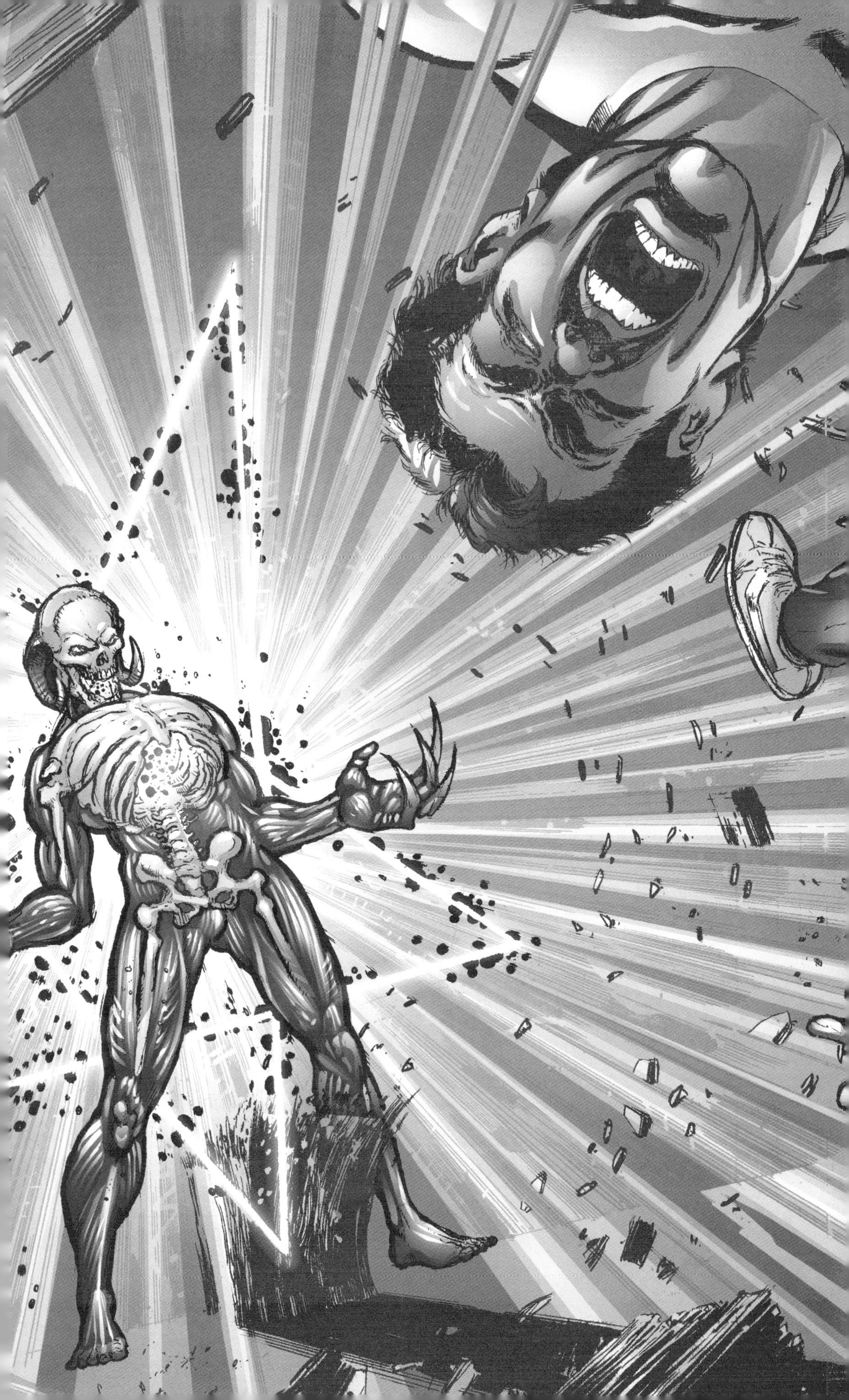

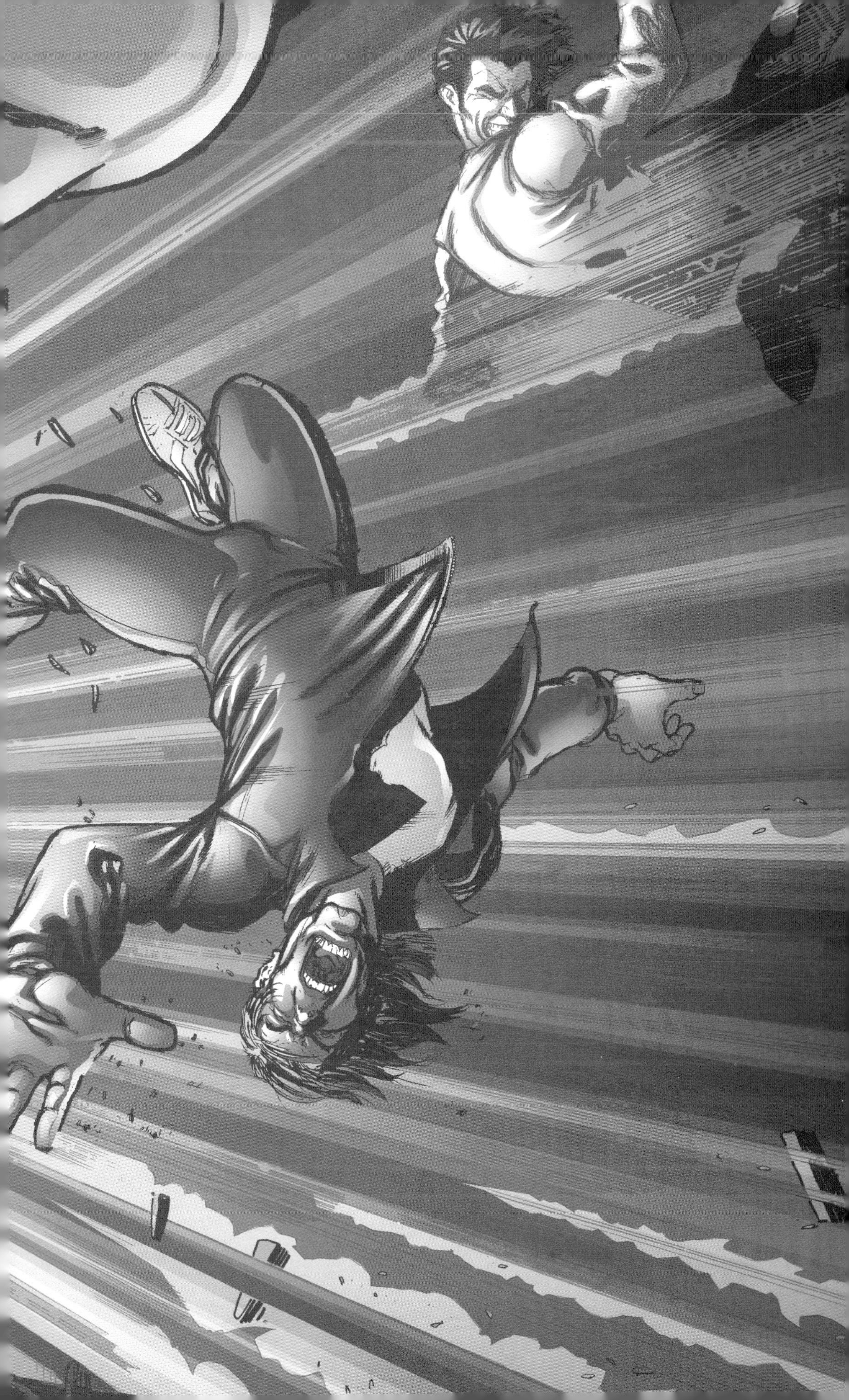

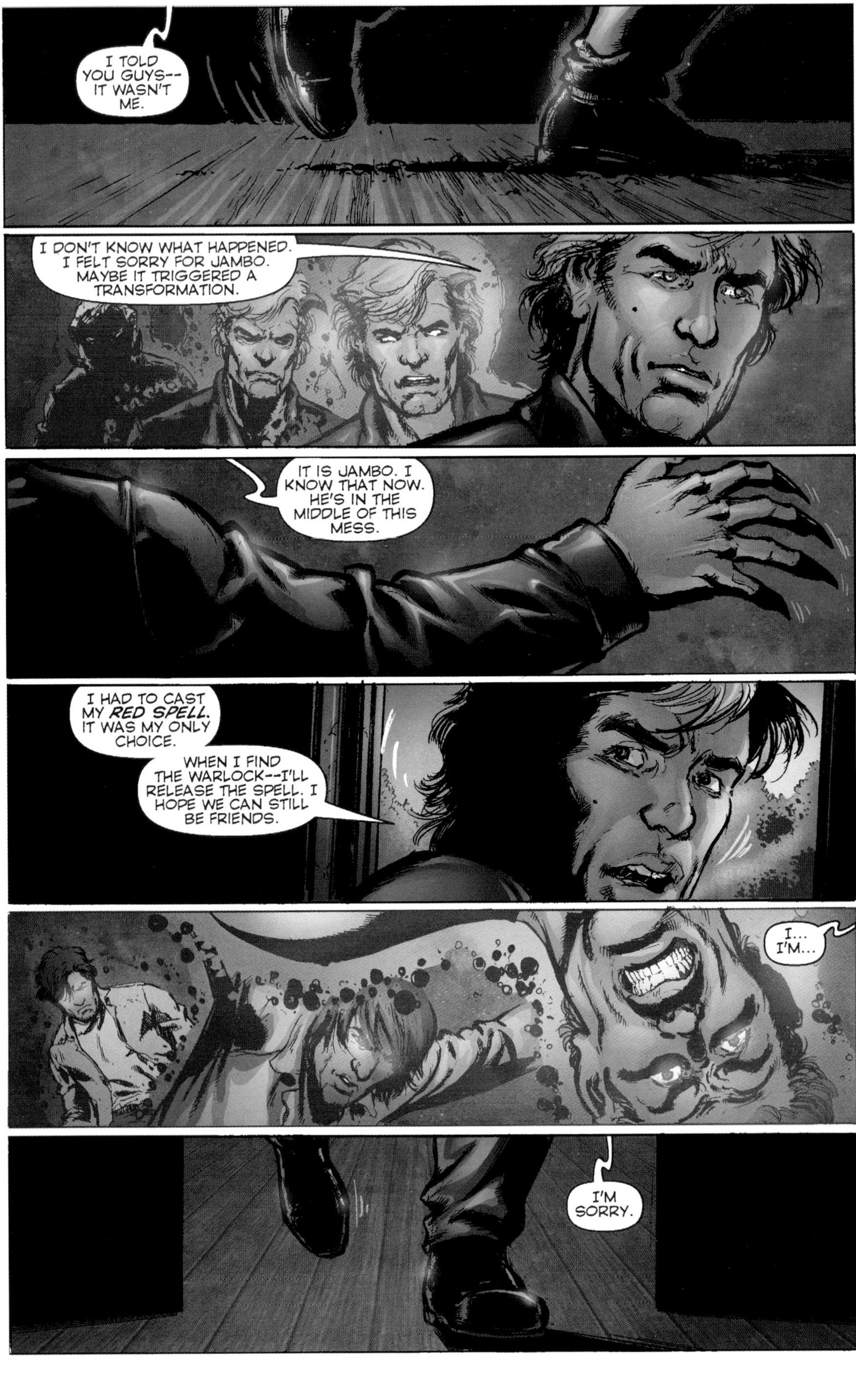
I TOLD YOU GUYS-- IT WASN'T ME.
I DON'T KNOW WHAT HAPPENED. I FELT SORRY FOR JAMBO. MAYBE IT TRIGGERED A TRANSFORMATION.
IT IS JAMBO. I KNOW THAT NOW. HE'S IN THE MIDDLE OF THIS MESS.
I HAD TO CAST MY *RED SPELL.* IT WAS MY ONLY CHOICE.
WHEN I FIND THE WARLOCK--I'LL RELEASE THE SPELL. I HOPE WE CAN STILL BE FRIENDS.
I... I'M...
I'M SORRY.

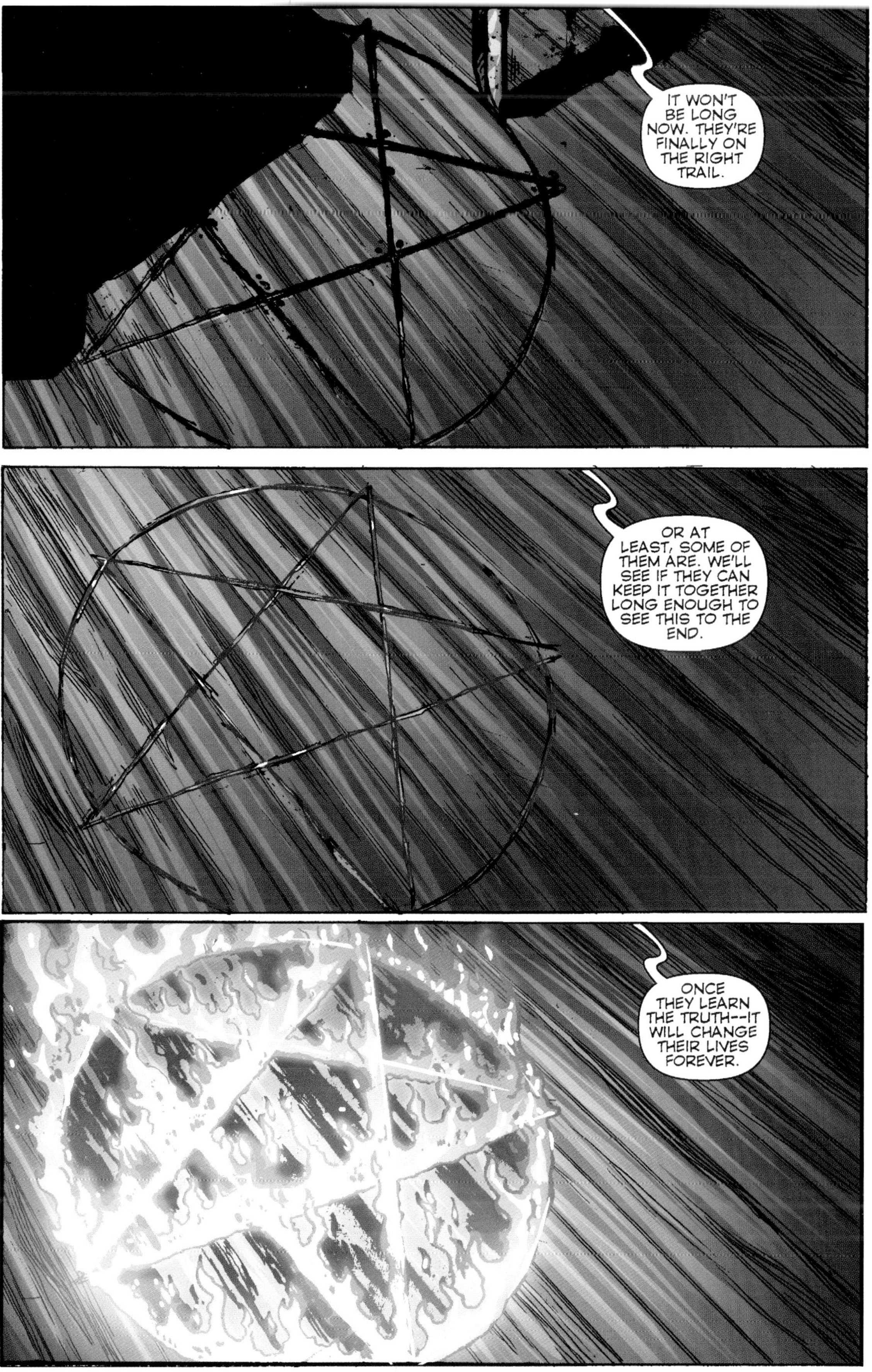
IT WON'T BE LONG NOW. THEY'RE FINALLY ON THE RIGHT TRAIL.
OR AT LEAST, SOME OF THEM ARE. WE'LL SEE IF THEY CAN KEEP IT TOGETHER LONG ENOUGH TO SEE THIS TO THE END.
ONCE THEY LEARN THE TRUTH--IT WILL CHANGE THEIR LIVES FOREVER.

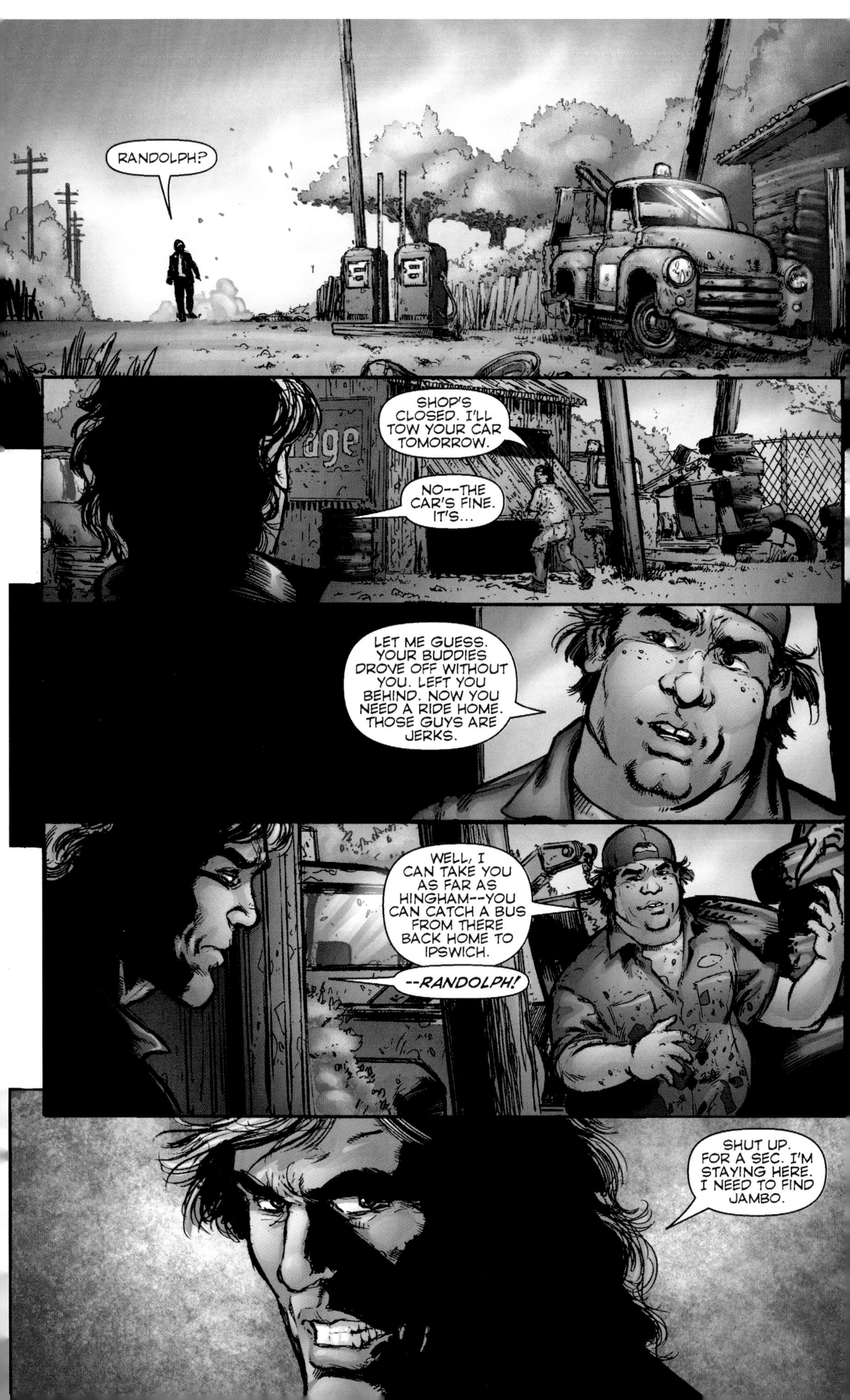
RANDOLPH?
SHOP'S CLOSED. I'LL TOW YOUR CAR TOMORROW.
NO--THE CAR'S FINE. IT'S...
LET ME GUESS. YOUR BUDDIES DROVE OFF WITHOUT YOU. LEFT YOU BEHIND. NOW YOU NEED A RIDE HOME. THOSE GUYS ARE JERKS.
WELL, I CAN TAKE YOU AS FAR AS HINGHAM--YOU CAN CATCH A BUS FROM THERE BACK HOME TO IPSWICH.
--RANDOLPH!
SHUT UP. FOR A SEC. I'M STAYING HERE. I NEED TO FIND JAMBO.

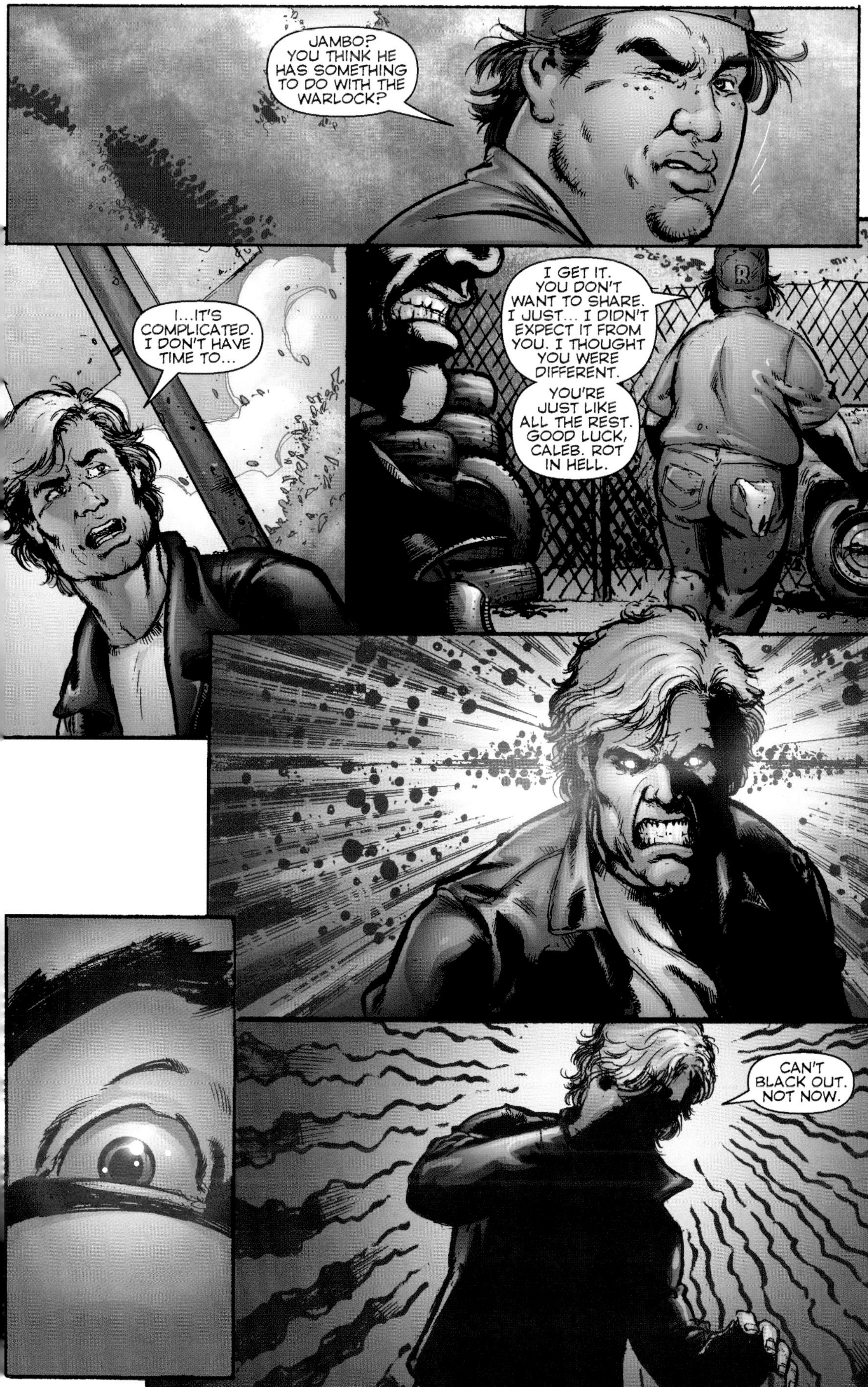
JAMBO? YOU THINK HE HAS SOMETHING TO DO WITH THE WARLOCK?
I...IT'S COMPLICATED. I DON'T HAVE TIME TO...
I GET IT. YOU DON'T WANT TO SHARE. I JUST... I DIDN'T EXPECT IT FROM YOU. I THOUGHT YOU WERE DIFFERENT.
YOU'RE JUST LIKE ALL THE REST. GOOD LUCK, CALEB. ROT IN HELL.
CAN'T BLACK OUT. NOT NOW.

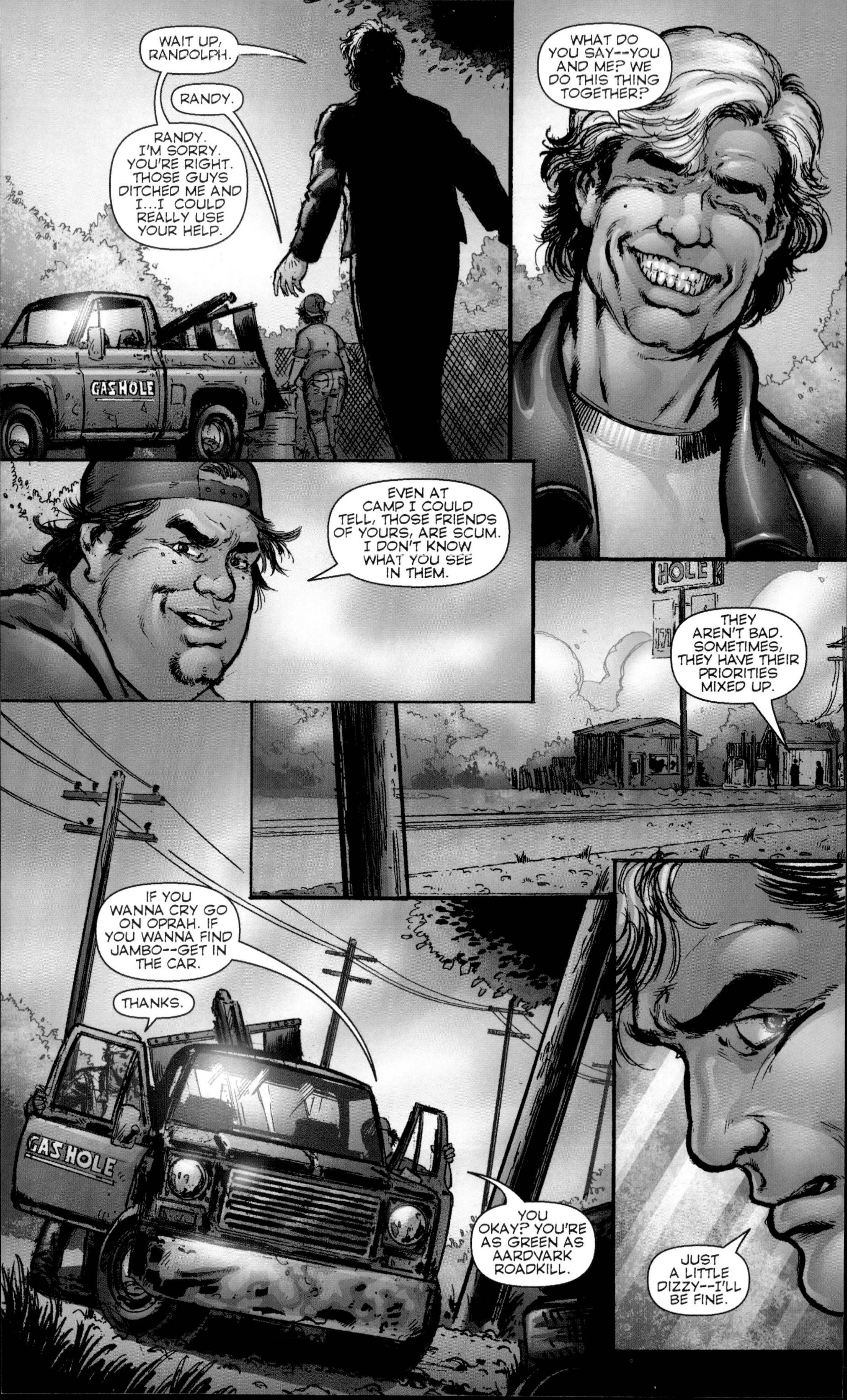
WAIT UP, RANDOLPH.
RANDY.
RANDY. I'M SORRY. YOU'RE RIGHT. THOSE GUYS DITCHED ME AND I...I COULD REALLY USE YOUR HELP.
GASHOLE
WHAT DO YOU SAY--YOU AND ME? WE DO THIS THING TOGETHER?
EVEN AT CAMP I COULD TELL, THOSE FRIENDS OF YOURS, ARE SCUM. I DON'T KNOW WHAT YOU SEE IN THEM.
HOLE
THEY AREN'T BAD. SOMETIMES, THEY HAVE THEIR PRIORITIES MIXED UP.
IF YOU WANNA CRY GO ON OPRAH. IF YOU WANNA FIND JAMBO--GET IN THE CAR.
THANKS.
GASHOLE
YOU OKAY? YOU'RE AS GREEN AS AARDVARK ROADKILL.
JUST A LITTLE DIZZY--I'LL BE FINE.

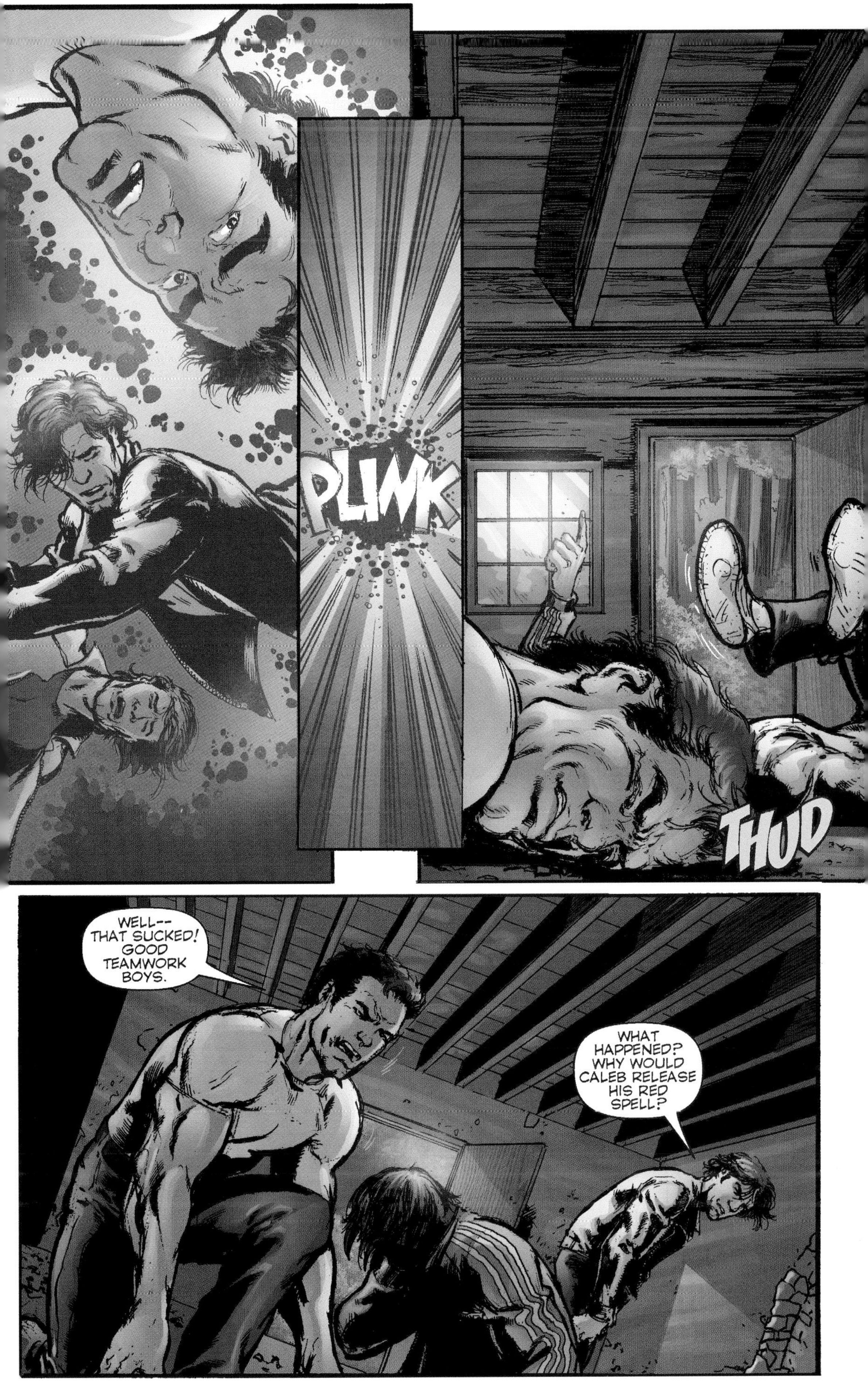
PLINK
THUD
WELL-- THAT SUCKED! GOOD TEAMWORK BOYS.
WHAT HAPPENED? WHY WOULD CALEB RELEASE HIS RED SPELL?

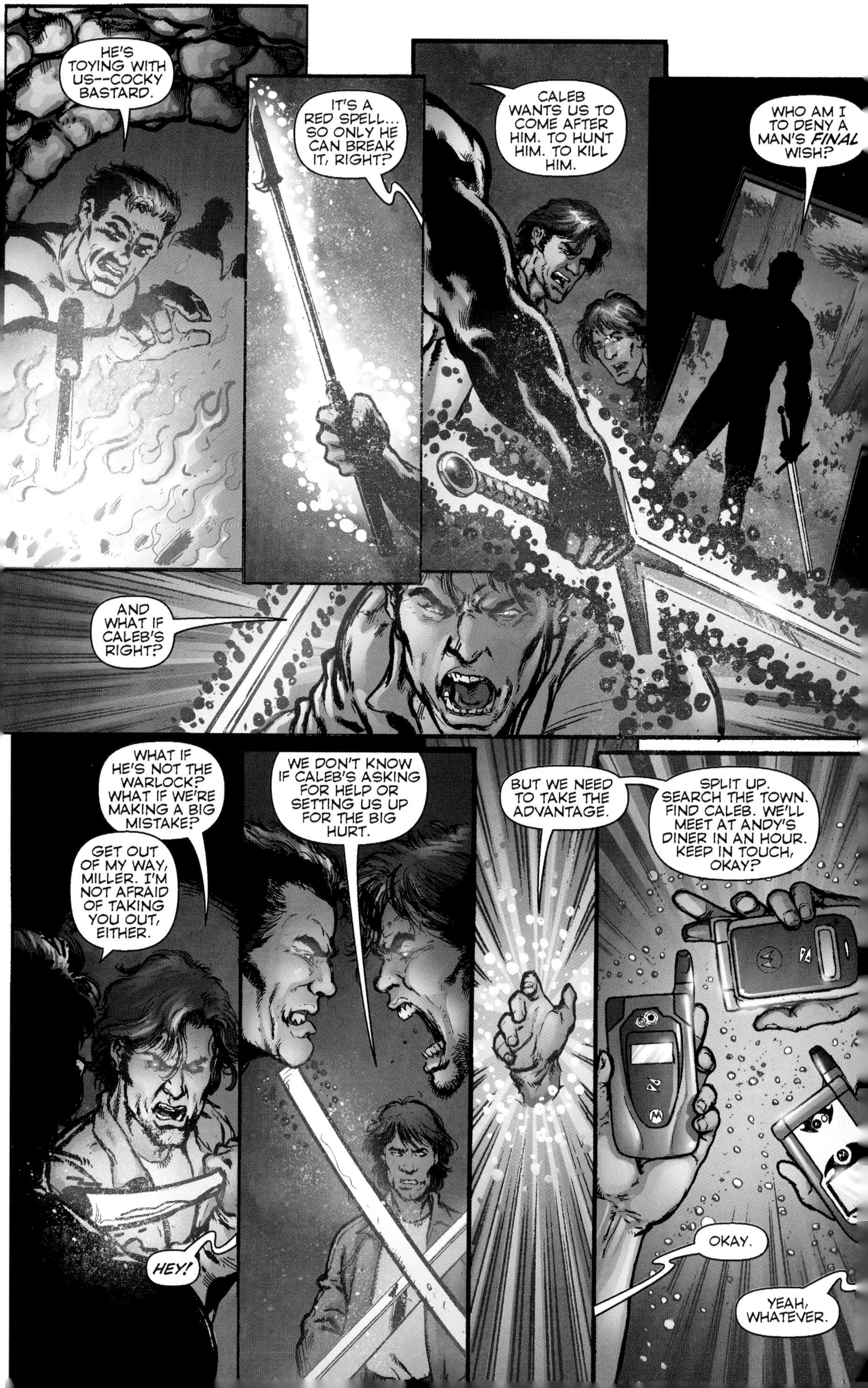
HE'S TOYING WITH US--COCKY BASTARD.
IT'S A RED SPELL... SO ONLY HE CAN BREAK IT, RIGHT?
CALEB WANTS US TO COME AFTER HIM. TO HUNT HIM. TO KILL HIM.
WHO AM I TO DENY A MAN'S *FINAL* WISH?
AND WHAT IF CALEB'S RIGHT?
WHAT IF HE'S NOT THE WARLOCK? WHAT IF WE'RE MAKING A BIG MISTAKE?
GET OUT OF MY WAY, MILLER. I'M NOT AFRAID OF TAKING YOU OUT, EITHER.
HEY!
WE DON'T KNOW IF CALEB'S ASKING FOR HELP OR SETTING US UP FOR THE BIG HURT.
BUT WE NEED TO TAKE THE ADVANTAGE.
SPLIT UP. SEARCH THE TOWN. FIND CALEB. WE'LL MEET AT ANDY'S DINER IN AN HOUR. KEEP IN TOUCH, OKAY?
OKAY.
YEAH, WHATEVER.

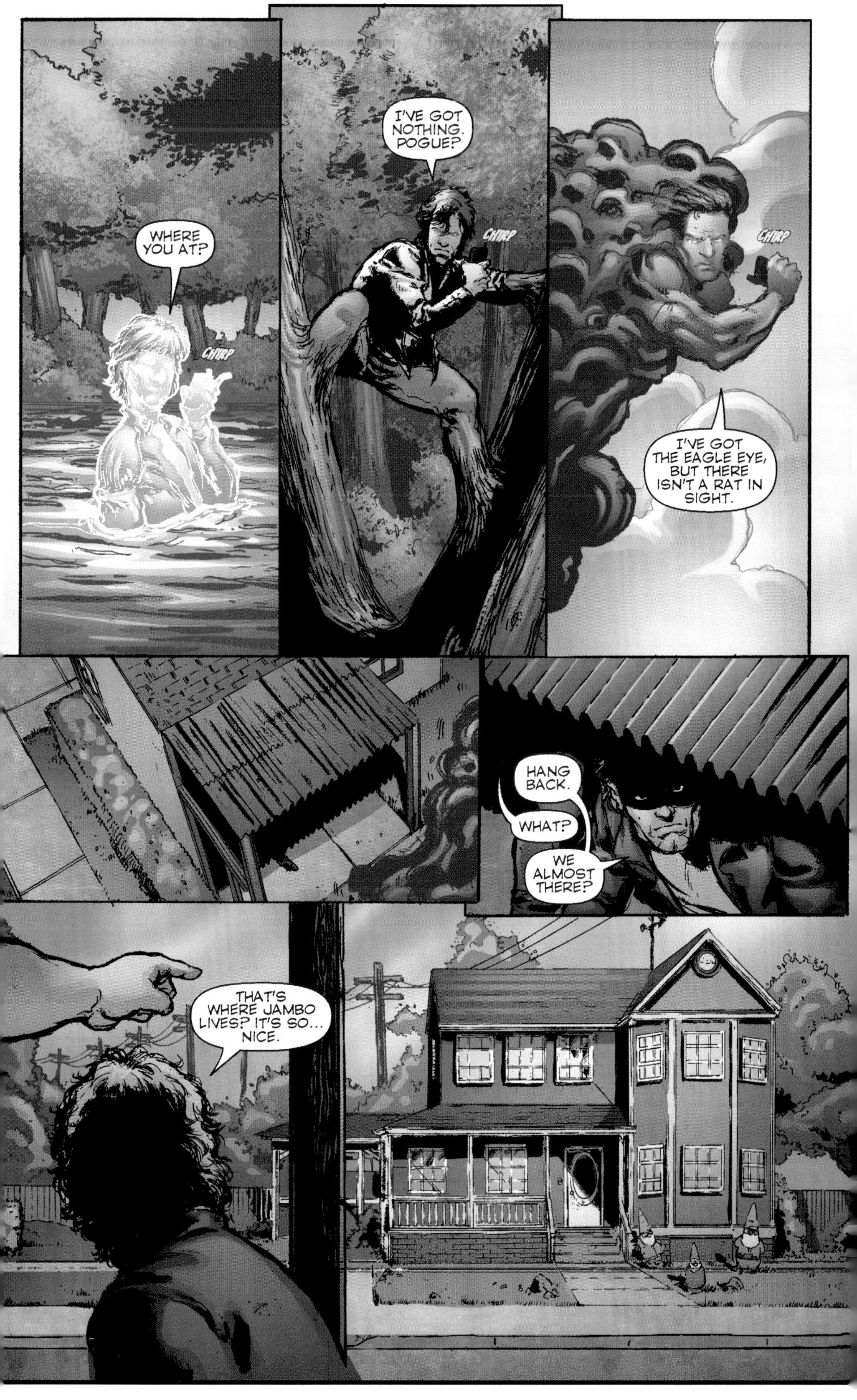
WHERE YOU AT?
CHIRP
I'VE GOT NOTHING. POGUE?
CHIRP
CHIRP
I'VE GOT THE EAGLE EYE, BUT THERE ISN'T A RAT IN SIGHT.
HANG BACK.
WHAT?
WE ALMOST THERE?
THAT'S WHERE JAMBO LIVES? IT'S SO... NICE.

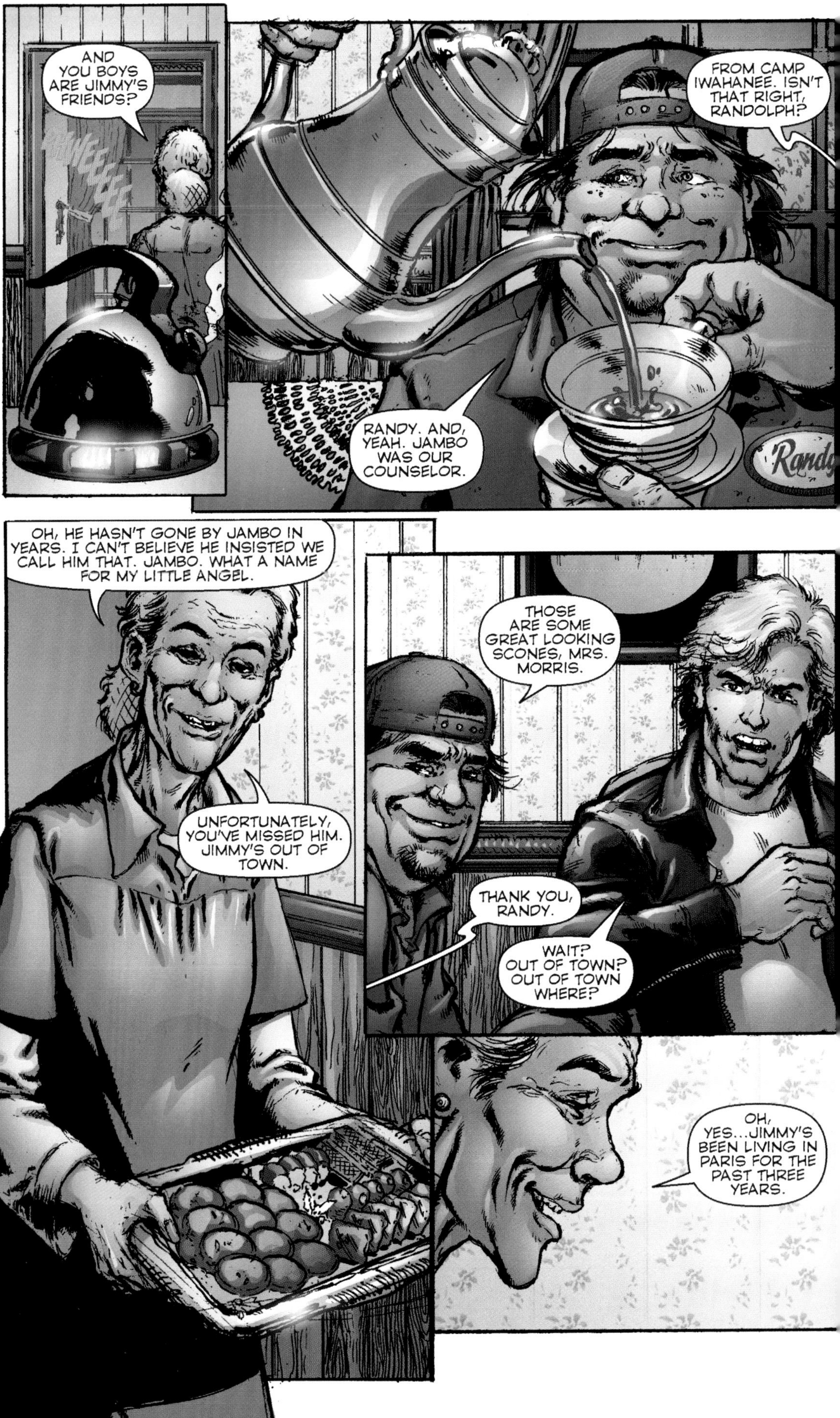

AND YOU BOYS ARE JIMMY'S FRIENDS?
FROM CAMP IWAHANEE. ISN'T THAT RIGHT, RANDOLPH?
RANDY. AND, YEAH. JAMBO WAS OUR COUNSELOR.
OH, HE HASN'T GONE BY JAMBO IN YEARS. I CAN'T BELIEVE HE INSISTED WE CALL HIM THAT. JAMBO. WHAT A NAME FOR MY LITTLE ANGEL.
UNFORTUNATELY, YOU'VE MISSED HIM. JIMMY'S OUT OF TOWN.
THOSE ARE SOME GREAT LOOKING SCONES, MRS. MORRIS.
THANK YOU, RANDY.
WAIT? OUT OF TOWN? OUT OF TOWN WHERE?
OH, YES...JIMMY'S BEEN LIVING IN PARIS FOR THE PAST THREE YEARS.

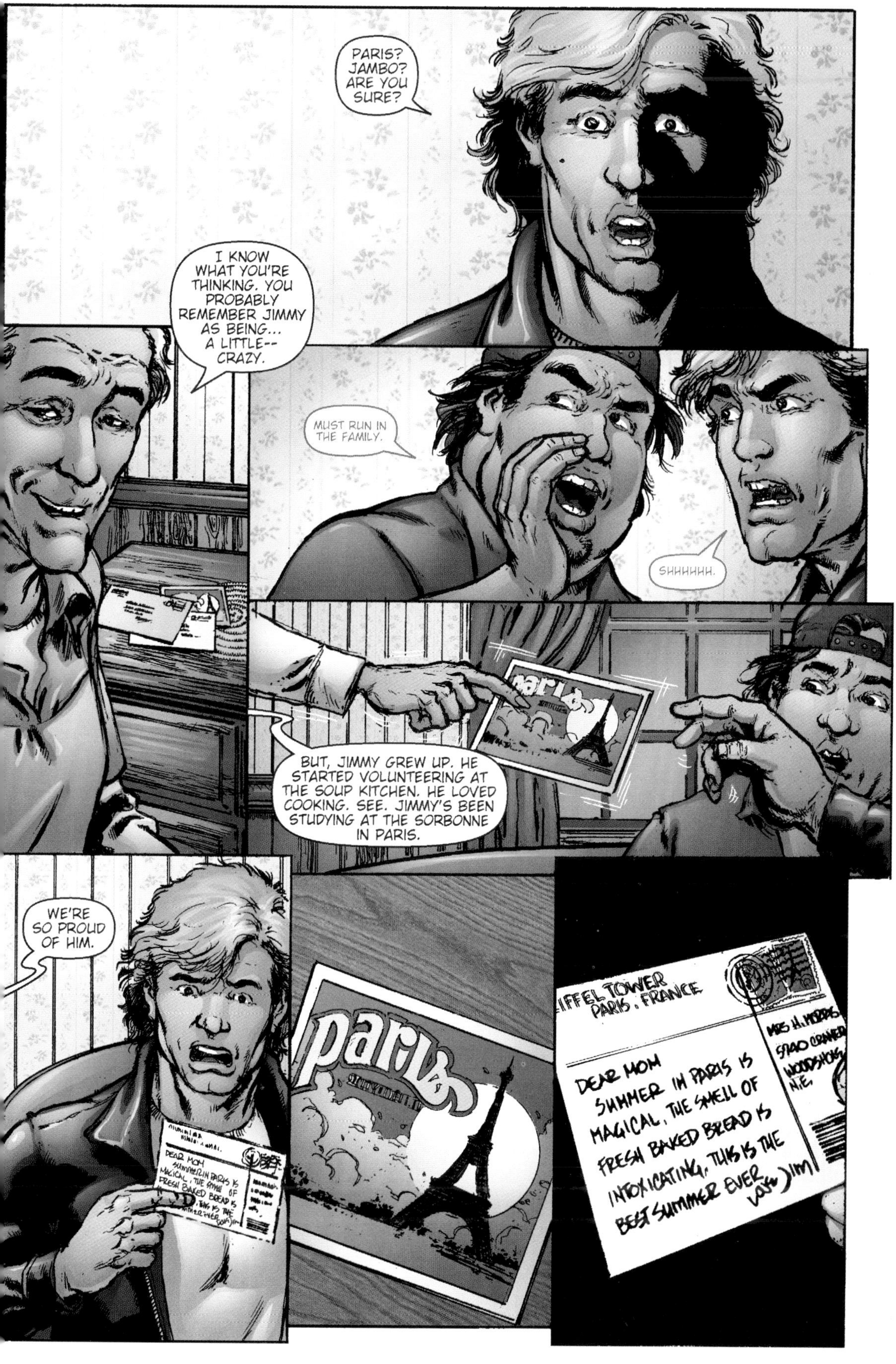
PARIS? JAMBO? ARE YOU SURE?
I KNOW WHAT YOU'RE THINKING. YOU PROBABLY REMEMBER JIMMY AS BEING... A LITTLE-- CRAZY.
MUST RUN IN THE FAMILY.
SHHHHHH.
BUT, JIMMY GREW UP. HE STARTED VOLUNTEERING AT THE SOUP KITCHEN. HE LOVED COOKING. SEE. JIMMY'S BEEN STUDYING AT THE SORBONNE IN PARIS.
WE'RE SO PROUD OF HIM.
paris
IFFEL TOWER
PARIS . FRANCE
DEAR MOM
SUMMER IN PARIS IS MAGICAL. THE SMELL OF FRESH BAKED BREAD IS INTOXICATING. THIS IS THE BEST SUMMER EVER
LOVE JIM

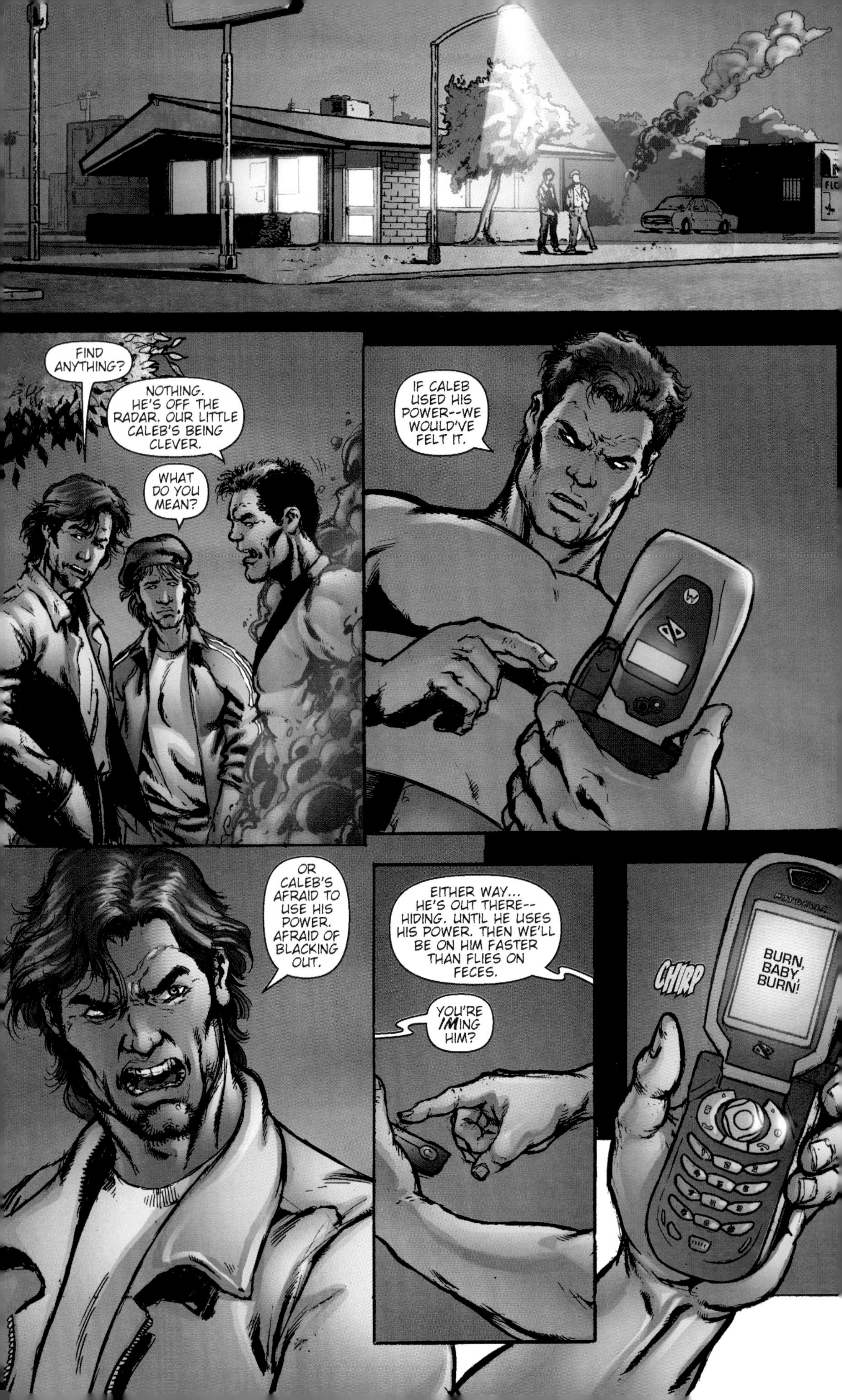
FIND ANYTHING?
NOTHING. HE'S OFF THE RADAR. OUR LITTLE CALEB'S BEING CLEVER.
WHAT DO YOU MEAN?
IF CALEB USED HIS POWER--WE WOULD'VE FELT IT.
OR CALEB'S AFRAID TO USE HIS POWER. AFRAID OF BLACKING OUT.
EITHER WAY... HE'S OUT THERE--HIDING. UNTIL HE USES HIS POWER. THEN WE'LL BE ON HIM FASTER THAN FLIES ON FECES.
YOU'RE IMING HIM?
CHIRP
BURN, BABY, BURN!

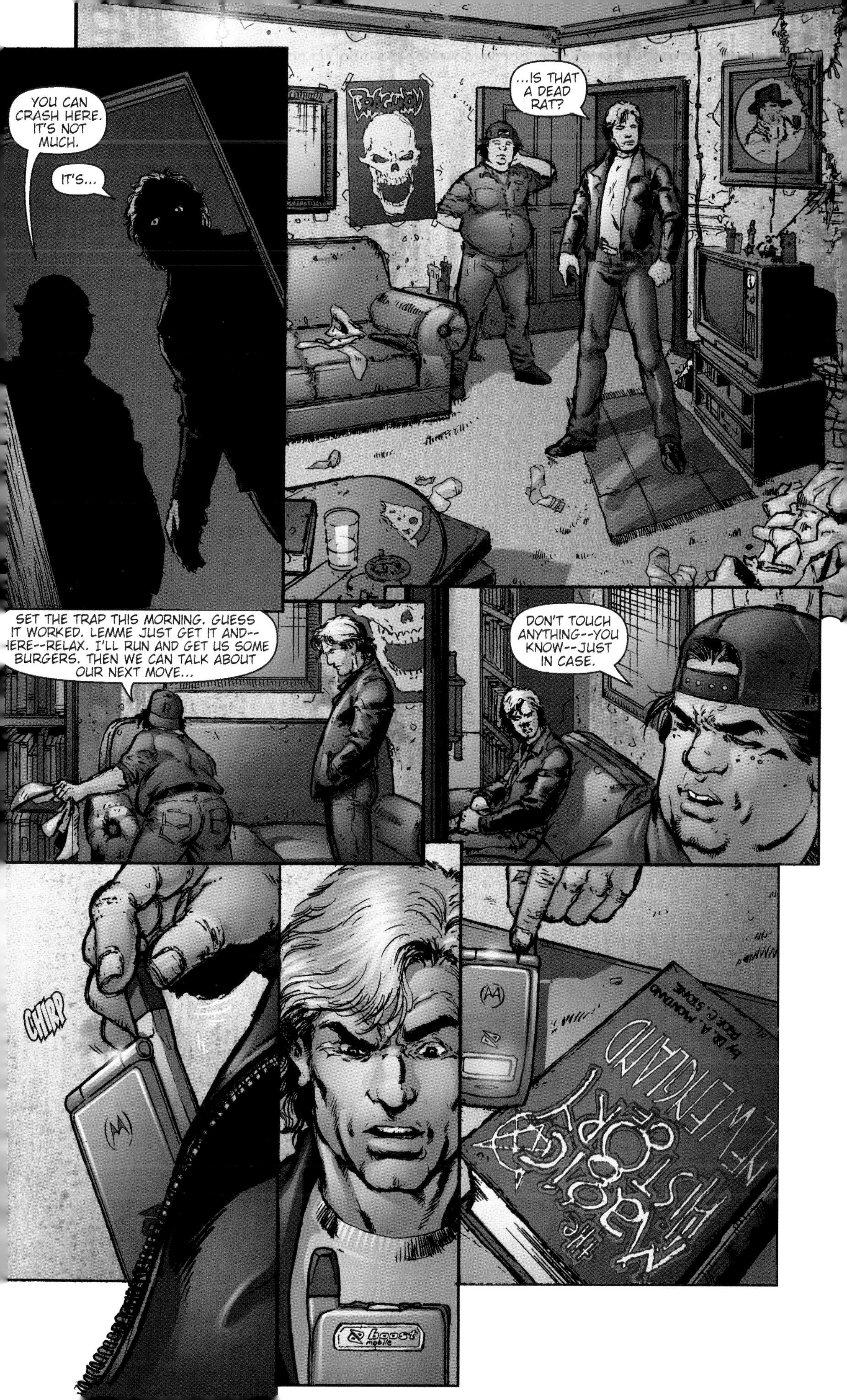
YOU CAN CRASH HERE. IT'S NOT MUCH.
IT'S...
...IS THAT A DEAD RAT?
SET THE TRAP THIS MORNING. GUESS IT WORKED. LEMME JUST GET IT AND-- ERE--RELAX. I'LL RUN AND GET US SOME BURGERS. THEN WE CAN TALK ABOUT OUR NEXT MOVE...
DON'T TOUCH ANYTHING--YOU KNOW--JUST IN CASE.
CHIRP

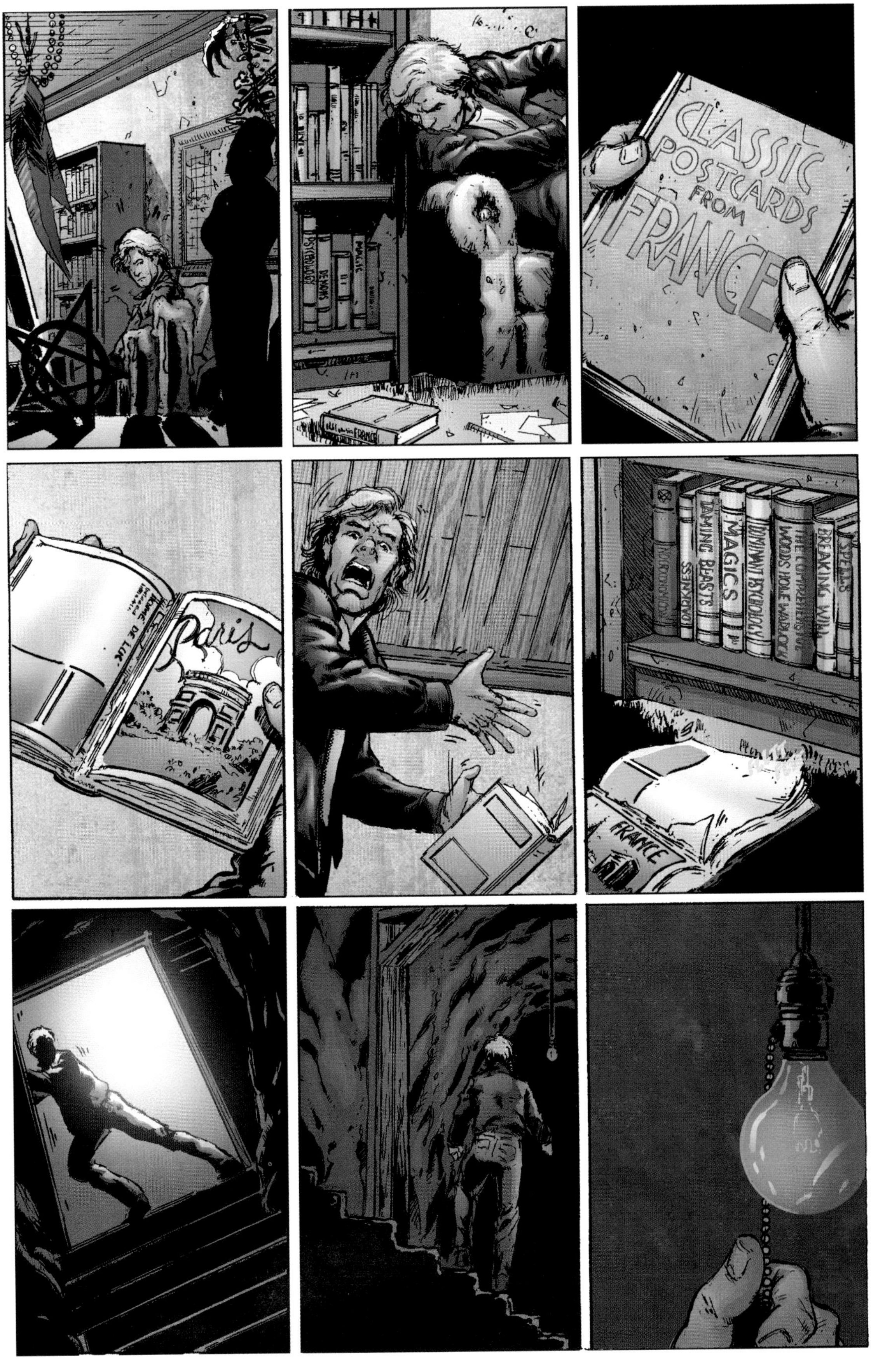

CLASSIC POSTCARDS FROM FRANCE
Paris
DARKNESS
DAMNING BEASTS
MAGICS
BREAKING WILL
SPELLS
FRANCE

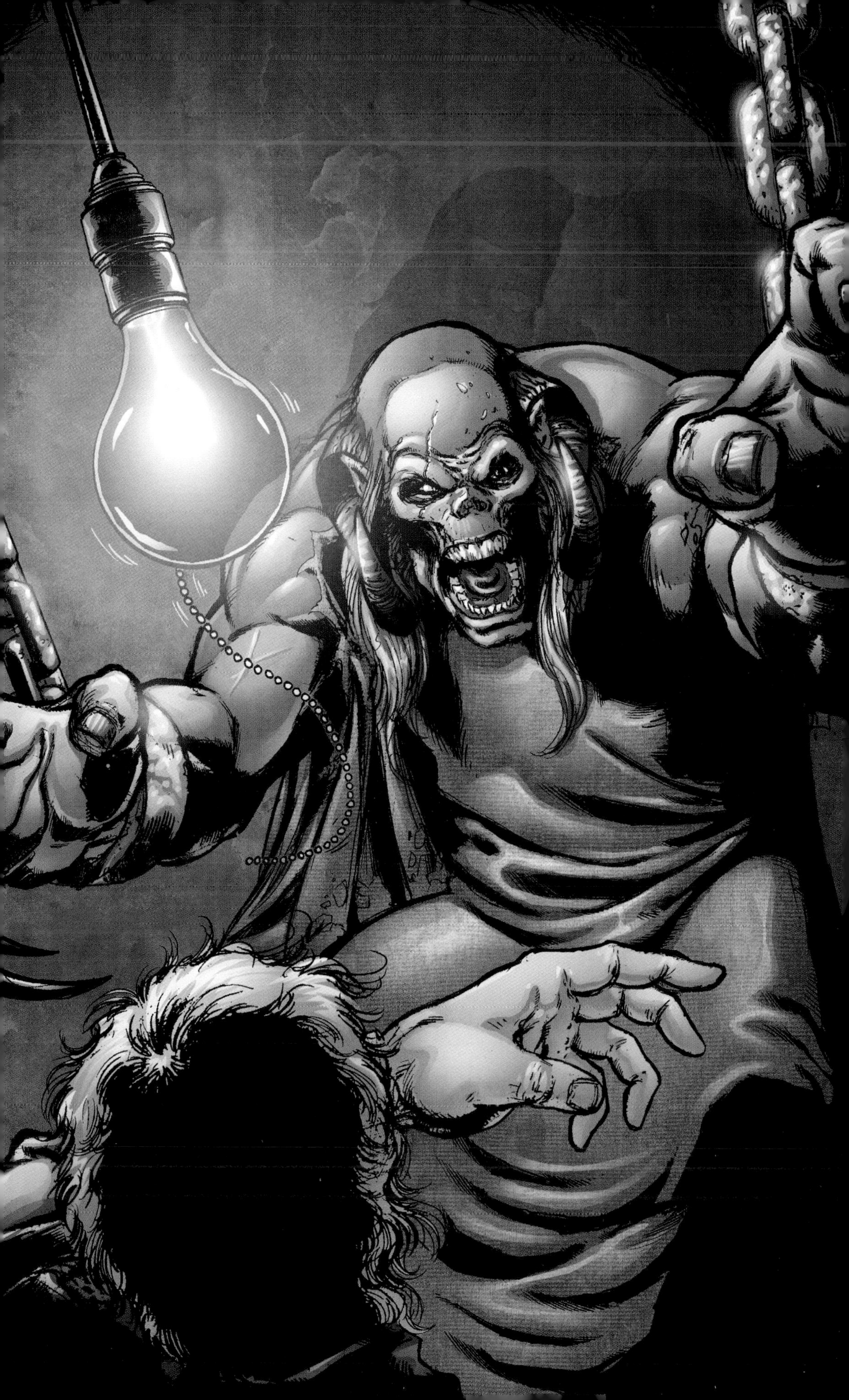

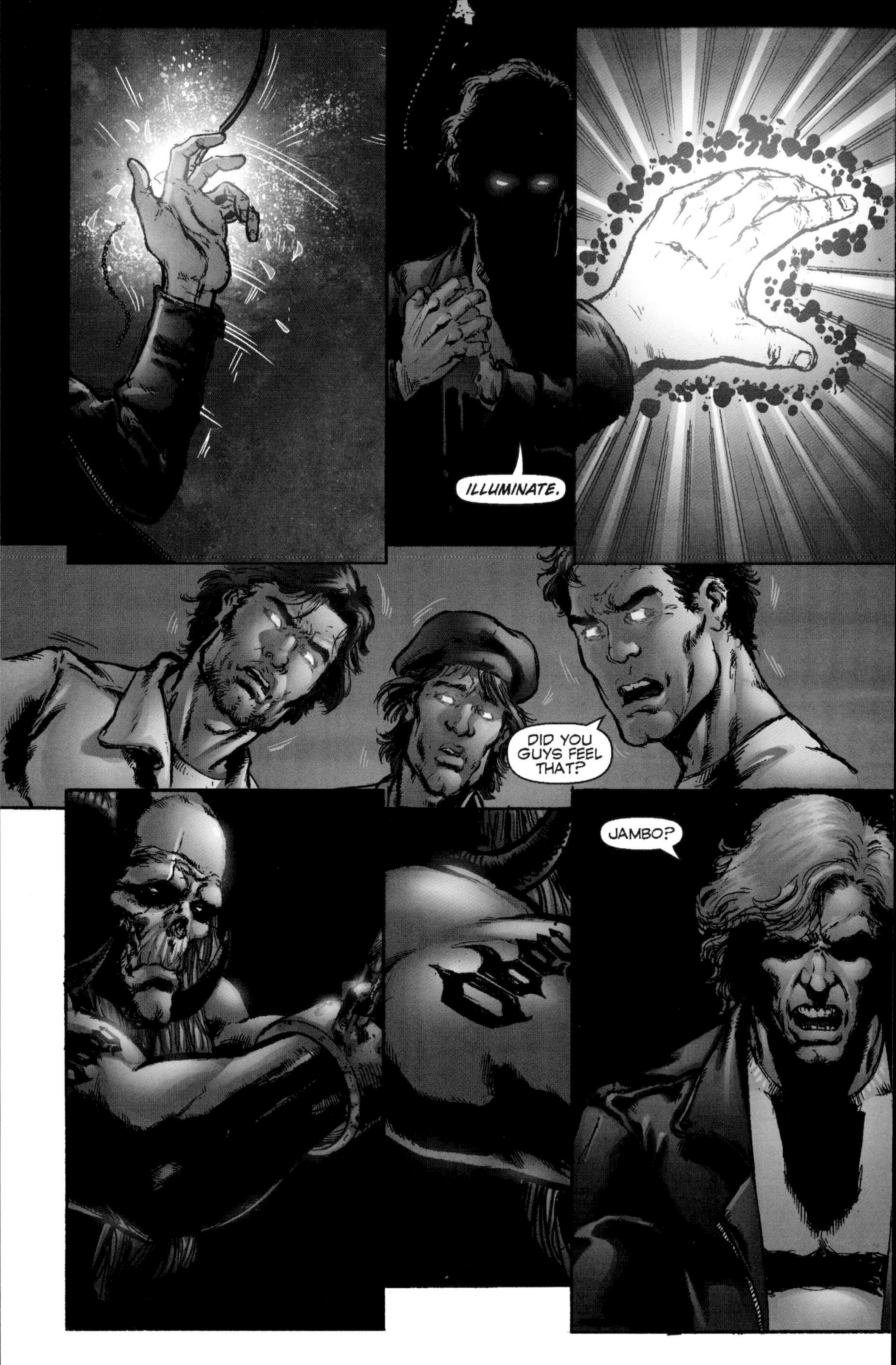
ILLUMINATE.
DID YOU GUYS FEEL THAT?
JAMBO?

Art by: Jason Badower

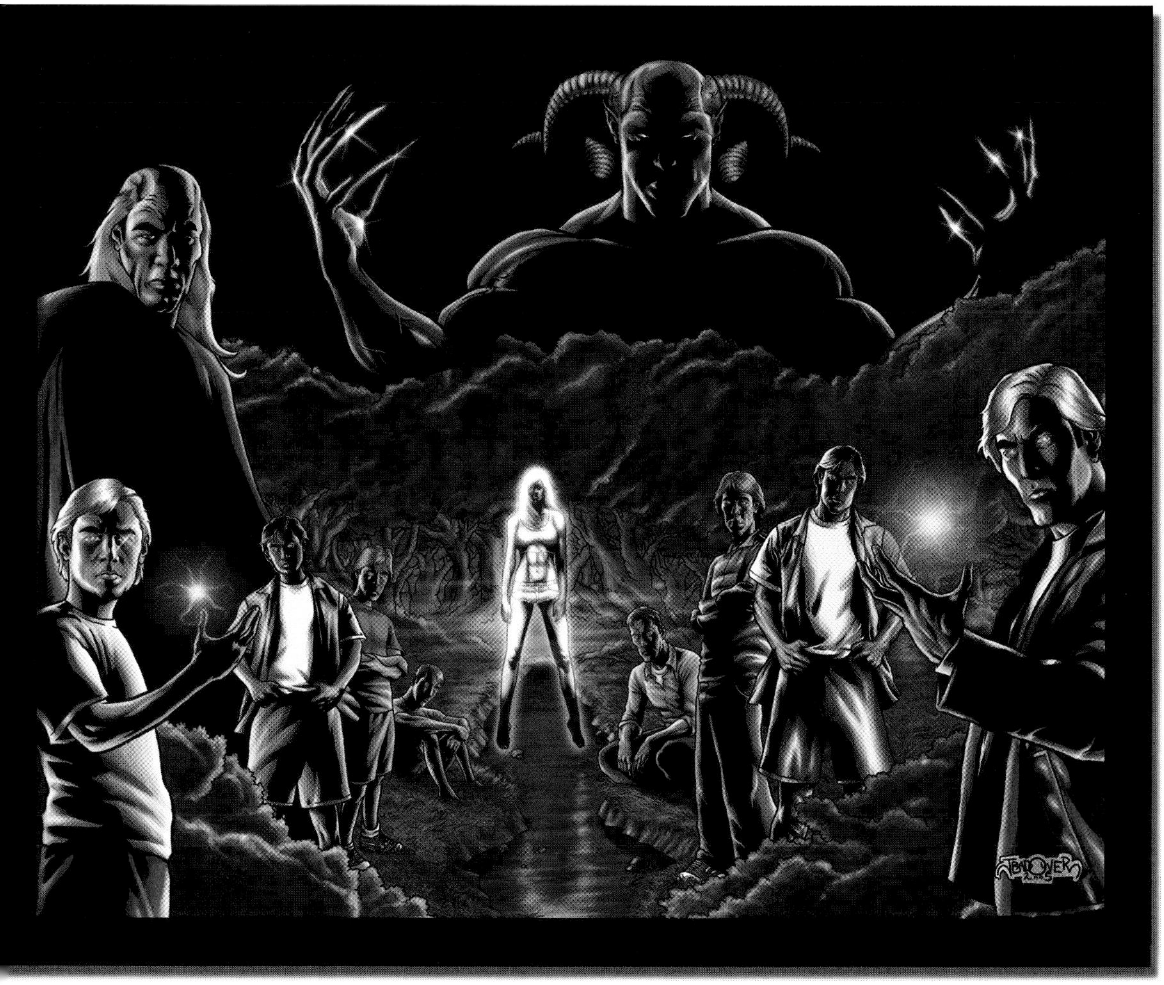

# Chapter 4

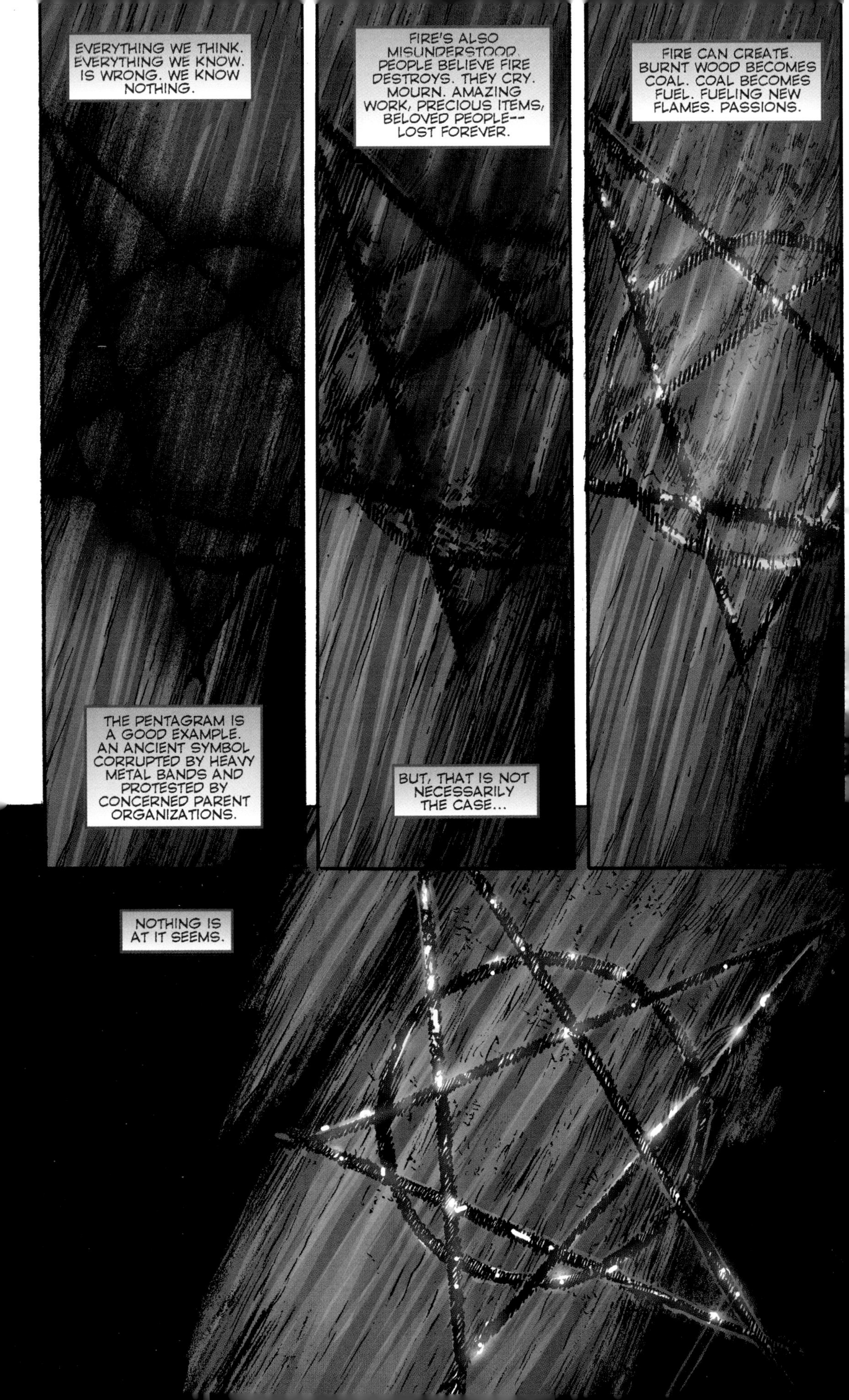
EVERYTHING WE THINK. EVERYTHING WE KNOW. IS WRONG. WE KNOW NOTHING.
THE PENTAGRAM IS A GOOD EXAMPLE. AN ANCIENT SYMBOL CORRUPTED BY HEAVY METAL BANDS AND PROTESTED BY CONCERNED PARENT ORGANIZATIONS.
FIRE'S ALSO MISUNDERSTOOD. PEOPLE BELIEVE FIRE DESTROYS. THEY CRY. MOURN. AMAZING WORK, PRECIOUS ITEMS, BELOVED PEOPLE-- LOST FOREVER.
BUT, THAT IS NOT NECESSARILY THE CASE...
FIRE CAN CREATE. BURNT WOOD BECOMES COAL. COAL BECOMES FUEL. FUELING NEW FLAMES. PASSIONS.
NOTHING IS AT IT SEEMS.

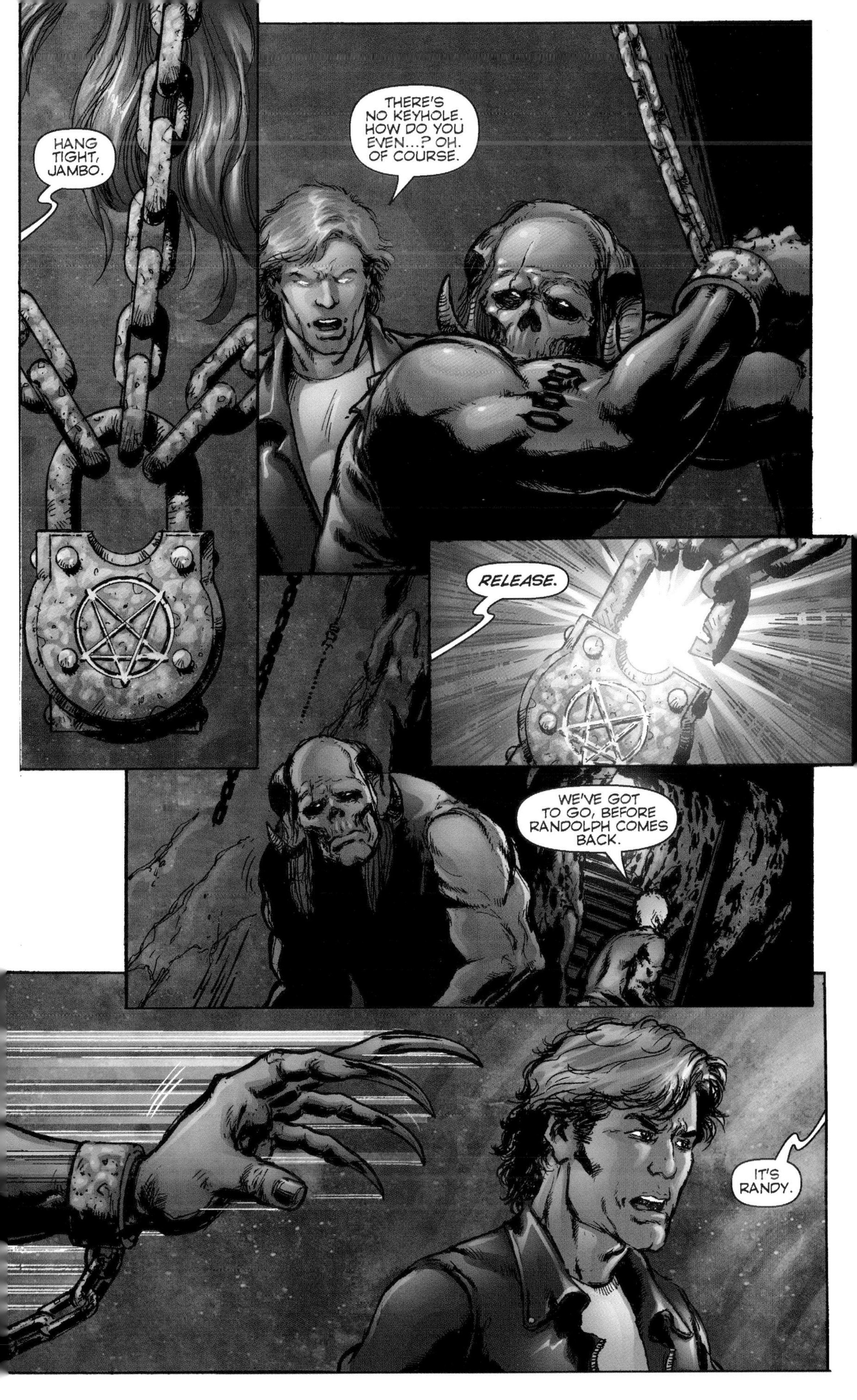

HANG TIGHT, JAMBO.
THERE'S NO KEYHOLE. HOW DO YOU EVEN...? OH. OF COURSE.
RELEASE.
WE'VE GOT TO GO, BEFORE RANDOLPH COMES BACK.
IT'S RANDY.

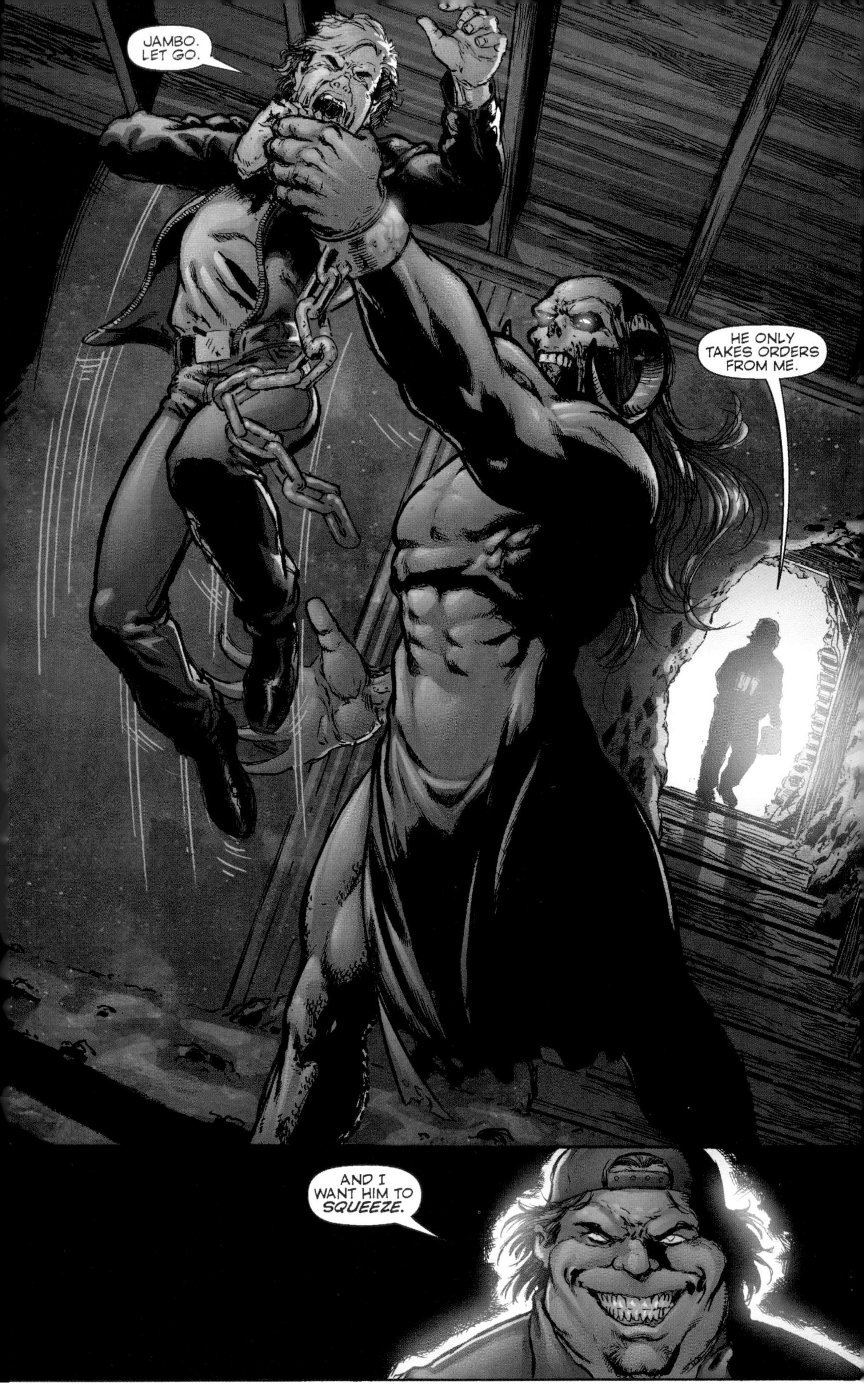
JAMBO. LET GO.
HE ONLY TAKES ORDERS FROM ME.
AND I WANT HIM TO SQUEEZE.

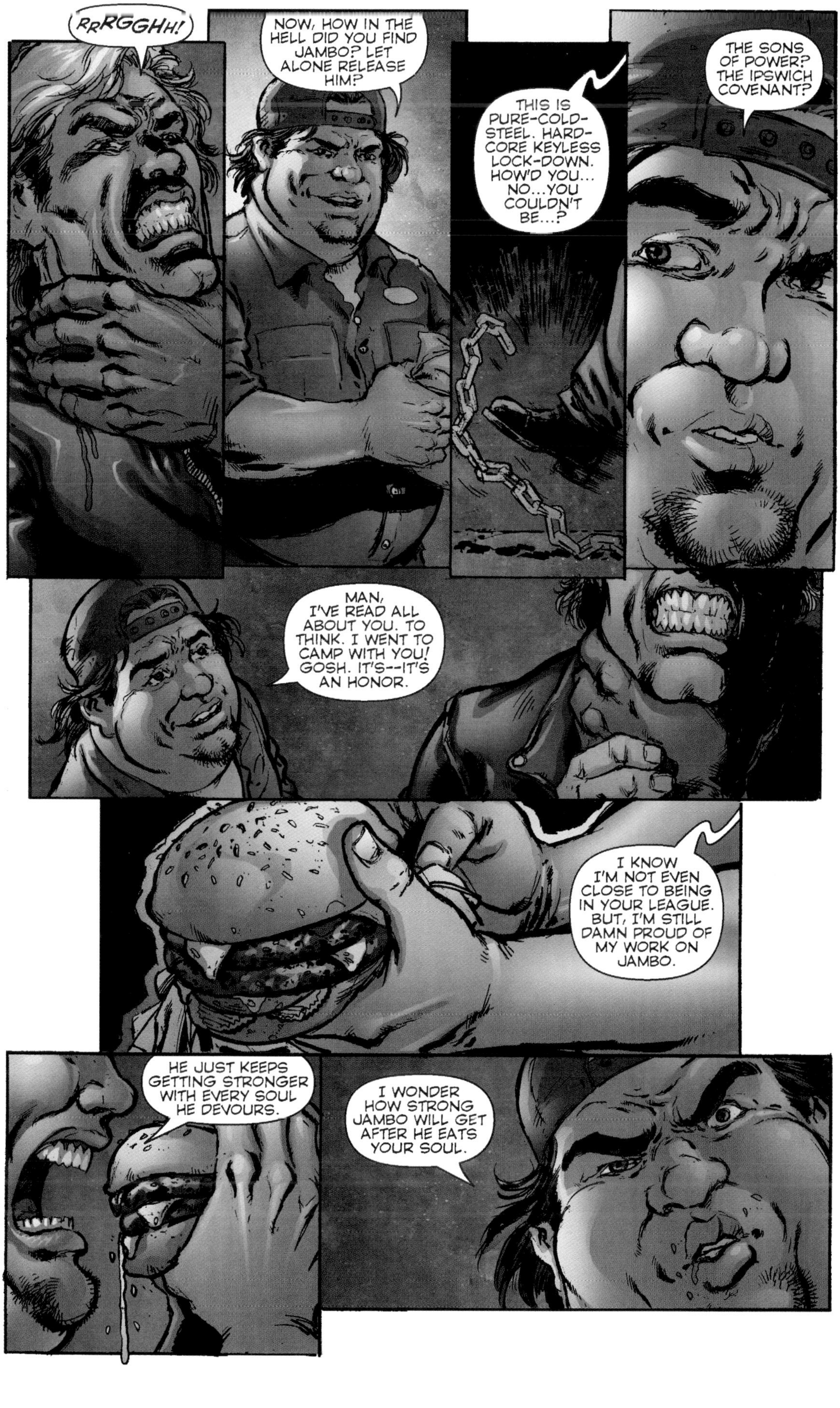
RRRGGHH!
NOW, HOW IN THE HELL DID YOU FIND JAMBO? LET ALONE RELEASE HIM?
THIS IS PURE-COLD-STEEL. HARD-CORE KEYLESS LOCK-DOWN. HOW'D YOU... NO...YOU COULDN'T BE...?
THE SONS OF POWER? THE IPSWICH COVENANT?
MAN, I'VE READ ALL ABOUT YOU. TO THINK. I WENT TO CAMP WITH YOU! GOSH. IT'S--IT'S AN HONOR.
I KNOW I'M NOT EVEN CLOSE TO BEING IN YOUR LEAGUE. BUT, I'M STILL DAMN PROUD OF MY WORK ON JAMBO.
HE JUST KEEPS GETTING STRONGER WITH EVERY SOUL HE DEVOURS.
I WONDER HOW STRONG JAMBO WILL GET AFTER HE EATS YOUR SOUL.

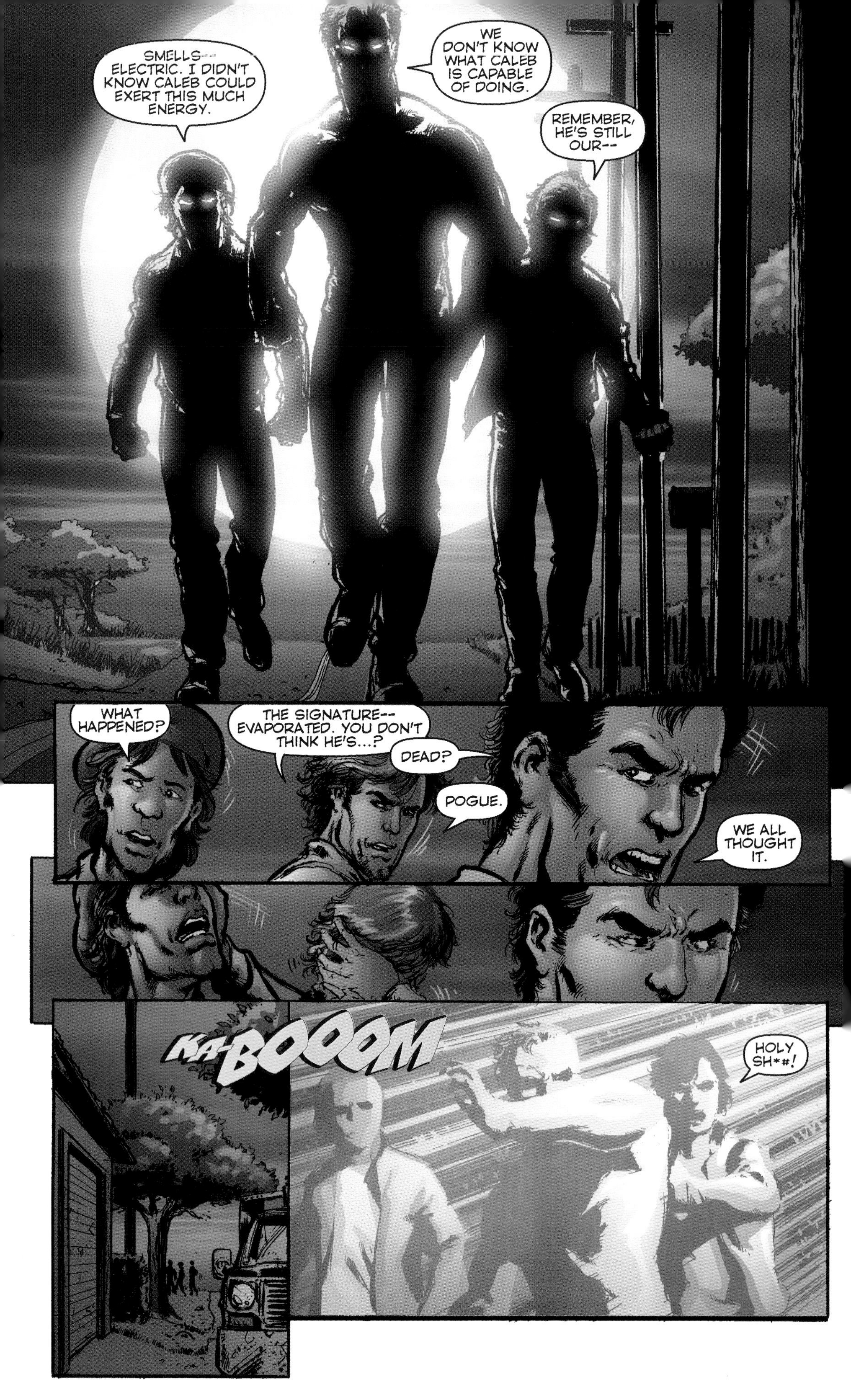
SMELLS... ELECTRIC. I DIDN'T KNOW CALEB COULD EXERT THIS MUCH ENERGY.
WE DON'T KNOW WHAT CALEB IS CAPABLE OF DOING.
REMEMBER, HE'S STILL OUR--
WHAT HAPPENED?
THE SIGNATURE--EVAPORATED. YOU DON'T THINK HE'S...?
DEAD?
POGUE.
WE ALL THOUGHT IT.
KA-BOOOM
HOLY SH*#!

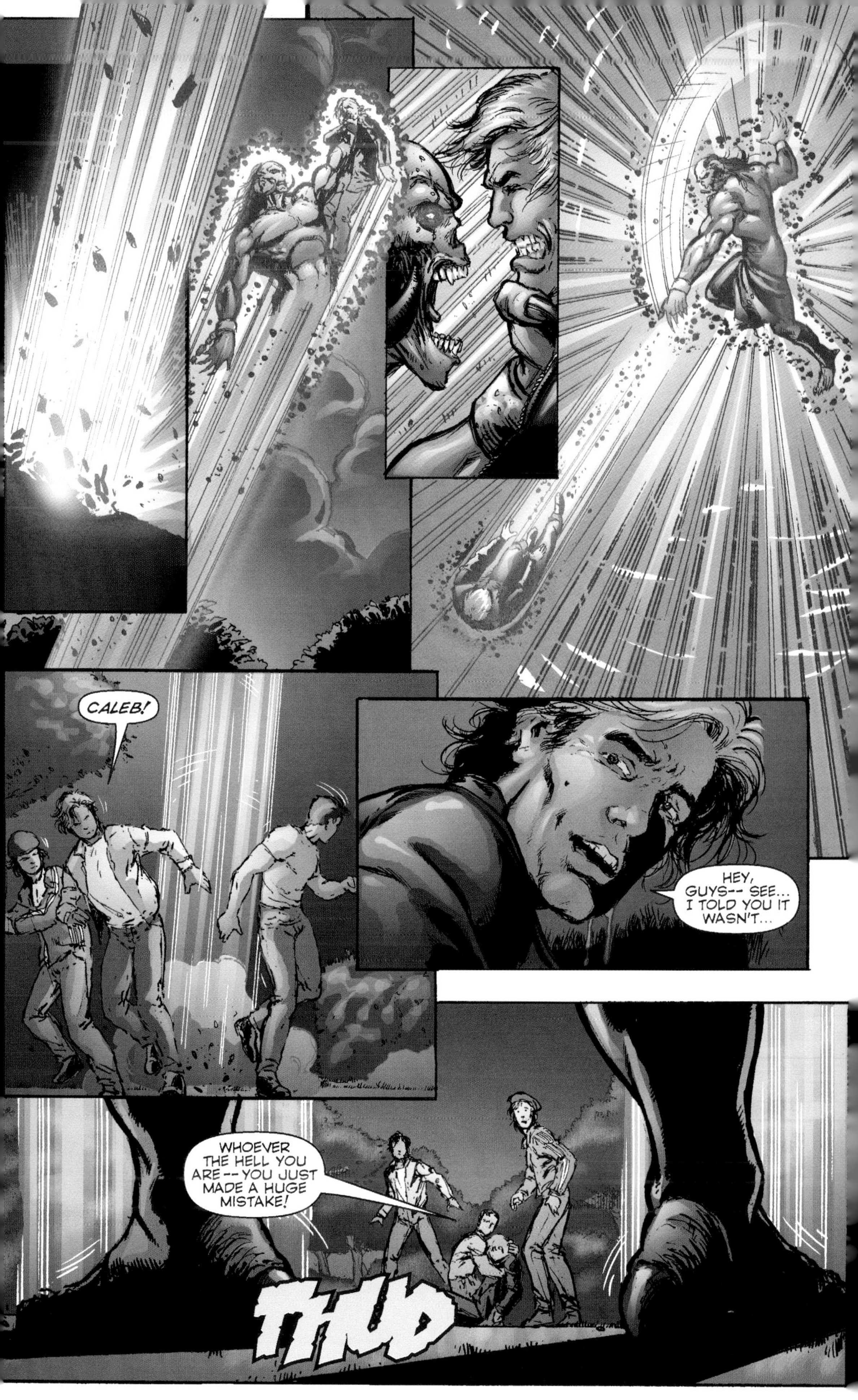
CALEB!
HEY, GUYS-- SEE... I TOLD YOU IT WASN'T...
WHOEVER THE HELL YOU ARE--YOU JUST MADE A HUGE MISTAKE!
THUD

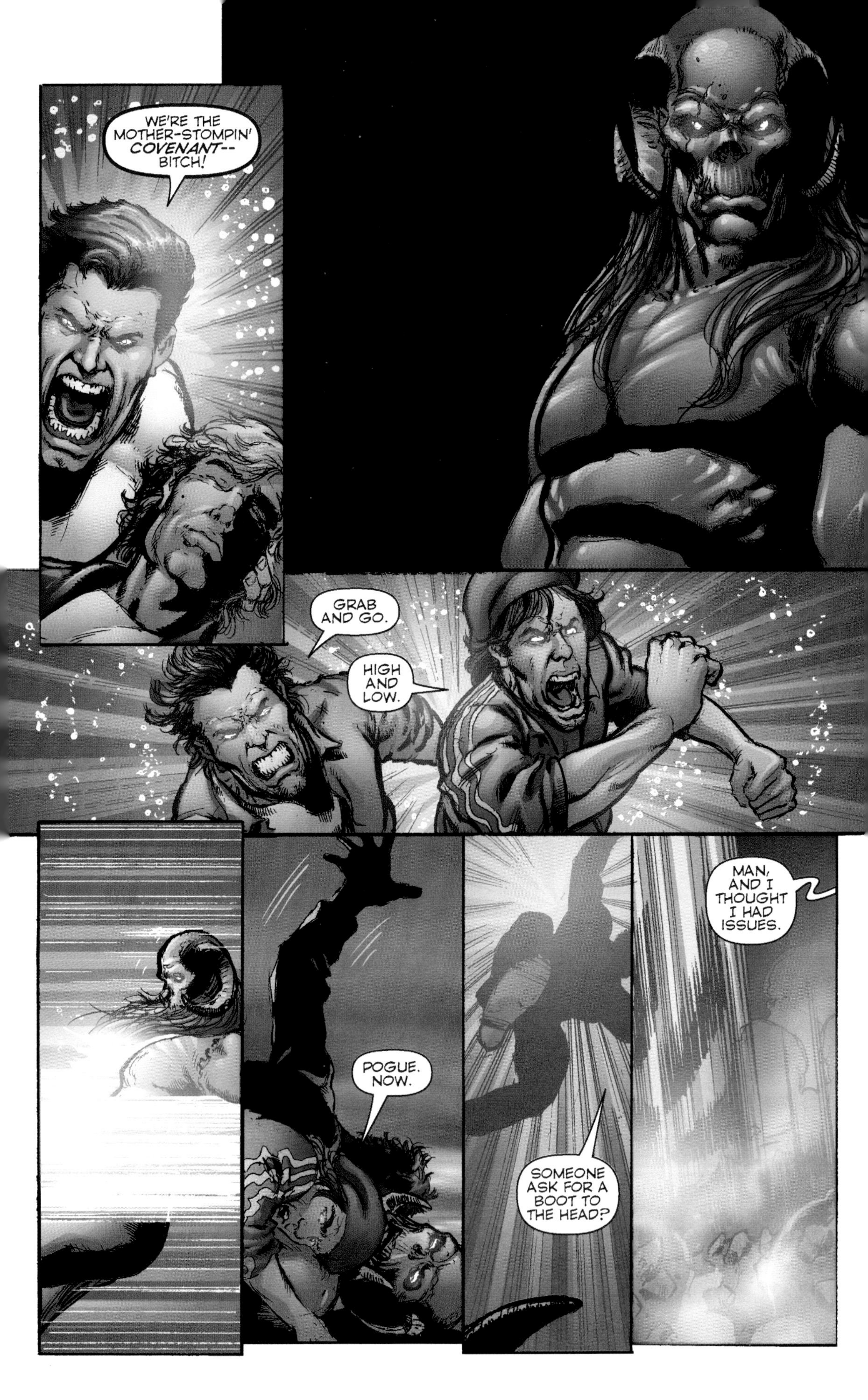

WE'RE THE MOTHER-STOMPIN' *COVENANT*-- BITCH!
GRAB AND GO.
HIGH AND LOW.
POGUE. NOW.
SOMEONE ASK FOR A BOOT TO THE HEAD?
MAN, AND I THOUGHT I HAD ISSUES.

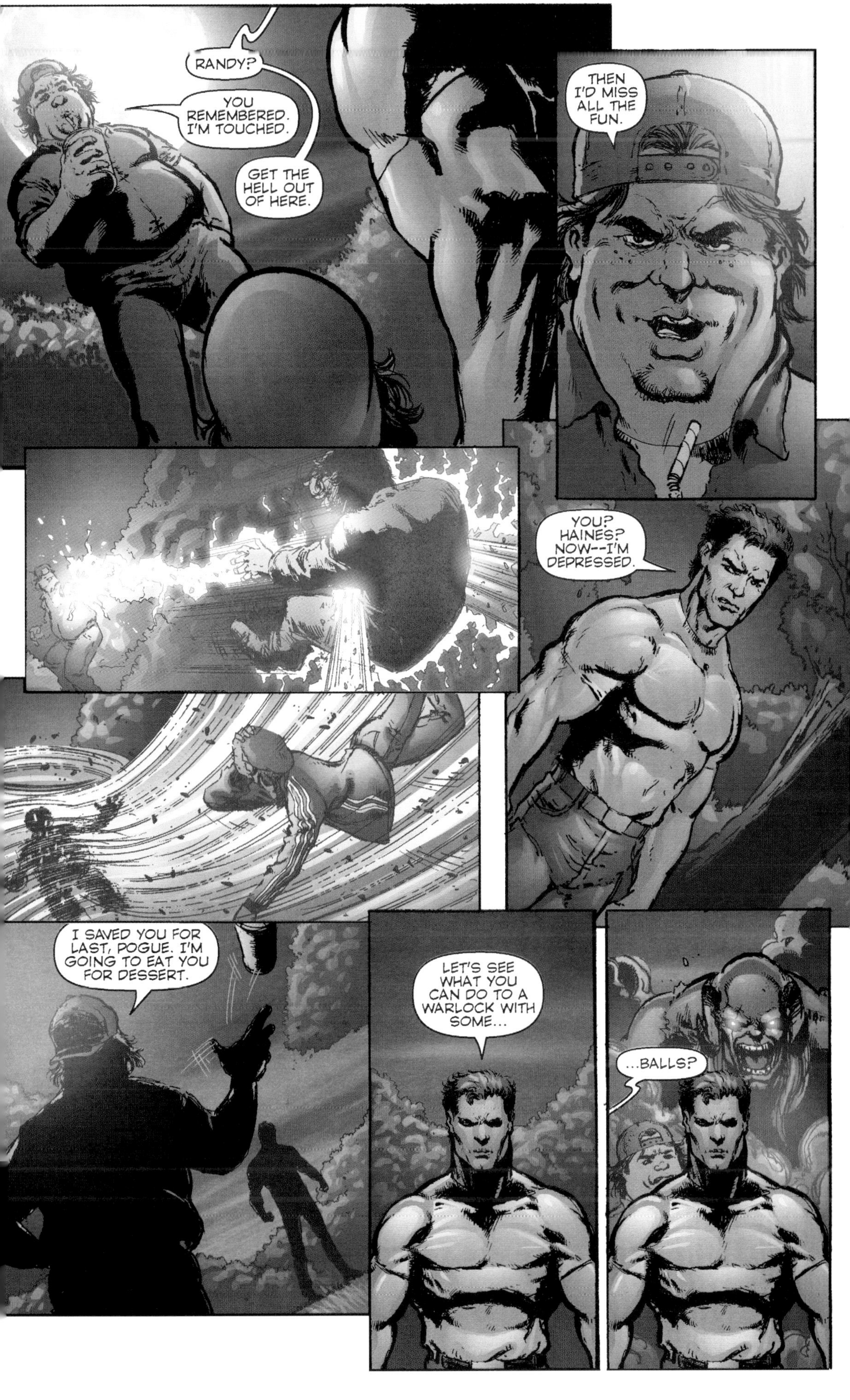
RANDY?
YOU REMEMBERED. I'M TOUCHED.
GET THE HELL OUT OF HERE.
THEN I'D MISS ALL THE FUN.
YOU? HAINES? NOW--I'M DEPRESSED.
I SAVED YOU FOR LAST, POGUE. I'M GOING TO EAT YOU FOR DESSERT.
LET'S SEE WHAT YOU CAN DO TO A WARLOCK WITH SOME...
...BALLS?

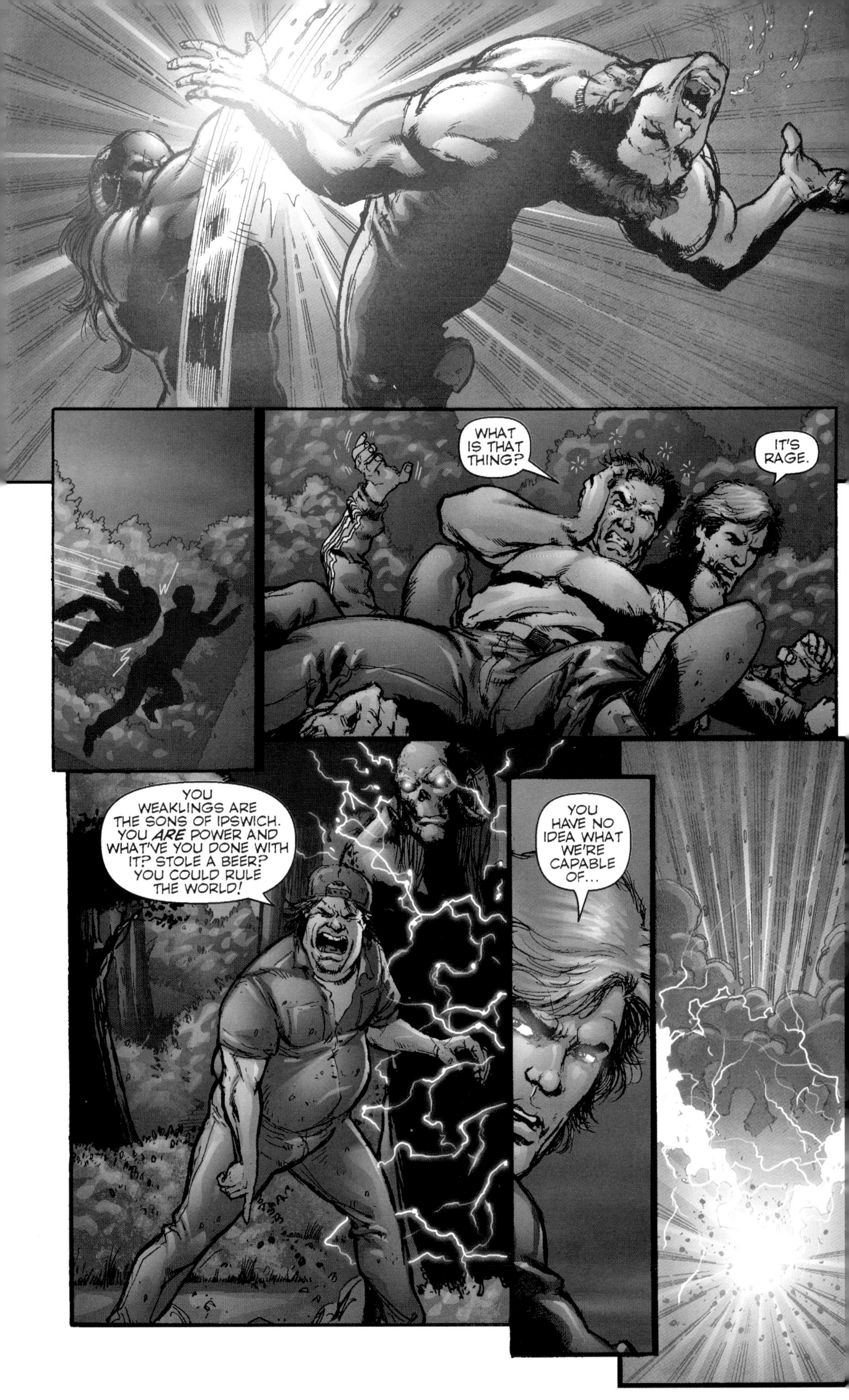
WHAT IS THAT THING?
IT'S RAGE.
YOU WEAKLINGS ARE THE SONS OF IPSWICH. YOU *ARE* POWER AND WHAT'VE YOU DONE WITH IT? STOLE A BEER? YOU COULD RULE THE WORLD!
YOU HAVE NO IDEA WHAT WE'RE CAPABLE OF...

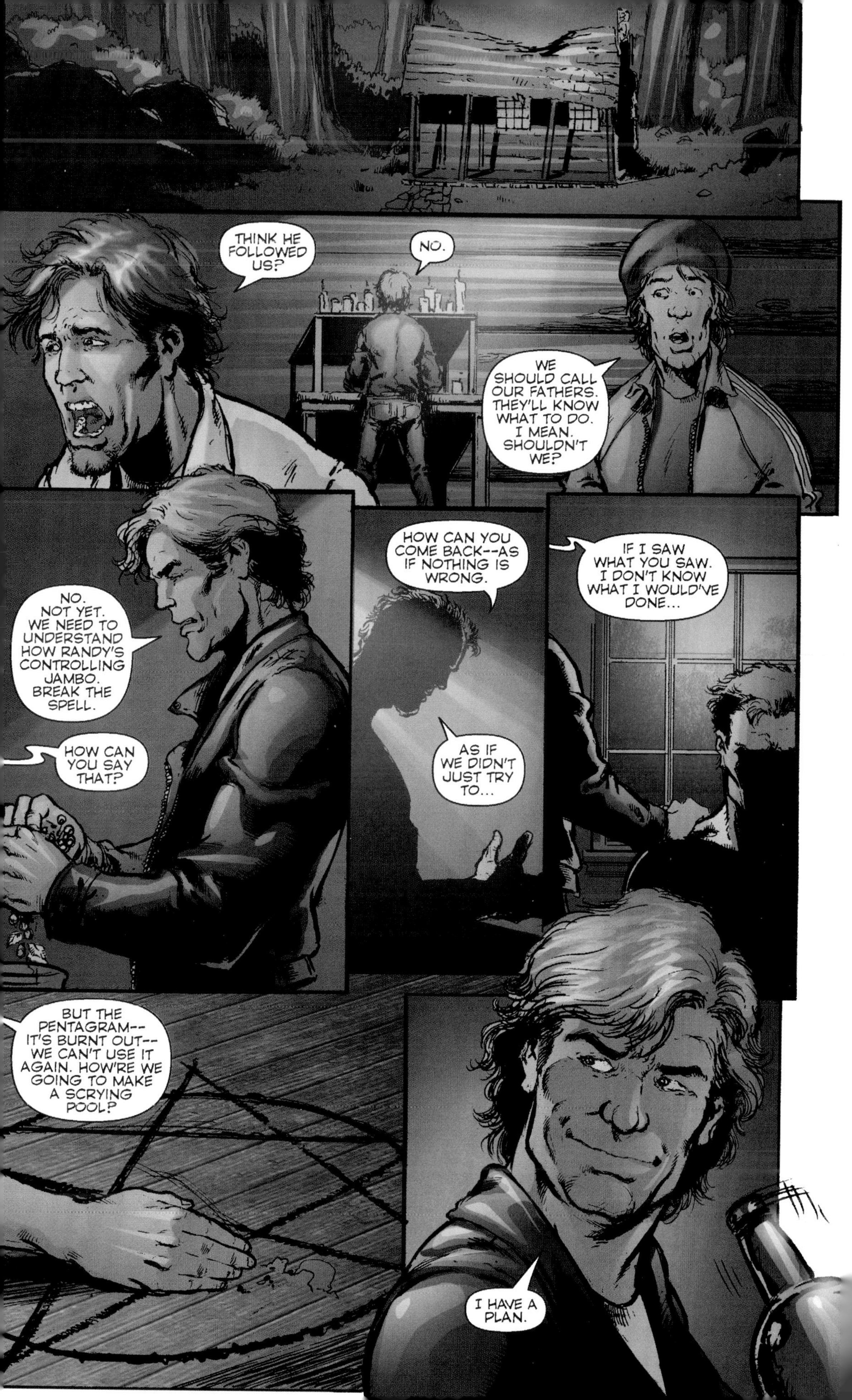
THINK HE FOLLOWED US?
NO.
WE SHOULD CALL OUR FATHERS. THEY'LL KNOW WHAT TO DO. I MEAN. SHOULDN'T WE?
NO. NOT YET. WE NEED TO UNDERSTAND HOW RANDY'S CONTROLLING JAMBO. BREAK THE SPELL.
HOW CAN YOU SAY THAT?
HOW CAN YOU COME BACK--AS IF NOTHING IS WRONG.
AS IF WE DIDN'T JUST TRY TO...
IF I SAW WHAT YOU SAW. I DON'T KNOW WHAT I WOULD'VE DONE...
BUT THE PENTAGRAM--IT'S BURNT OUT--WE CAN'T USE IT AGAIN. HOW'RE WE GOING TO MAKE A SCRYING POOL?
I HAVE A PLAN.

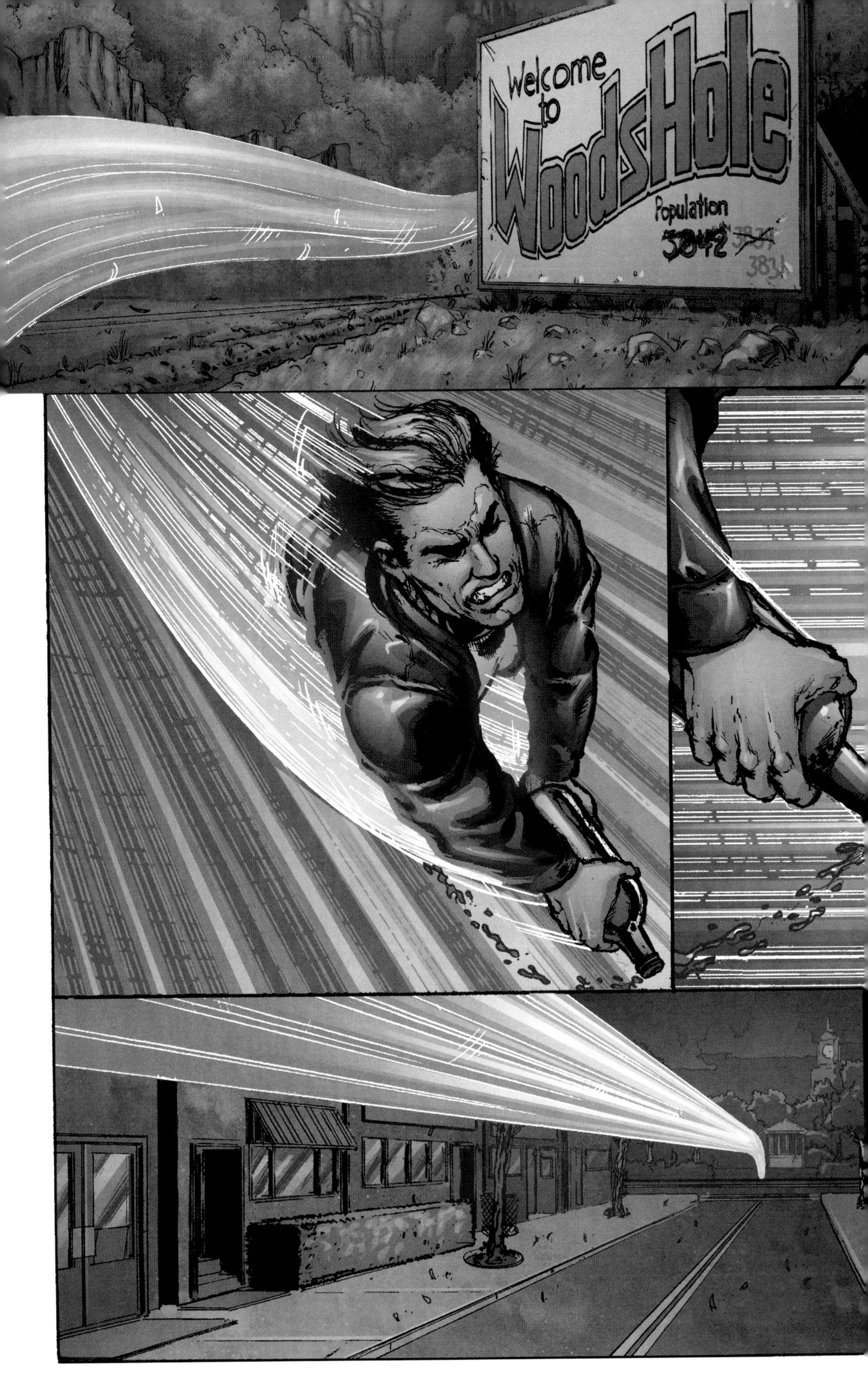
Welcome to
WoodsHole
Population
3842

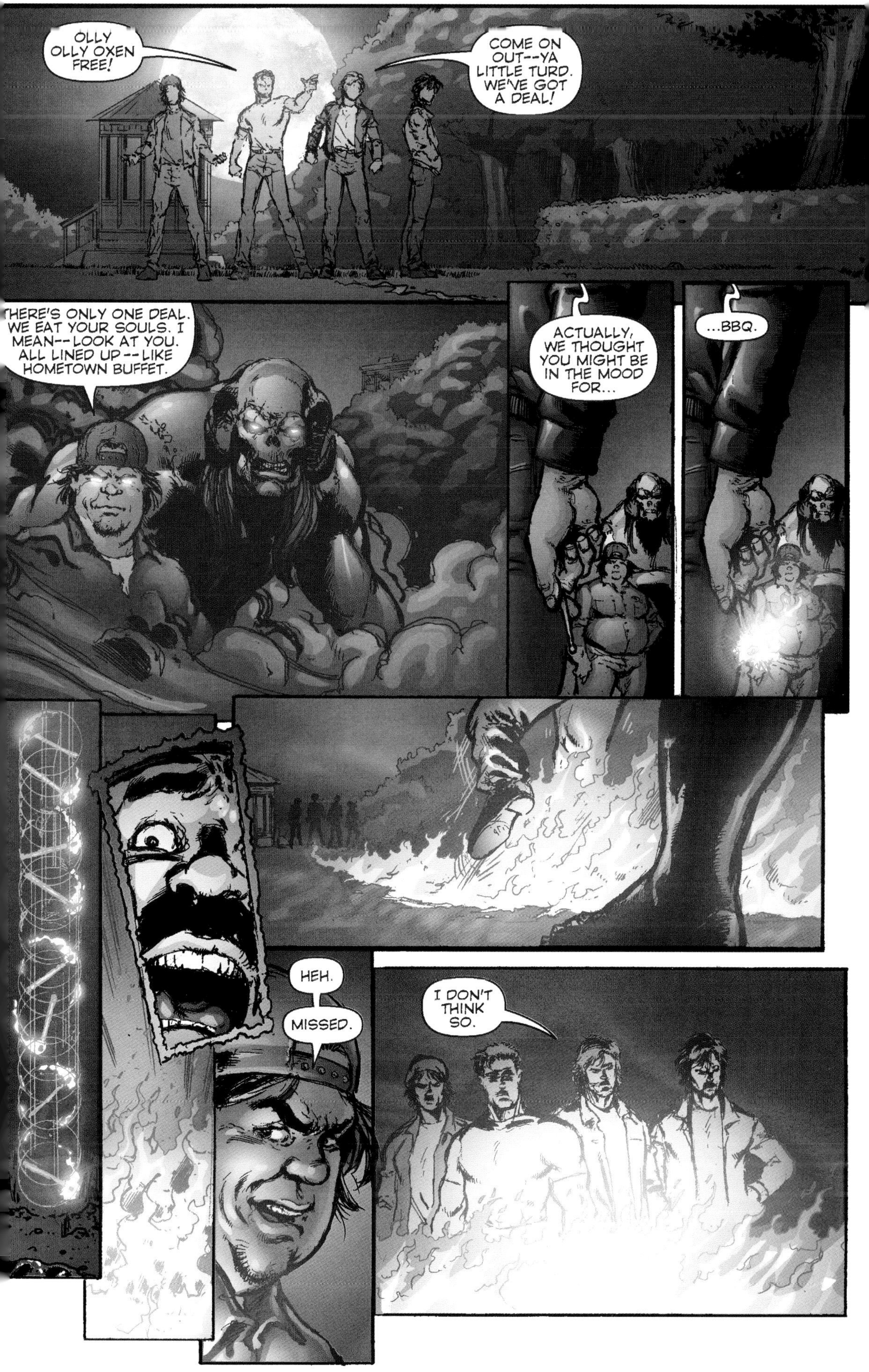
OLLY OLLY OXEN FREE!
COME ON OUT--YA LITTLE TURD. WE'VE GOT A DEAL!
THERE'S ONLY ONE DEAL. WE EAT YOUR SOULS. I MEAN--LOOK AT YOU. ALL LINED UP--LIKE HOMETOWN BUFFET.
ACTUALLY, WE THOUGHT YOU MIGHT BE IN THE MOOD FOR...
...BBQ.
HEH.
MISSED.
I DON'T THINK SO.

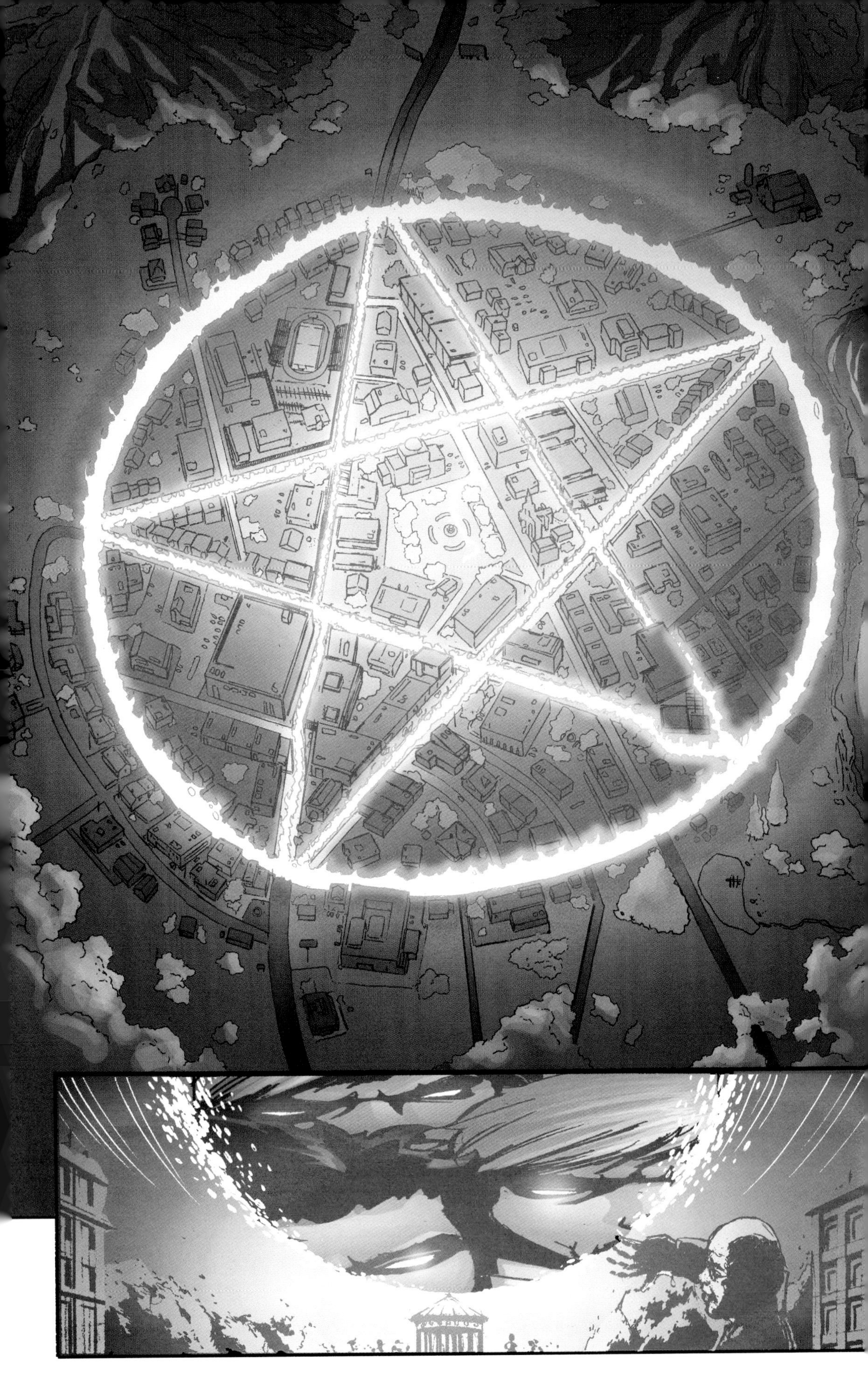

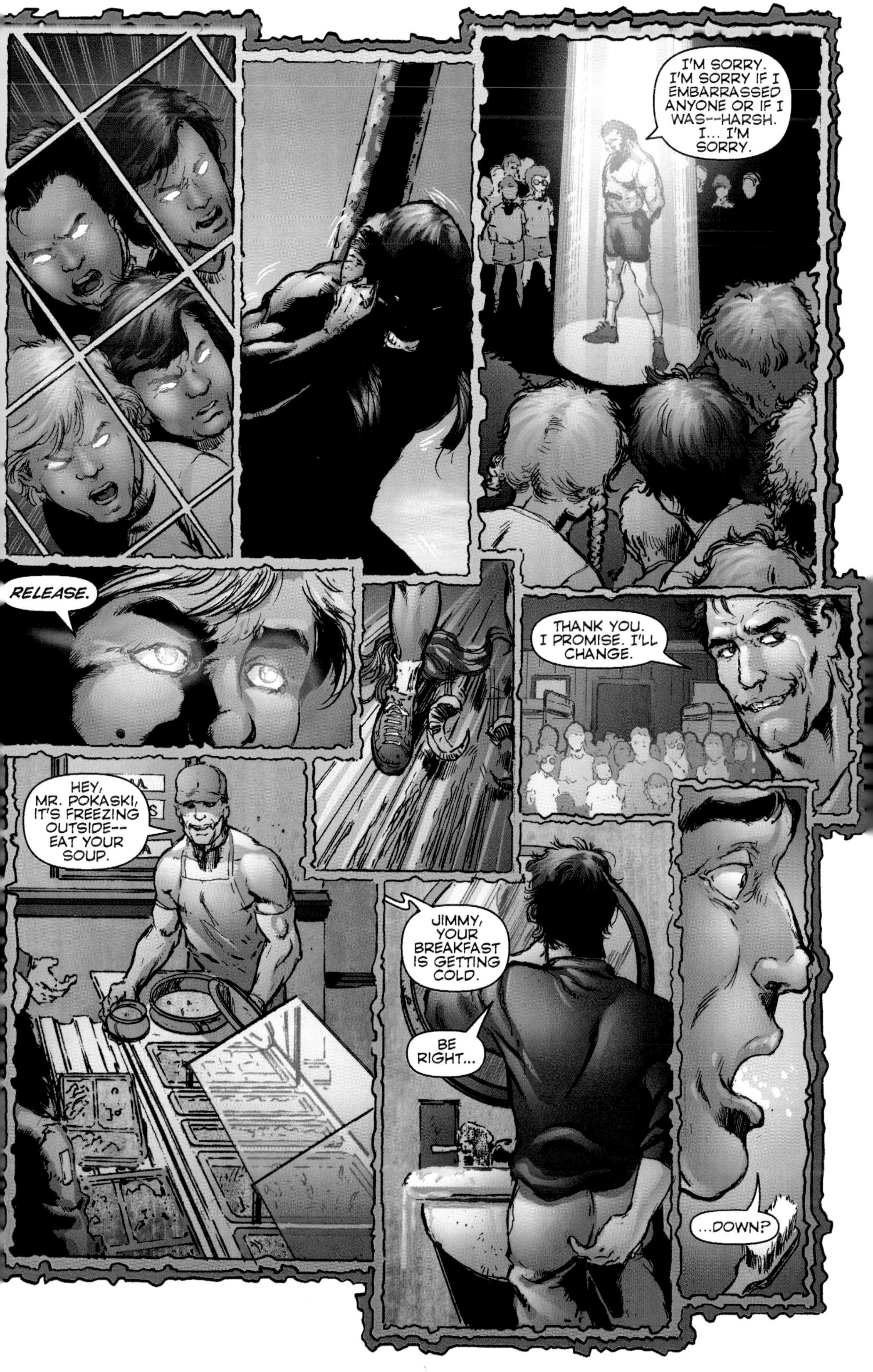
I'M SORRY. I'M SORRY IF I EMBARRASSED ANYONE OR IF I WAS--HARSH. I... I'M SORRY.
RELEASE.
THANK YOU. I PROMISE. I'LL CHANGE.
HEY, MR. POKASKI, IT'S FREEZING OUTSIDE-- EAT YOUR SOUP.
JIMMY, YOUR BREAKFAST IS GETTING COLD.
BE RIGHT...
...DOWN?

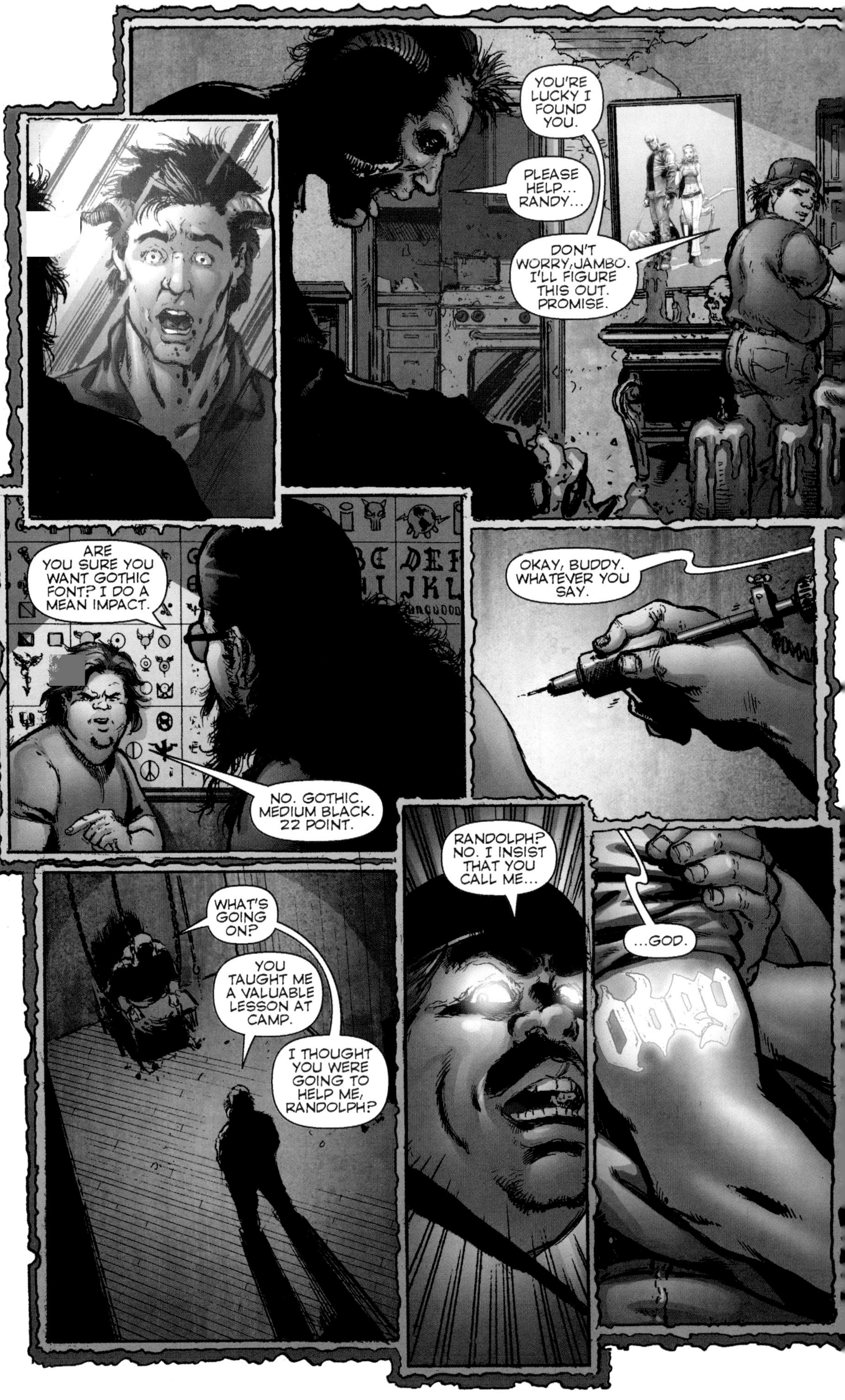
YOU'RE LUCKY I FOUND YOU.
PLEASE HELP... RANDY...
DON'T WORRY, JAMBO. I'LL FIGURE THIS OUT. PROMISE.
ARE YOU SURE YOU WANT GOTHIC FONT? I DO A MEAN IMPACT.
NO. GOTHIC. MEDIUM BLACK. 22 POINT.
OKAY, BUDDY. WHATEVER YOU SAY.
WHAT'S GOING ON?
YOU TAUGHT ME A VALUABLE LESSON AT CAMP.
I THOUGHT YOU WERE GOING TO HELP ME, RANDOLPH?
RANDOLPH? NO. I INSIST THAT YOU CALL ME...
...GOD.

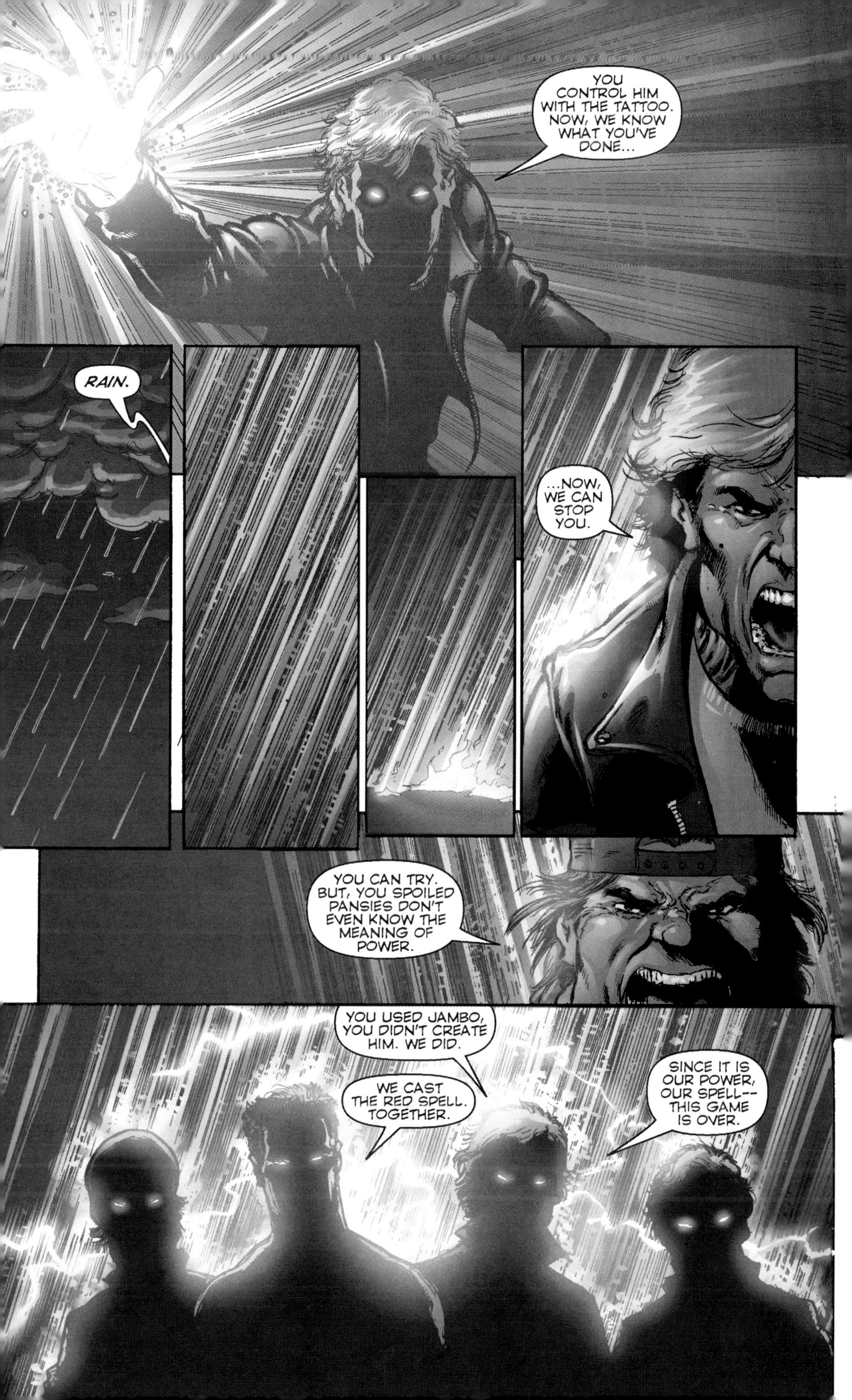
YOU CONTROL HIM WITH THE TATTOO. NOW, WE KNOW WHAT YOU'VE DONE...
RAIN.
...NOW, WE CAN STOP YOU.
YOU CAN TRY. BUT, YOU SPOILED PANSIES DON'T EVEN KNOW THE MEANING OF POWER.
YOU USED JAMBO, YOU DIDN'T CREATE HIM. WE DID.
WE CAST THE RED SPELL. TOGETHER.
SINCE IT IS OUR POWER, OUR SPELL-- THIS GAME IS OVER.

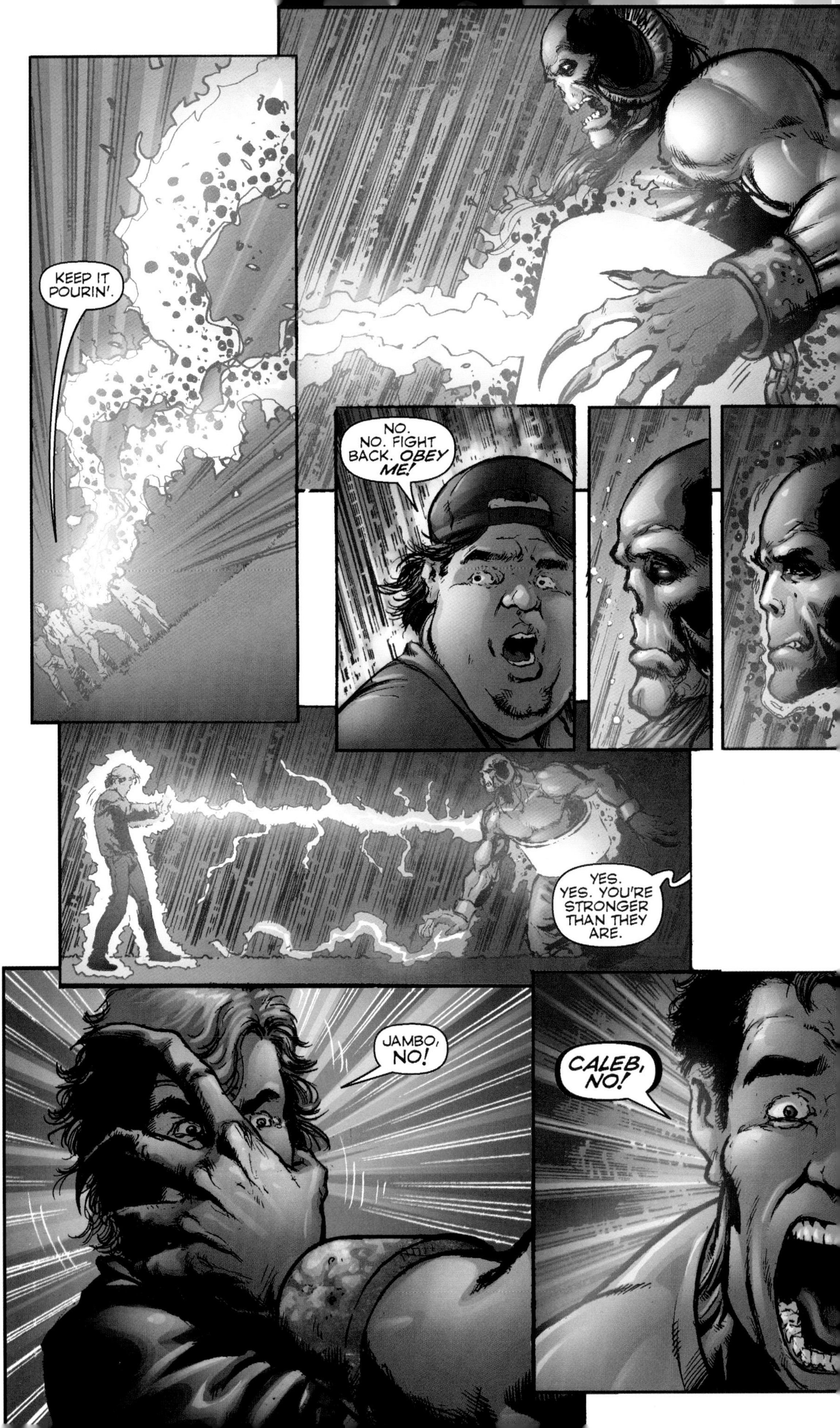
KEEP IT POURIN'.
NO. NO. FIGHT BACK. *OBEY ME!*
YES. YES. YOU'RE STRONGER THAN THEY ARE.
JAMBO, NO!
*CALEB, NO!*

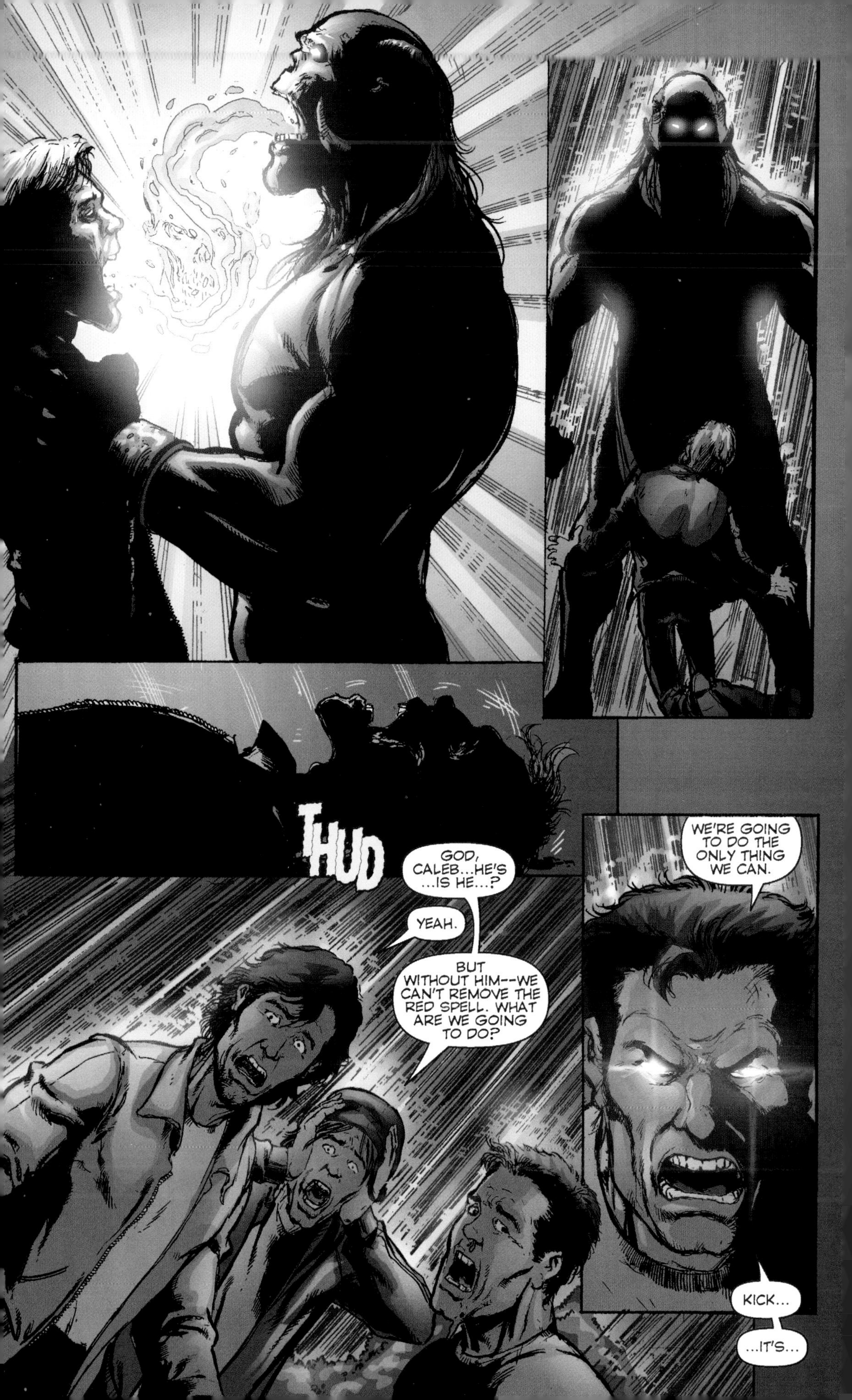
THUD
GOD, CALEB...HE'S ...IS HE...?
YEAH.
BUT WITHOUT HIM--WE CAN'T REMOVE THE RED SPELL. WHAT ARE WE GOING TO DO?
WE'RE GOING TO DO THE ONLY THING WE CAN.
KICK...
...IT'S...

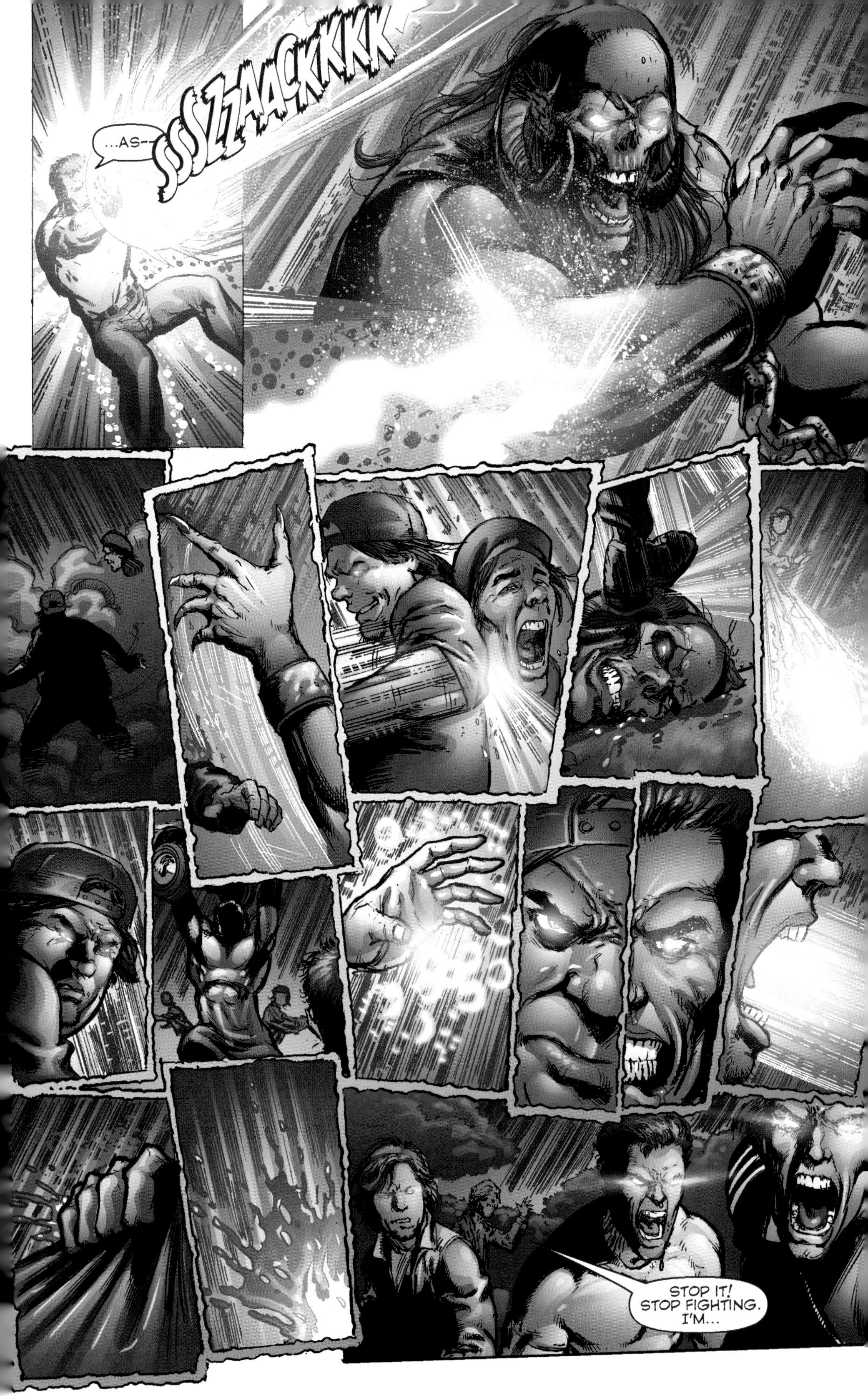
...AS--
SSSZZAACKKKK
STOP IT! STOP FIGHTING. I'M...

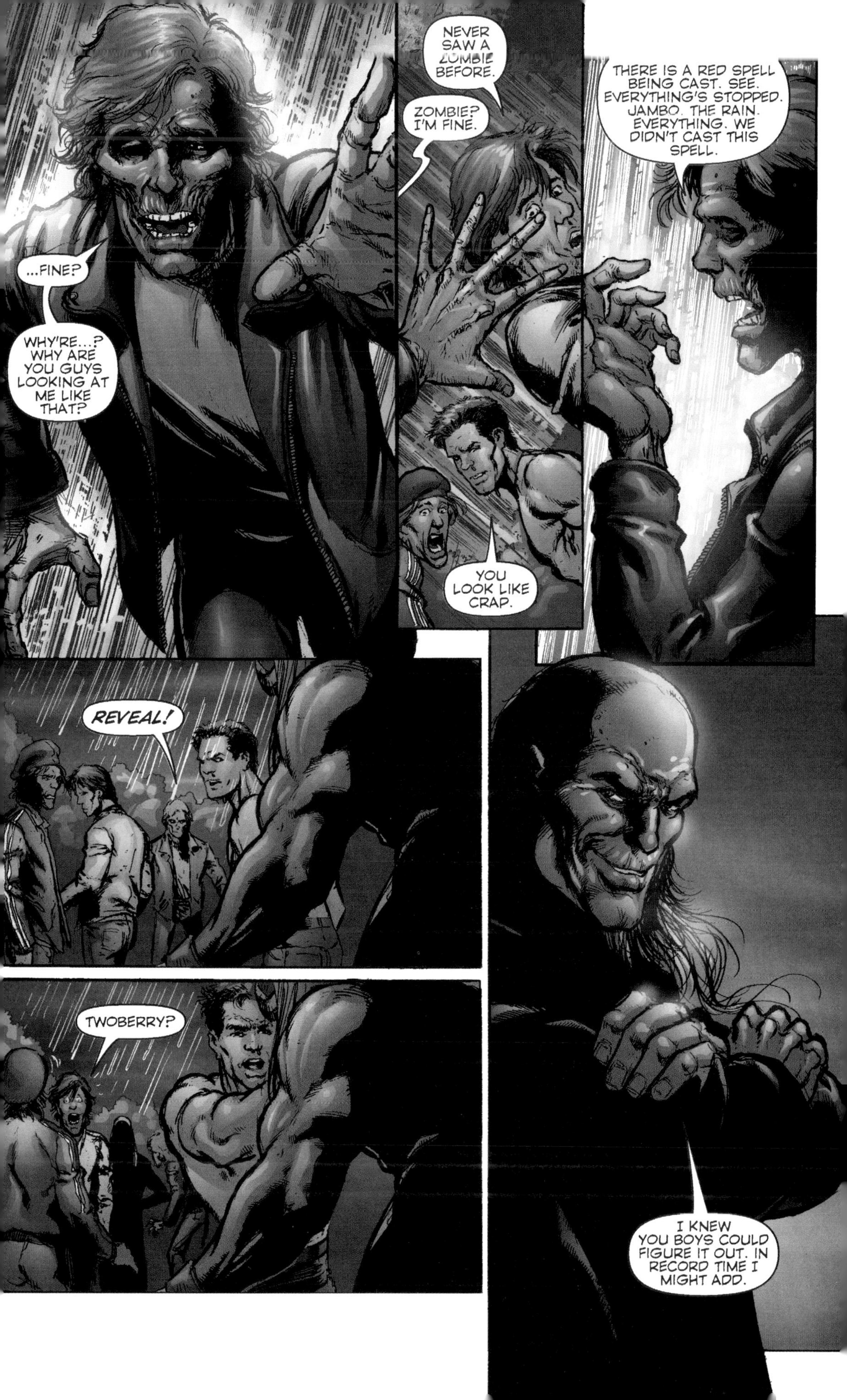
...FINE?
WHY'RE...? WHY ARE YOU GUYS LOOKING AT ME LIKE THAT?
NEVER SAW A ZOMBIE BEFORE.
ZOMBIE? I'M FINE.
YOU LOOK LIKE CRAP.
THERE IS A RED SPELL BEING CAST. SEE. EVERYTHING'S STOPPED. JAMBO. THE RAIN. EVERYTHING. WE DIDN'T CAST THIS SPELL.
REVEAL!
TWOBERRY?
I KNEW YOU BOYS COULD FIGURE IT OUT. IN RECORD TIME I MIGHT ADD.

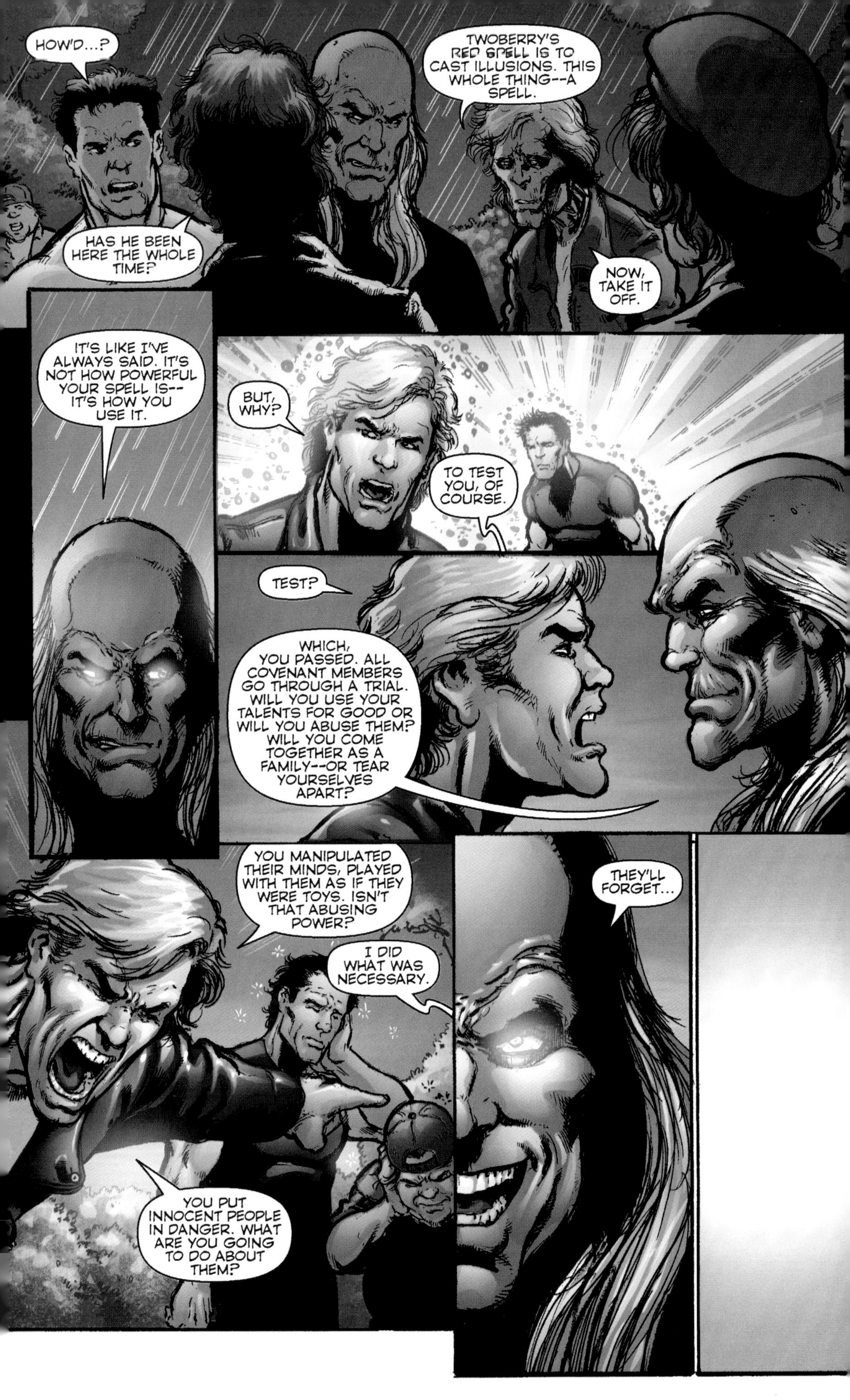
HOW'D...?
HAS HE BEEN HERE THE WHOLE TIME?
TWOBERRY'S RED SPELL IS TO CAST ILLUSIONS. THIS WHOLE THING--A SPELL.
NOW, TAKE IT OFF.
IT'S LIKE I'VE ALWAYS SAID. IT'S NOT HOW POWERFUL YOUR SPELL IS-- IT'S HOW YOU USE IT.
BUT, WHY?
TO TEST YOU, OF COURSE.
TEST?
WHICH, YOU PASSED. ALL COVENANT MEMBERS GO THROUGH A TRIAL. WILL YOU USE YOUR TALENTS FOR GOOD OR WILL YOU ABUSE THEM? WILL YOU COME TOGETHER AS A FAMILY--OR TEAR YOURSELVES APART?
YOU MANIPULATED THEIR MINDS, PLAYED WITH THEM AS IF THEY WERE TOYS. ISN'T THAT ABUSING POWER?
I DID WHAT WAS NECESSARY.
YOU PUT INNOCENT PEOPLE IN DANGER. WHAT ARE YOU GOING TO DO ABOUT THEM?
THEY'LL FORGET...

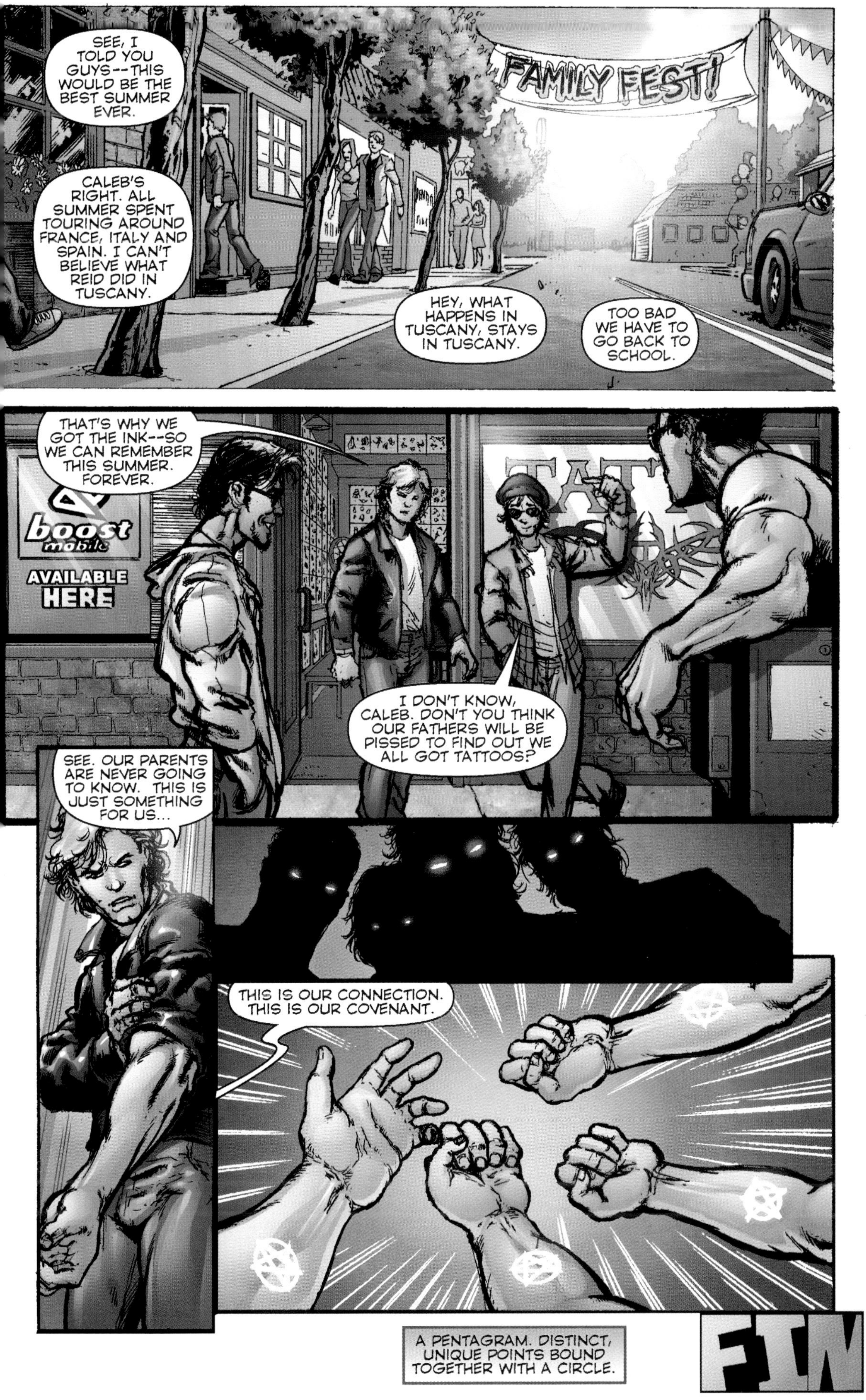
FAMILY FEST!
SEE, I TOLD YOU GUYS--THIS WOULD BE THE BEST SUMMER EVER.
CALEB'S RIGHT. ALL SUMMER SPENT TOURING AROUND FRANCE, ITALY AND SPAIN. I CAN'T BELIEVE WHAT REID DID IN TUSCANY.
HEY, WHAT HAPPENS IN TUSCANY, STAYS IN TUSCANY.
TOO BAD WE HAVE TO GO BACK TO SCHOOL.
THAT'S WHY WE GOT THE INK--SO WE CAN REMEMBER THIS SUMMER. FOREVER.
boost mobile
AVAILABLE HERE
I DON'T KNOW, CALEB. DON'T YOU THINK OUR FATHERS WILL BE PISSED TO FIND OUT WE ALL GOT TATTOOS?
SEE. OUR PARENTS ARE NEVER GOING TO KNOW. THIS IS JUST SOMETHING FOR US...
THIS IS OUR CONNECTION. THIS IS OUR COVENANT.
A PENTAGRAM. DISTINCT, UNIQUE POINTS BOUND TOGETHER WITH A CIRCLE.
FIN

ART BY: GREG LAUREN

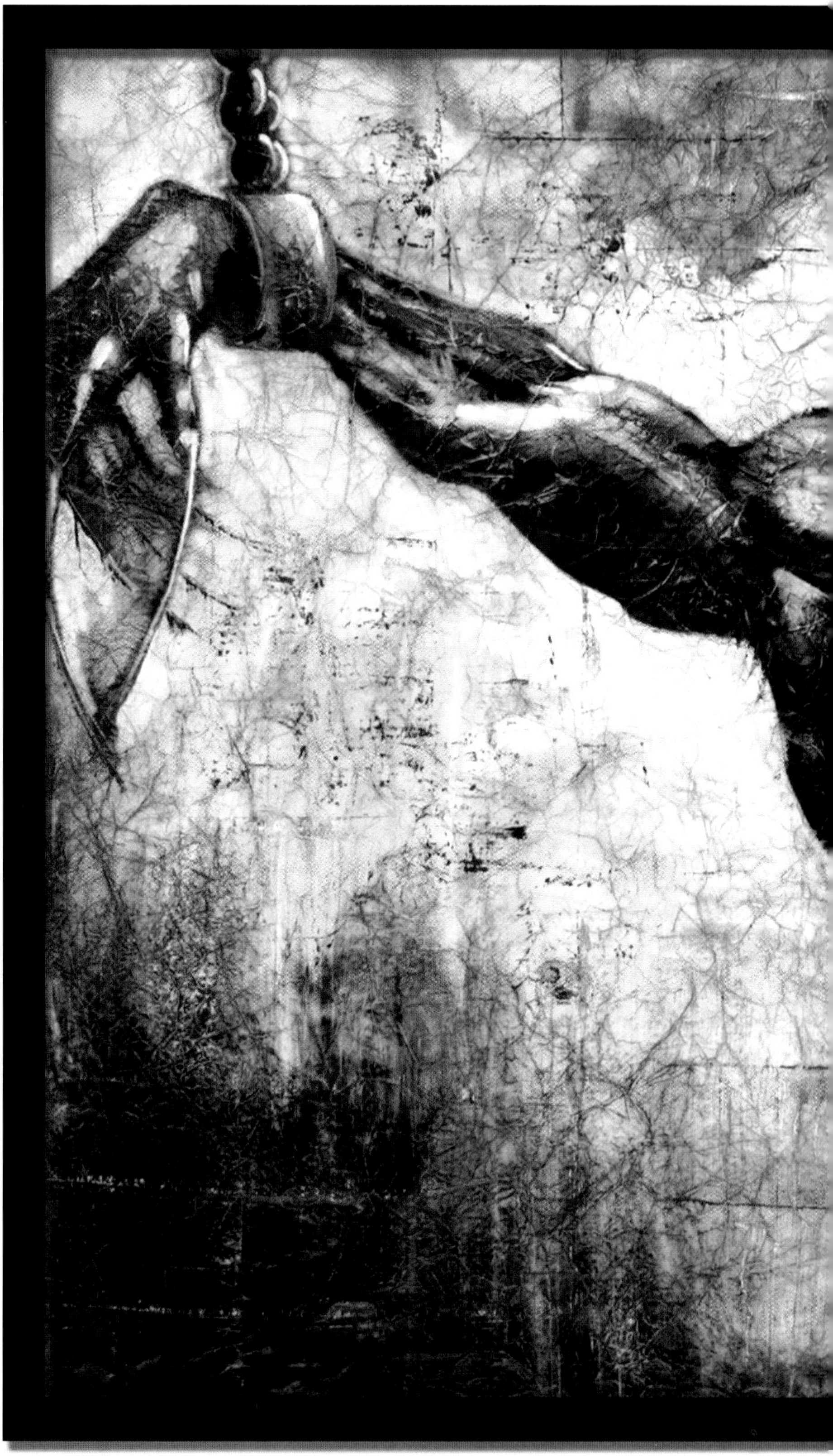

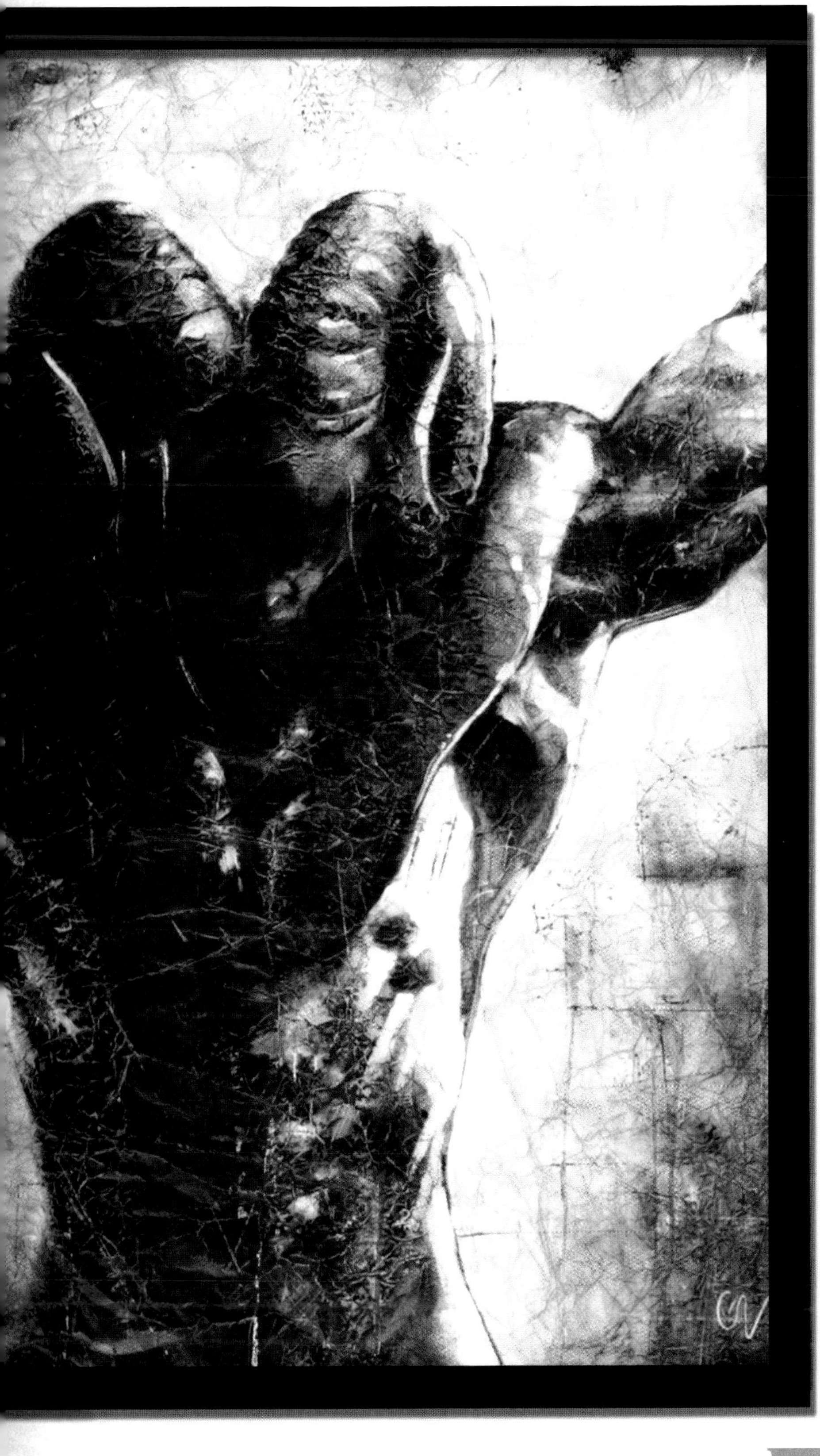

# FIN

SKETCHES AND CONCEPT ART

BY: TONE RODRIGUEZ

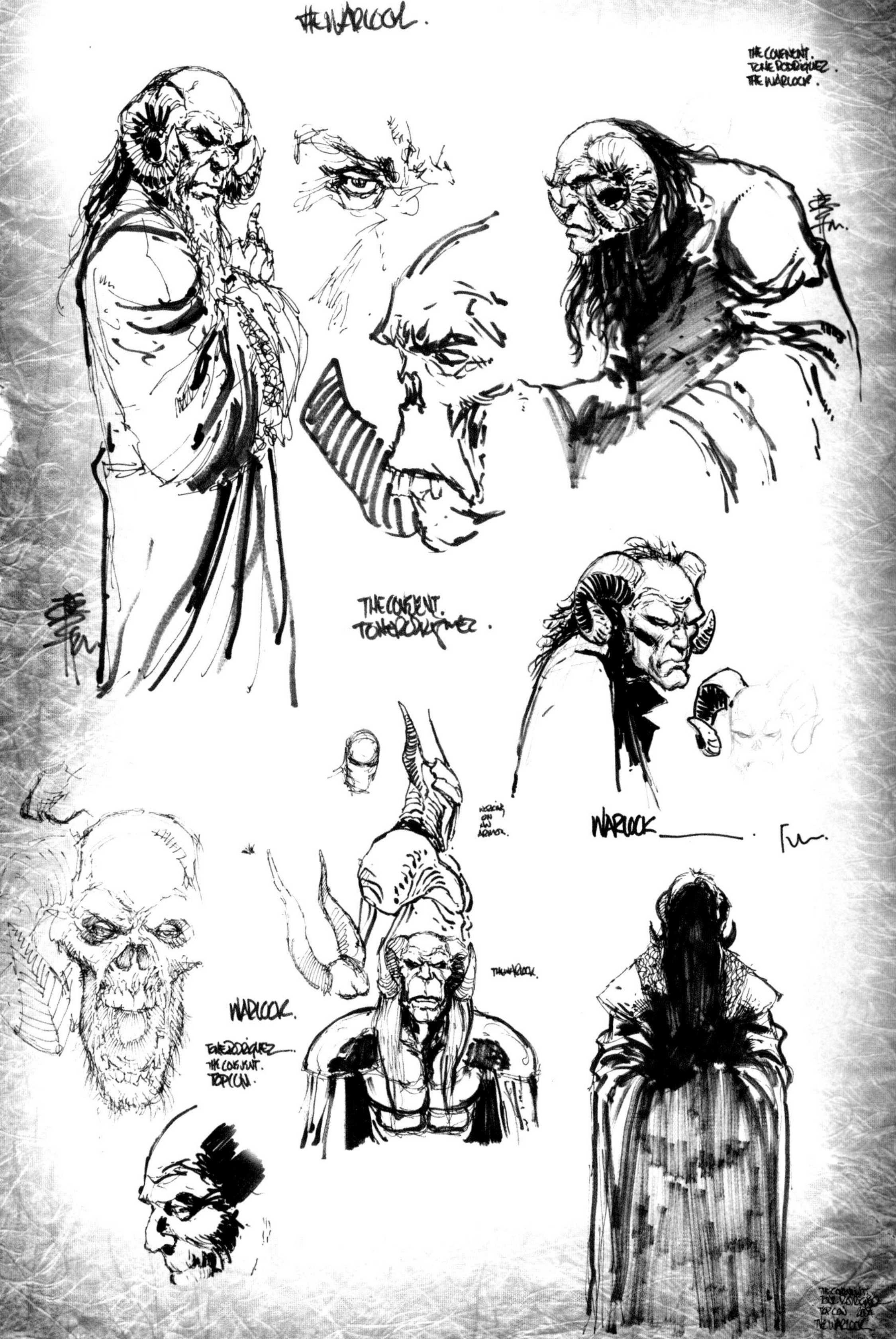
THE WARLOCK.
WARLOCK
WARLOCK.